Capital
Disasters

HOW LONDON HAS SURVIVED FIRE, FLOOD, DISEASE, RIOT AND WAR

John Withington

SUTTON PUBLISHING

First published in the United Kingdom in 2003 by
Sutton Publishing Limited · Phoenix Mill
Thrupp · Stroud · Gloucestershire · GL5 2BU

British Library Cataloguing in Publication Data
A catalogue record for this book is available from the British Library.

ISBN 0-7509-3317-8

Typeset in 11/14.5pt Sabon
Typesetting and origination by
Sutton Publishing Limited.
Printed and bound in England by
J.H. Haynes & Co. Ltd, Sparkford.

Contents

Acknowledgements

I would like to thank the library staffs of the Health and Safety Executive, the London Fire Brigade and the London Fire Brigade Museum for their help and their patience. Above all, I would like to thank my wife, Anne, for her constant support.

For my father

PART ONE

Hostile Action

ONE

War and Invasion

London did not have to wait long for its first disaster. The city was founded by the Romans as Londinium around AD 50; within a decade, it lay in ruins – the only time in its history that a disaster has completely destroyed it.

The Roman city was built around Cornhill and Ludgate. By AD 60, it had spread over about 30 acres and become a busy trading centre. The houses had timber frames and thatched roofs and most were probably owned by Romans, well-to-do Gauls and other foreigners. The chain of events that began Londinium's destruction started in modern-day Norfolk. There Prasutagus, King of the Iceni, had collaborated with the Romans and managed to construct a special relationship. His reward was to be allowed to remain semi-independent. Such arrangements, though, tended not to last beyond the death of the favoured individual.

In AD 61, the King died. He was survived by his widow Boudicca and two daughters. Prasutagus had hoped to safeguard their future by a will in which he left half of his considerable wealth to the Emperor Nero and half to his daughters. When he died, representatives of the procurator, the financial overlord of the province of Britain, appeared. They probably had instructions to seize the whole estate, but even if they did not, their arrogance and high-handedness provoked resistance.

The Romans responded brutally, flogging Boudicca and raping her daughters. It was not only the Iceni, though, whom they had alienated. The Iceni's neighbours, the Trinovantes, whose territory lay in Essex and southern Suffolk, were also in restless mood. They bitterly resented having their lands and houses handed over to Roman war veterans, as well as the Romans' efforts to make them worship the Emperor.

When the Britons went to war, the Roman Governor, Suetonius Paulinus, was campaigning far away in Anglesey with the XIVth Legion. In his absence, Boudicca's host sacked and looted Colchester, massacring its Roman colonists, and destroyed part of a Roman legion that had tried to come to their rescue. When Suetonius heard the news, he raced down to London. His cavalry probably made it in three or four days, but the infantry was left far behind. With his depleted force, he decided that if he was to save the province, he had to abandon the city. So, in the words of the Roman historian Tacitus, 'undeflected by the prayers and tears of those who begged for his help', he led his soldiers off to the north, taking with him those Roman Londoners fit and willing to escape. The rest he abandoned to their fate. Some may have escaped into the territory of neighbouring tribes still friendly to Rome, but many were reluctant to leave, and the old and infirm could not.

When Boudicca's army entered the city, the inhabitants were slaughtered. Tacitus complained the rebels did not want to take prisoners and make money from ransoms, they just wished to kill – cutting throats, hanging and crucifying 'with a headlong fury'. They also burned down the city. The fearful intensity of the fire is clear from the way a heap of Roman coins found near the northern end of London Bridge have been partially melted together, and in the Museum of London, there are remains of coins and pottery burned as the city was destroyed. The ruins of Roman London also contain reddish fire debris 18 inches thick, another tangible reminder of the city's first disaster.

Boudicca's followers carried the destruction across the river to the settlement at Southwark, then they swung back north and meted out similar treatment to St Albans. Tacitus claims they killed 70,000 people in all. The figure is almost certainly a gross exaggeration, but the massacre was nonetheless a terrible one. The campaign, though, was to end in another massacre, this time of Boudicca's host. It may have been 80,000 strong, but it was hampered by a long, unwieldy tail of women and children. Suetonius had probably gathered together a force of about 10,000, but its discipline and tactical sophistication enabled it to win a devastating victory. Tens of thousands of Britons were killed against just 400 Romans. Boudicca took poison rather than fall into the hands of her enemies.

Tradition has placed the fatal battle at a number of sites around London, like Stanmore Common to the north, or Honor Oak in the south. The favourite was Battle Bridge, near King's Cross, with the body of Boudicca said to be buried at a site now occupied by one of the platforms of King's Cross station, or under an ancient tumulus at Parliament Hill. No sign of the Queen was found, however, when the mound was excavated, and the view of historians nowadays is that the decisive battle probably took place in the Midlands.

Although Roman London was to encounter disaster from fire (see Chapter 5), in the two centuries after the defeat of Boudicca, it seems to have remained free from attack. Towards the end of the second century, however, work was begun on a major defensive wall and ditch on the landward side of the city, perhaps reflecting a fear that more turbulent times were on the way.

In 286, Marcus Carausius declared himself Emperor of Britain and for ten years he and Allectus, who eventually deposed and murdered him, defied the Roman Empire. Then, in 296, Constantius Chlorus appeared to defeat and kill Allectus and win back Britain for Rome. Frankish mercenaries who had been hired by the rebel 'emperor', took refuge in London and began plundering the city. Fortunately for the citizens, some of Constantius's ships sailed up the Thames. When the Franks saw them, they tried to escape, but, according to a contemporary account, the Romans 'slew them in the streets'.

There was more trouble in 367 when the Saxons overran London. They were leaving loaded with plunder, driving prisoners in chains and cattle before them, when they were caught by the Roman general Theodosius, who had been despatched by the emperor. The Roman army routed the marauders and, when Theodosius entered the city, he was received with all the jubilation of a Roman triumph. Theodosius may also have strengthened London's defences, and more work seems to have been done in the last decade of the fourth century too, but the barbarian tide could not be checked indefinitely, and besides, Rome was facing problems much nearer home, which meant it could no longer afford to protect outposts of the empire.

In the early years of the fifth century, the last Roman troops were withdrawn and, in 410, the Emperor Honorius warned Londinium it would have to look after itself. By this time, the citizens were probably hiring German mercenaries to protect them, perhaps giving them land to farm as payment. After the Romans left, Londinium and Southwark seem to have been largely abandoned, with the Anglo-Saxons initially settling outside the city walls, but, by the ninth century, they were moving back inside because of attacks from a new and fearsome enemy.

In 842, there was, according to some accounts, 'great slaughter' as the Vikings attacked London for the first time. In 851, they returned to kill once more, leaving the city a smouldering wreck. Then, in 871, London was occupied by the Danish Great Army, which probably stayed until 886 when Alfred the Great conquered the city. There followed a period of relative peace until 994 when the Norsemen, led by Svein Forkbeard, King of Denmark, and the future King of Norway, Olaf Tryggvason, invaded England with a fleet of ninety-four ships. They sailed up the Thames and set fire to London, but stubborn resistance from the defenders drove them off, and the city repulsed a further attack in 1009. In 1014, London submitted to Svein, but he died the same year and King Ethelred the Unready returned in alliance with another King Olaf of Norway. This one was known as Olaf the Fat during his lifetime, and after his death as a saint.

Seeing the Danes had massed their soldiers on the bridge between Southwark and London, Ethelred and Olaf tied ropes from their ships to the posts holding it up, and pulled it into the river, taking the soldiers with it. They then reconquered Southwark, and London capitulated. Two years later Ethelred died, and the kingdom fell to Svein Forkbeard's son, Cnut, but London would face one more foreign invader before this tangled tale of dynastic rivalries reached its conclusion.

Cnut was succeeded in turn by his son, Harthacnut. Meanwhile, across the Channel, one of Ethelred's sons, Edward, was living in exile with the Dukes of Normandy. Harthacnut invited him to return to England and on his death Edward became King, earning the nickname 'the Confessor' for his great piety. Edward's Norman connections, though, led to more trouble. On his death, he left the throne to the English earl Harold Godwinson, but Duke William of Normandy, the future William the Conqueror, claimed that both Edward and Harold had promised it to him.

Determined to take England, William sailed across the Channel with his army. After defeating and killing Harold at the Battle of Hastings in 1066, William spent a month subduing the south-east before turning his attentions to London. He began by burning down Southwark. In response, London's defenders crossed the bridge to take on the invader. They rather got the worst of the encounter, but London had a formidable garrison and William was reluctant to face the possibility of a bloody battle, so he withdrew to the west, devastating the country as he went.

London was spared further destruction when the Anglo-Saxon nobles submitted to the conquering Duke at Berkhamsted. His coronation, though, proved the most disastrous in London's history. When William was crowned on Christmas Day 1066, the crowd outside Westminster Abbey shouted its acclamation of him as King. Hearing the noise, the Norman soldiers inside believed it heralded the start of a revolt so they ran out into the street, setting fire to houses and hacking down the supposed rebels. In view of the turbulence of the previous 200 years, perhaps the most surprising thing was that what now followed for London were nearly 900 years of freedom from enemy attack.

TWO

Rebellion and Riot

London may have been free from foreign attack, but it would sometimes face death and destruction at the hands of Englishmen. By 1381, the country had been enmeshed in the Hundred Years' War with France for forty-four years. Hostilities, as ever, proved expensive, and in 1377 the government levied a poll tax, which had to be paid by even the poorest peasants. The countryside seethed with anger, and in Kent an ex-soldier named Wat Tyler emerged as leader. His right-hand man was a renegade egalitarian priest, John Ball, who asked the famous rhyming question: 'When Adam delved, and Eve span / Who was then the gentleman?' By June, Tyler had gathered a band of 10,000 Kentish peasants and decided to lead them to London. On the way, they plundered Rochester and Canterbury. At the same time, another group of like-minded men set out from Essex. The Kentish rebels went to Blackheath to await a meeting with the King, while the Essex men camped at Mile End.

On 13 June, King Richard II, then aged fourteen, set off from the Tower with his advisers in the royal barge, intending to meet Tyler. But when he saw the angry crowd of peasants, he turned back, so the rebels got to work on Southwark, burning down the Marshalsea Prison, freeing the inmates and plundering Lambeth Palace. The Mayor, William Walworth, was sufficiently alarmed to order that the drawbridge on London Bridge be raised and secured to stop the rebels crossing the river. Confined to the south bank, they wrecked the highly profitable Bankside brothels, most of which were owned by the Bishop of Winchester, though some belonged to Walworth.

Then Tyler threatened to burn down houses on London Bridge if the drawbridge was not lowered. The alderman in charge,

8

apparently refusing help from armed volunteers among the citizenry, promptly lowered it, and the rebels streamed across. They were soon reinforced by Jack Straw's men from Essex and others from Surrey, as well as large numbers of Londoners, from vagrants to master craftsmen, with whom the poll tax was also deeply unpopular. One chronicler even believed the revolts in Kent and Essex had been incited from London. Soon the rebels were running riot in the City. In the mayhem that followed the inmates in the Fleet Prison were released, and legal records were burned at the Temple.

A key target was the King's uncle, John of Gaunt, Duke of Lancaster, seen as the power behind the throne. The rebels attacked his opulent Savoy Palace, killing some of his servants and throwing furnishings, clothes, jewels and plate into the Thames. Tyler had insisted there should be no looting, but some of the rebels clearly thought that drinking the Duke's wine did not count, and a number were killed when they had had rather too much, and were trapped in the cellars as the Palace burned above them.

By now the rebels were becoming an increasingly threatening and disorderly mob. They killed tax collectors, and some carried on sticks the heads of foreigners they had murdered; the decapitated bodies of Flemish merchants were said to have been piled forty high. In Cheapside, the mob summarily executed lawyers. Then Newgate was emptied of prisoners. They also managed to gain control of the Tower, and seized their arch-enemy, Simon Sudbury, Archbishop of Canterbury and Chancellor, the man widely seen as responsible for the government's financial mismanagement. They also captured the King's Treasurer, Robert Hales, Prior of the Hospital of St John, Clerkenwell, and executed them both on Tower Hill. For good measure, they burned down the priory too. The Archbishop's cap was nailed to his skull and paraded through the streets, then displayed on London Bridge. There was a massacre in the City, and the mob burned down buildings at Westminster and along Holborn.

There followed King Richard's finest hour. The rest of his reign might turn out a disaster, culminating in his being deposed and murdered, but now the fourteen-year-old showed astonishing coolness and courage, not to mention duplicity and ruthlessness.

While one band of rebels led by Jack Straw was attacking the Treasurer's house at Highbury, Richard went with his courtiers to talk to another group at Mile End. He agreed to abolish their obligation to do feudal service and made a series of other concessions, as well as promising an amnesty to the insurgents. Charters guaranteeing these concessions were drawn up, and the Essex men began to disperse. The following day, Richard went to Smithfield, then a large open space west of the City wall, where Tyler's men were gathered, to resume negotiations with them.

When they met, Tyler is supposed to have shaken Richard's hand and said, 'Brother, be of good cheer', which was not how you were meant to speak to the King. William Walworth promptly stabbed him, and dragged him to the ground, while another of the King's party finished him off. Richard then rode up to the wavering, confused rebels and offered himself as their leader. He took them to St John's Fields, Clerkenwell, where the City militia had been raised. There the rebels were surrounded and persuaded to disperse without bloodshed. As the Kentish peasants were returning home, on London Bridge they would have seen the heads of Tyler and Straw, who had been executed, in the place where the Archbishop's had been only a few hours earlier. Their exploits in London were followed by risings in four counties, but by the end of June, the revolt had been crushed and most of its local leaders killed. The concessions made by the King were quietly forgotten, though the poll tax was abolished.

Sixty-nine years later, the Hundred Years' War was still being fought, but it was about to end in ignominy, with the loss of virtually all England's possessions in France. The throne was occupied by the pious, well-meaning, but feeble-minded Henry VI, who founded Eton College and King's College, Cambridge. By 1450, the government was bankrupt and once again it was the people of Kent whose patience snapped first. A man named Jack Cade led tens of thousands of them, including a number of gentry, to Blackheath, where they camped on 29 June 1450.

Ignoring an urgent appeal from the Lord Mayor to stay, the King fled north and left the City to defend itself. A hero of Agincourt,

10

Sir John Fastolf, helped mount guards on the gates and along the wharves, and deploy projectile-throwing machines. He also sent his servant, John Payne, to Blackheath to find out what exactly it was the rebels wanted. They decided to behead him, and fetched an axe and block, but he managed to persuade them to let him go back and report their grievances instead. Their complaints about the selfishness and incompetence of the 'kitchen' cabinet surrounding the King would be calculated to appeal to many Londoners.

Payne delivered the message, and also told Fastolf about the size of Cade's force, at which point his master retreated to the Tower. Cade's men promptly took possession of Southwark on 1 July, making their headquarters at the White Hart Inn in Borough High Street. The next day, they cut the ropes of the drawbridge on London Bridge so that it could not be raised against them, and crossed the river. They caught Lord Saye and Sele, the Lord Treasurer of England, and decided to put him on trial. He refused to plead, so the rebels beheaded him in Cheapside and stuck his head on a spear. Then they tied his body to a horse's tail and dragged it across the bridge to Southwark, where it was put on a gallows and quartered. His son-in-law, William Crowmer, the Sheriff of Kent, was also captured, and beheaded at Mile End; some twenty royal servants and a few other unpopular characters met a similar fate.

Cade had given a warning that any of his followers caught plundering would be executed, but with a force of 25,000 inside the City, there was soon looting of rich folk's houses, assault, robbery and rape, and sympathy for the rebels began to evaporate. On 5 July, after they had retired to their Southwark headquarters for the night, another veteran of Henry V's wars against the French got to work. Captain Matthew Gough took a group of men, killed Cade's sentries, and occupied London Bridge. When the rebels heard the news, they rushed to the bridge and a fierce fight ensued, raging back and forth over its entire length. By now, a few of the inhabitants had fled, but most had stayed behind to try to protect their property. Some of them were now burned alive as Cade's men set fire to their houses. Others were cut down in the street, and others still fell into the river and drowned. The battle raged for ten hours, and about two hundred were killed, including Gough himself. Then at eight in the morning, both sides agreed to a truce.

Many of the rebels were now inclined to head home with their booty, and the offer of a general pardon was enough to buy them off. Once Cade was out of town, though, the government offered a reward for him, dead or alive, and he was quickly run to ground in Sussex. Wounded, he was bundled into a cart, but died on the way back to London, where his naked corpse was mutilated and dragged on a hurdle over London Bridge to Newgate. His skull, in the time-honoured fashion, was displayed on the bridge, and, general pardon or not, dozens of rebels were rounded up and executed in Kent.

The most disastrous riot in London's history would come more than 300 years later in response to a modest dilution of the laws discriminating against Roman Catholics. Lord George Gordon, a young MP on the make, spotted a way to advance his career. He became President of the Protestant Association, which got up a huge petition against the new law. On Friday 2 June 1780, he drew a crowd of 50,000 people to St George's Fields in Lambeth and urged them to come with him to Parliament to present it. This was not a rabble; rather they were 'the better sort of tradesmen' – journeymen, apprentices, small employers. Indeed, a great deal of 'respectable' opinion was against the new law and the government of the City, the Court of Common Council, had asked for it to be repealed.

It was a very hot day, with the sun beating down, but Gordon told his supporters to dress in their 'Sabbath day clothes'. The protesters marched three abreast and the main column was 4 miles long. At Westminster, they raised a great yell and invaded the parliamentary lobbies, carrying the petition into the chamber of the House of Commons. The mob terrorised Lords and MPs until the rumour got about that armed soldiers were on their way, at which point they dispersed. A body of Horse Guards did capture some of the protestors and took them off to Newgate, but that evening the mob gathered again, and people began to bar doors and windows, fearing the worst.

Obvious Catholic targets were soon under attack. The Bavarian Embassy was ransacked and the Sardinian Embassy burned to the ground. When the mob arrived at his chapel in Lincoln's Inn Fields, the Sardinian ambassador offered them 500 guineas not to damage a portrait of Christ, and 1,000 guineas to spare the organ. Both were destroyed as the building was burned down. On Saturday, the rioters took a day off, but on Sunday they descended on Moorfields and gutted a Catholic chapel, coming back the next day to wreck the schoolhouse and some priests' houses nearby. The mob broke into groups and the violence spread. Some attacked Catholic buildings. Others turned on magistrates who had imprisoned rioters, and politicians who had supported pro-Catholic legislation. Irish districts were a particular target, because Irish immigrants were believed to be stealing jobs from Londoners. Sometimes, houses were attacked just to settle scores, and sometimes mistakes were made, as French Protestants, who had fled to England to escape persecution by Catholics, found themselves under attack. In Houndsditch, Jewish householders thought it prudent to put up notices saying 'This house is true Protestant'.

All over the City, rioters were roaming the streets with blue cockades in their hats to show their allegiance, and houses flew blue 'No Popery' flags. Up to now, the City authorities had shown little inclination to act, although some soldiers were stationed at vantage points, but on Tuesday, the crowd began to select more alarming targets. They returned to Westminster, where Parliament adjourned after hearing reports that the rioters were armed. They also attacked Bow Street police office, and then assembled in front of Newgate Prison, demanding that the gates be opened. They burned down the house of the keeper, then piled furniture against the prison gate and set fire to it. Other rioters scaled the walls and threw burning torches onto the roof. When constables came to try to help the keeper, the mob trapped them. By now, the rioters had broken through the roof and climbed down on ladders, while many prisoners feared they would be burned alive. Then the fire did its work and the gate began to give way. The crowd forced its way in and dragged out more than three hundred inmates, some of whom had been awaiting imminent execution. They also opened Clerkenwell Bridewell Prison.

The mob attacked the home of the Lord Chief Justice in Bloomsbury Square, burning his furniture, his paintings and his law library. Another judge's house in Red Lion Square was also wrecked. By Wednesday, Gordon had completely lost control. Catholic shops, taverns and houses all over London were destroyed; the Fleet and King's Bench Prisons were forced open, freeing about sixteen hundred debtors. The Clink was burned down, never to be rebuilt. A gin distillery owned by a Roman Catholic in Holborn was set on fire, taking with it twenty houses and several looters who got drunk and fell into the flames. The Bank of England was attacked. According to one story, the rioters were beaten back by clerks using bullets made from melted-down ink wells, but the authorities decided that in future they would take no chances. From then on, it was patrolled by a platoon of guards in ceremonial bearskins. There were also threats to the Mint, the Royal Arsenal and even royal palaces.

Now the City began to regret its earlier relaxed attitude. The militia and the Honourable Artillery Company were called out. Even the great radical John Wilkes took up arms against the mob. The government brought 10,000 troops into London. They were ordered to fire on the crowd and, by Thursday night, 285 rioters lay dead or dying. Order was finally restored, but, according to some estimates, more property was destroyed in London during the Gordon riots than in Paris during the week following the storming of the Bastille.

One week after the great procession to Parliament, a warrant was issued for the arrest of Lord George Gordon. He surrendered quietly, and was cleared of high treason. Many of his followers paid a heavier price: 25 were hanged in addition to those shot down in the streets. Estimates of the number killed or injured during the riots range up to 850. Gordon lived another thirteen years, finding time to be converted to Judaism, and to libel Marie Antoinette, an offence for which he was sent to the rebuilt Newgate Prison, where he died.

THREE

Air Raids

In bright moonlight, just before midnight on 31 May 1915, nearly nine centuries of immunity from enemy attack ended in London as the German Zeppelin LZ38 flew over the docks and the East End. A new kind of war had arrived, but for many Londoners the main surprise was how long it had taken to get there.

British aircraft had bombed Cologne railway station as early as September 1914 and, ever since the opening weeks of the First World War, the capital had been expecting attacks by the Zeppelins, gas-filled airships that cruised at more than 50 miles an hour at a height of between 10,000 and 15,000 feet. The government had taken the precaution of ordering a blackout. Street lamps had to be dimmed and domestic lights must not be visible through curtains. It was said that in the West End people bought thicker drapes, while in the East End, they turned down the gas lights, or lit the room with a single candle.

At first, the Germans were reluctant to sanction attacks on civilians, and as the raids that had been feared failed to materialise, vigilance in London began to relax. Then, in 1915, the Kaiser decided to authorise raids on 'military' targets in London such as the docks. On the night of that first raid, the blackout was ineffective. The Zeppelin commander easily identified Commercial Road, and headed for the docks. At 10,000 feet, he was beyond the range of anti-aircraft fire or night fighters. Fortunately, the 120 bombs he dropped were quite small: 90 were incendiaries, and the rest were little more than grenades. Although seven people were killed, relatively little damage was done. There was no panic, but London was already seething with anger after the sinking of the *Lusitania* earlier in the month. Physical attacks followed on foreign-owned

15

shops and verbal attacks on the Admiralty, which at the time had the job of protecting London from bombardment.

Further raids followed, with the Zeppelins invariably coming at night. On 7 and 8 September, a total of thirty-two people were killed. The raid of 8 September did an estimated £½ million worth of damage and brought the City's first bomb, which exploded in Fenchurch Street. A raid the following month killed seventy-one people at Woolwich.

The warning system was fairly primitive. Policemen would wear placards and blow whistles to sound the alert, while boy scouts on bicycles would blow bugles for the all-clear. Another way of raising the alarm was to set off loud fireworks called maroons, usually from police stations. The problem was that these were sometimes mistaken for the sound of falling bombs. During the winter of 1915/16, the government began to set up more searchlights and anti-aircraft batteries, but progress was not quick enough for many Londoners. On one occasion when the City was under attack, the only available gun had to be transported all the way from Wormwood Scrubs. The issue of air defence dominated a parliamentary by-election at Mile End in January 1916, and the coalition government candidate came within 400 votes of defeat.

Altogether, there were ten airship raids on London in 1915 and 1916, but on 3 September 1916, the defenders had their first success against the enemy after an air chase across London and the Home Counties, when a wooden-framed Schutte-Lanz airship was shot down in flames at Cuffley in Hertfordshire, near enough for East Enders to see the fireball.

It was a sign that the tide was about to turn. Within a month, two more airships were shot down by aircraft after being picked out in the beams of searchlights. In the second incident, on 1 October, the Germans' most successful London raider, Heinrich Mathy, was killed with his crew. The growing cost led the Germans to abandon Zeppelin raids on London, and the last came in October 1917, causing casualties in a number of areas including Camberwell and Hither Green, and hitting Swan & Edgar's store in Piccadilly.

Before that final airship raid though, a more deadly foe had already made its first appearance in the skies over the capital. One lone aircraft had attacked the East End on 6 May 1916, then, more than six months later, another dropped six small bombs near Victoria station. It was in the following year, however, that the real raids began, conducted by the 'England Squadron' of Gotha biplane bombers based at two airfields in Belgian territory occupied by the Germans. Because the aeroplanes had a shorter range than the airships, more raids were concentrated on London.

At half past eleven on the morning of 13 June 1917, seventeen Gothas flew in tight formation over the Essex countryside. They dropped their first bombs on East Ham, then hit the front carriages of the Cambridge express at Liverpool Street station. One witness was the soldier and poet Siegfried Sassoon. He wrote: 'an invisible enemy sent destruction spinning down from a fine weather sky; poor old men bought a railway ticket and were trundled away again dead on a barrow; wounded women lay about in the station groaning'. They attacked other streets around the station, and at Spitalfields, bomb fragments broke a window at Commercial Street School. As the news spread, parents ran to save their children. Some even scaled the school walls in the rush to get them out. In the afternoon, fewer than 250 out of 900 pupils turned up for lessons.

Only a few minutes later and less than 3 miles away, it was a 110-lb bomb, not stray pieces of shrapnel, that struck Upper North Street School at Poplar. It hit the infants' class, killing fifteen children outright. Another three died later from their injuries, and twenty-seven more were maimed for life. Because it was a daylight raid, Londoners understandably assumed that the school must have been deliberately targeted, but it could just have been a tragic mistake. The school was only half a mile from quayside warehouses and railway sidings for the docks, which may have been the squadron's real targets.

Bombs also fell near the London Hospital in Whitechapel and around Aldgate. Casualties were rushed into the hospital in ambulances, tradesmen's vans and on hand-carts, or carried on stretchers and shutters. A bus that had been hit simply drove in with the casualties still on board. Altogether, more than 200 arrived in the space of one hour, and soon stretchers were blocking the corridors. Of the injured, 44 died, while 30 people were brought in dead.

Whether the civilian casualties were a mistake or not, the effect was devastating. That day, the Gothas killed 162 people and injured another 432 – nearly twice as many as in any other raid during the First World War. Not a single Gotha was shot down. Those who could afford it or who had friends or relatives outside London, began to get their children away from the capital, though there was no official evacuation.

Three weeks later, on 7 July, the Gothas were back. This time twenty-two of them hit Shoreditch, St Pancras and the City, destroying the Ironmongers' Hall in Fenchurch Street, the only City livery hall to suffer this fate during the First World War. The writer V.S. Pritchett reported seeing walls stripped off houses, carts overturned and dead horses among the crowds, as 57 people were killed and 193 injured.

As the atmosphere in the capital grew more and more jumpy, there were false alarms too. Twelve days later, all seventy-nine fire stations in the London area, now linked by special emergency telephone lines, set off their ear-splitting maroons. Londoners leapt from their beds and ran for cover. Enemy aircraft had been sighted over the Essex coast, but they never made it to London. On 24 September though, the alarm was all too real. A 110-lb bomb dropped outside the Bedford Hotel in Southampton Row; it killed 13 people and injured 26.

In December, for the first time the Germans tried systematic fire-raising on a major scale; 6 aircraft dropped 276 incendiary bombs and started 52 fires. Fire crews had to race in from as far away as Wembley and Twickenham to help their London colleagues. They managed to contain casualties so that only two died and six were injured. Disturbingly for the fire-fighters, it was clear that the bombers sometimes returned to deliberately target them as they struggled to get the flames under control.

In the face of this new onslaught, the government shook up air defence, putting the whole operation under a single commander, who established a line of anti-aircraft guns 20 miles east of London and trained pilots to patrol in formation and coordinate their fire-power with that of the guns on the ground. Other changes were made on the home front too. Professional firemen who had been conscripted into the forces were brought back to London where their expertise was sorely needed. The improved defences forced the Germans to turn to night raids, and approach from different directions to avoid the guns. The capital was attacked for seven nights at the end of September and the beginning of October 1917, with districts like Paddington and Westminster now finding themselves in the front line.

Soon the Germans had a new weapon. Before the end of 1917, the Gothas were joined by a four-engined bomber, the Staaken R-39, the biggest aircraft used against London in either world war, capable of carrying huge 600-lb bombs. Some Londoners took refuge in nearby open countryside like Epping Forest. Others got out altogether. Brighton was a favourite bolt hole, and East End clothing companies began to complain about how many machinists they were losing, but most Londoners stayed in the city. They sought safety underground, often in designated public shelters in the basements of buildings where families would settle in with bedding and even pets. One was at the Odhams printing works at Long Acre in Covent Garden. Early on the morning of 29 January 1918, a Staaken scored a direct hit on the works with one of its 600-lb bombs. Thirty-eight people lost their lives. Another twenty-nine died in other parts of London during the raid.

Another refuge was the Tube where, by autumn 1917, there could sometimes be more than a quarter of a million people taking shelter. The government was at best ambivalent. There was a fear that once people had gone underground, it might be difficult to get them out again; a fear that would resurface during the Second World War. Lloyd George complained in his memoirs that there was growing panic in the East End, especially after the raid of 7 July 1917, and that at the slightest rumour of approaching aeroplanes, Tube tunnels would be packed with panic-stricken citizens, and that every night London's commons were black with people, though other observers commented on the fortitude of the population. Certainly, there was some evidence of panic. A few hours before the bomb was dropped on Odhams, the firing of maroons was mistaken for the sound of falling bombs, and people stampeded for shelter at Bishopsgate goods depot and Mile End station. Fourteen were killed in the crush.

In fact, that night saw the last major bombing raid of the war in London. By 1918, air defences had been strengthened yet again, with Sopwith Camels stationed at six airfields in Essex to try to intercept the raiders. Bombing London was becoming an ever more hazardous activity, and on 19 May 1918, six German planes were shot down. After that, the raids were called off.

Altogether during the First World War there were 12 airship raids on London out of a total of 53 over the entire United Kingdom, and 27 by aircraft, with nearly 1,000 tons of incendiary and high-explosive bombs dropped. The dead numbered 670 (out of 1,413 across the country), with 1,960 injured. Damage to property was estimated at £2 million. The Kaiser may have wished to limit attacks to 'military' targets like the docks or railway lines, but bombs were simply not that accurate, and the houses of those living near the targets were just as likely to be hit as the targets themselves. The degree to which the docks were successfully targeted can be gauged from the fact that the total bill for war damage to the Port of London Authority's property all the way up to Teddington was only £3,000.

Just five years after the end of the First World War, the British Fire Prevention Committee wrote: 'Take it for granted that in the next war, cities will be bombed without warning; what has been done in the past will be altogether eclipsed by the horrors of future aerial bombardments.' At the time, nobody wanted to think a 'next war' might be on the way, but the government did appoint Wing Commander E.J. Hodsoll, a former Royal Flying Corps officer, as Special Assistant to the Home Secretary to consider what precautions might be necessary in the almost unthinkable event of further air attack. By the early 1930s, it was said there were cupboards full of his reports, few of which anyone had ever read. But even if the threat were taken seriously, what could be done? Many shared the view of three-times Prime Minister Stanley Baldwin that 'the bomber will always get through'.

Shortly after the end of the First World War, the RAF had attacked dissident Afghan tribesmen from the air and bombed the grounds of the Amir of Afghanistan's palace. During the 'low, dishonest decade' of the 1930s, the spectre grew ever more frightening. In 1936 Mussolini dropped poison gas on the Abyssinians. The following year, during the Spanish Civil War, the Germans and Italians dive-bombed cities, hitting Guernica on market day, and Bertrand Russell predicted that air raids on London would turn it into 'one vast raving bedlam'. By the late 1930s, the Air Staff believed that in an all-out 24-hour raid, 3,500 tons of bombs would be dropped and 58,000 Londoners might perish.

During the crisis over Czechoslovakia in 1938, when war sometimes seemed inevitable, many mothers left London for the country with their children, returning when the Munich agreement was reached, but the respite was short. By 1939, Hitler was demanding Danzig from Poland, whose safety Britain was pledged to guarantee. That summer, gas masks were handed out, and Londoners were given corrugated steel sheets to make primitive 'Anderson' air-raid shelters in their back gardens. Then, on 1 September, Hitler invaded Poland. London's railway stations were filled with children being evacuated, air-raid precautions began, the new Auxiliary Fire Service was mobilised, and at eleven on the morning of Sunday 3 September, Prime Minister Neville Chamberlain announced that Britain was at war with Germany.

Twenty-eight minutes later, London heard its first air-raid siren of the war. After half an hour, the 'all-clear' sounded. The alert had been caused by the sighting of an unidentified aircraft over the Channel. At a quarter to three the next morning, the same thing happened again. Many false alarms punctuated the first weeks of the war, but gradually they became a rarity. What actually transpired was not the dreaded air raids, but the so-called 'phoney war'. Hitler was wary of attacking London because he feared retaliation, so the first bombs of the Second World War in the capital came not from the Germans, but from the IRA (see Chapter 4).

Still, nearly 1½ million people, mainly women and children, left Greater London in September 1939. Some soon got miserable in unwelcoming billets, others were bored by the countryside, and many were not convinced that the places they had gone to, either near the east coast or close to important factories in Hertfordshire, would be any safer than London. So by Christmas, half had returned. Some unhappy East End children even made their way back on foot from Oxfordshire and Dorset.

London children may have found the countryside dull, but the capital to which they returned was probably quieter and more subdued than it had been at any time since the Great Plague. The Control of Noises (Defence) Act forbade the sounding of sirens, factory hooters and whistles, and even church bells. Then there was the blackout. At first, people just complained about getting lost, but during the long winter nights of December 1939, there were eight times as many fatal road accidents as there had been in pre-war London. When an elderly man was knocked down and killed in Epping, the coroner commented: 'I am convinced that a man of 82 has no right to be out at that time of night', but as the bombers stayed away, the regulations began to be eased. By the New Year, cars were allowed to use one screened headlight, people were permitted to carry torches of a sort, and West End shops could shine small lights on items at the back of their premises.

Such was the state of public nervousness, though, that relaxation of the rules was unpopular with many. When lights were provided at the entrance to a public shelter in Bethnal Green, they were sabotaged. A German-Swiss resident of Kensington was accused of using a lighted cigar to signal to enemy aircraft. An 83-year-old man in Kentish Town who showed a light had a mob pounding on his door and had to be taken into custody for his own protection, and an air-raid warden drew his pistol and shot out a light in a shop window.

By the summer of 1940, the 'phoney war' was drawing to its close. On 6 Jxune, the London region received its first bomb. It fell in open country in Addington. Two weeks later bombs fell in a field at Colney, and the region sustained its first casualty, a goat. When France fell, the Luftwaffe was able to move aircraft to just the other side of the Channel and while Hitler remained wary of targeting London itself, Londoners got used to the sound of bombs as airfields around the capital were attacked. When Croydon Airport was hit, ground staff said the bombers flew so low they could recognise the pilots as men who had flown Lufthansa airliners to the airport before the war.

Other targets included railway junctions and, on 16 August, a raid on the Wimbledon area left fouteeen dead and fifty-nine injured. Eight days later, the first bombs fell on the East End, dropped by mistake by a single aircraft, probably looking for the oil depot at Thames Haven near the mouth of the river. Churchill immediately ordered the RAF to retaliate, and forty bombers hit Berlin. The next night, the first bombs fell on central London, hitting Fore Street in the City, and almost completely destroying the ancient church of St Giles without Cripplegate.

Then at four o'clock in the bright afternoon sunshine of Saturday 7 September, the Luftwaffe flew in force over London. There were 320 bombers escorted by 600 fighters. Some observers could not help admiring their 'majestic orderliness'. They attacked Woolwich Arsenal, Beckton gasworks, West Ham power station and docks on both sides of the river. By day, or even on the darkest night, the Thames was always a wonderful aid to navigation, and high explosives and incendiaries rained down on the wharves and quays and on road and railway links. Inevitably, the terraced houses and blocks of flats among them were hit too. German intelligence had discovered that huge amounts of wooden scaffolding had been stored by the docks to help repair houses that might be damaged in air raids. The Luftwaffe attacked with oil bombs, 6-feet-long metal drums containing up to 50 gallons, that could throw burning oil over an area of 1,500 square feet and start enormous fires, and with small magnesium incendiaries that slid into every nook and cranny.

Soon a giant bonfire was blazing, which was not only enormously destructive but also acted as a beacon to draw in other bombers. The heat was so intense that telegraph poles would catch fire from top to bottom even though the nearest flames were yards away.

The wooden block road surface caught fire, and firemen, in danger of being cut off, had to run for their lives and abandon their equipment. The 'all-clear' sounded after a couple of hours, but the fires were still burning fiercely when the bombers returned two hours later. Wave after wave pounded the East End until after four o'clock on Sunday morning. Nine major fires were burning in East and West Ham. One fireman sent back a message to his control: 'Send every bloody pump you've got. The whole bloody world's on fire.'

Bombs fell on Victoria too, but the main damage was in the east, where destruction spread over Stepney, Whitechapel, Poplar, Bow and Shoreditch; the Ford works at Dagenham was also attacked. Worst hit of all was Silvertown. During the First World War, a factory explosion had flattened a large part of the area (see Chapter 9), but now it was enemy bombs. For hours the area was cut off by the inferno in the docks. Families desperately seeking shelter headed for the Thames hoping to find safety on floating barges. Some people took cover at the municipal swimming pool only to be killed when it sustained a direct hit. Water supplies were contaminated by a breach in the main sewer; gas mains, power cables and telephone wires were all knocked out of action. Virtually every fire engine in London went to the docks, and crews and vehicles poured in from as far away as Birmingham, Nottingham and Swindon. As was to happen often when fire engines were in short supply, London taxis and private cars were pressed into service to pull mobile fire pumps. At the peak of the blaze, 1,000 pumps were deployed at Surrey Docks, 100 others elsewhere in the docks, and 200 at Woolwich Arsenal. Witnesses said half a mile of the Surrey shore was ablaze. The Blitz had begun.

The death toll from that first attack was 430, with 1,600 seriously injured. One East Ender, seeing the destruction the bombers brought, exclaimed: 'Blimey, we've lost the war.' Then, at half past seven on Sunday evening, 200 bombers resumed the onslaught. For the next two months, apart from one November night when the weather was too bad for bombing, there would be no respite. Sunday night's raid killed another 400 people. As the bombing had begun on Saturday, several hundred families had been taken to

South Hallsville Road School in Canning Town to wait for evacuation to the suburbs. The school was close to a big power station and the Royal Victoria Dock. On Monday, a convoy of buses was due to take them to safer places, but, in the confusion, the drivers seem to have gone to Camden Town by mistake. Then they were hampered in their journey eastwards by blocked roads and diversions, and they did not arrive. The families settled down for another night at the school. The buses were to try again the next day, but before they could reach the school, the Luftwaffe came. At ten to four on Tuesday morning, it suffered a direct hit, and 400 people died in the rubble. No other single bomb that landed on Britain killed so many.

On 9 September, bombers had attacked London by day and by night, and killed another 370 people. The next night, flames leapt 200 feet in the air as St Katherine's Dock was gutted. By now, morale was low. A main sewer had been breached, contaminating the River Lea, and there were demands in West Ham for the evacuation of the whole borough. Even if people's homes were still standing, there was often no gas, water, or electricity, and basic services, such as milk deliveries, had broken down. Streets were roped off, and thousands had to leave their homes and take refuge in rest centres because of unexploded bombs. On mild nights, 5,000 people used to trek out to Epping and camp in the forest and fields of Winston Churchill's constituency. Others would have to pack into trenches in Victoria Park with water seeping up through the duckboards. At the same time, West End hotels offered wealthy visitors safe dormitory shelters. Not surprisingly, this fuelled resentment.

The Savoy was only 3 miles from London's biggest public shelter, the 'Tilbury', an underground goods yard off the Commercial Road, where up to 16,000 people would pass the night in filthy and grossly overcrowded conditions. Eight days after the Blitz began, 100 East Enders marched on the luxury hotel, and demanded admittance to its shelter. One of their leaders was Phil Piratin, who would win Mile End as England's only Communist MP at the 1945 general election. After a discussion, they were allowed in. The East Enders are said to have behaved politely, and some even tipped the hall porter as they left, but the protest sent a shiver of apprehension through the Establishment.

Less than forty-eight hours after the bombing began, a government intelligence report had noted: 'In dockside areas, the population is showing visible signs of its nerve cracking from constant ordeals', but the Home Secretary, Sir John Anderson, after whom the Anderson shelter was named, said he could see no sign of panic, and Churchill was reassured when he toured Stepney and Poplar. On 12 September, an 800-lb bomb, powerful enough to destroy the whole façade of St Paul's, landed in front of the building. It penetrated deep into the earth, but failed to explode. Very gingerly, it was removed and taken to Hackney Marshes. When it was exploded, it left a crater 100 feet across, and shattered windows half a mile away.

Public shelters were often unpleasant and insanitary, and in areas like Barking and Dagenham they were few in number, so most people had to rely on Anderson and Morrison shelters, steel tables with sides of wire mesh, which could not protect shelterers against a direct hit. The authorities, however, were reluctant to let people shelter in the Tube as they had in the First World War. It was that persistent fear that once Londoners had taken refuge below ground, they would never come up again, and London Transport posted notices at stations saying: 'During air-raids, passengers only admitted.' One evening, a big crowd gathered outside Liverpool Street station, demanding admittance. Soldiers were called to support the Tube staff, but the crowd would not disperse. Suddenly, the doors were flung open, the people entered, and eventually nearly eighty stations were used as shelters.

At Bethnal Green, uncompleted tracks that now form the Central Line were fitted out with bunks and became a refuge for 10,000 people. When there was heavy bombing, it was not unusual for more than 100,000 people to shelter on the Underground. One night when a count was taken, the number recorded was 177,000. Shelterers had to buy tickets. They were not allowed in before four in the afternoon, they could not bring blankets before half past seven, and they had to be away again by six in the morning.

It was not particularly comfortable. Mosquitoes were always a nuisance, and fierce winds would send bedclothes flying. Nor was there any guarantee of safety. The week after the stations were opened, 17 people died when a bomb penetrated Marble Arch station. In October, a direct hit on Balham Tube station sent a torrent of sludge and water onto the platform, burying 65 people alive. Three months later, a bomb bounced down the escalator at Bank and exploded on the platform, killing more than 100. In the first month of the Blitz, 5,730 people were killed and nearly 10,000 badly injured.

An average of 160 bombers would attack London each night, but the RAF soon made daylight raids too costly, and by mid-October the bombers were generally restricted to night operations. That first daylight raid proved to be the biggest of the war. Initially, the East End was worst hit, and some East Enders sought refuge in the west, but many returned quickly, because they felt unwelcome, or because more and more bombs were starting to fall on the West End. On 13 September Buckingham Palace was hit for the first time, and the King and Queen would probably have been seriously injured had it not been for the warm weather, which meant the windows were open, so lessening the blast. The BBC's headquarters at Broadcasting House was hit several times. On 15 October a bomb exploded outside the music library, killing six people. The newsreader paused for a moment to brush the dust off his script, then carried on reading. Madame Tussaud's lay in ruins, as did John Lewis. Bourne & Hollingsworth's store in Oxford Street was devastated too, though within days it was open again and serving customers among the ruins.

The devastation grew worse with the introduction of parachute mines, which usually exploded at rooftop level and caused more damage than conventional bombs. Some got caught in trees or were left hanging unexploded from street lamps or telegraph poles, bringing dreadful disruption. Then there were 'Molotov Breadbaskets', hollow metal shells carrying up to fifty incendiary bombs designed to detonate 100 feet above the ground, scattering them far and wide. Some incendiaries emitted a shriek as they fell, to terrify those on the ground.

At first, anti-aircraft guns were not used much against the bombers, the theory being that this left the skies open for night fighters, but hardly any German aircraft were shot down. In fact, over the course of the war, anti-aircraft fire killed many more Londoners than it did German pilots, through shrapnel or unexploded shells falling back to earth, but the government noted that morale improved when the guns kept up a steady barrage, and, besides, they soon became more effective. In September 1940, it took 30,000 shells to destroy a single enemy aircraft; by January 1941, the ratio had come down to 4,000, and the night fighters were withdrawn, so the gunners could blaze away. Unfortunately, as defences improved, enemy aircraft had to fly higher, and became less accurate, meaning they were even less likely to be able to hit docks or railway stations, and the homes around them were put at greater risk.

While the number of people killed by the bombing was far fewer than the government had feared, what had been underestimated was the destruction and the number of people who would be made homeless. Thousands who had been 'bombed out' were arriving at rest centres, usually set up in schools or church halls, in their night clothes, in shock, having lost everything. In addition, there were those who had to be compulsorily evacuated from their homes because of unexploded bombs. During the first six weeks of the Blitz, 16,000 houses were destroyed, with 60,000 seriously damaged, and more than 300,000 people needed rehousing. By mid-November, 40 per cent of all the houses in Stepney had been destroyed or damaged. In fact, during 1940 and 1941, one Londoner in six was made homeless for a time. Initially, repair work was mainly left to individual boroughs, but after the first six weeks of bombardment, they had only managed to rehouse 7,000 people. Sometimes the homeless were treated with extreme insensitivity by bureaucrats, and in the East End a priest had to break into an official food store to hand out rations.

No provision had been made in rest centres for a stay of more than a few hours. Clothing and blankets were in short supply, food and cooking equipment completely inadequate, and sanitation dreadful. In one centre at Stepney, 300 people had to sleep on the floor, there were 10 pails and coal scuttles for lavatories, 7 washbasins with cold water, and the only lighting was from hurricane lamps. No wonder the authorities feared outbreaks of disease.

Things improved when the government gave the London County Council a freer hand, and eventually 780 much better equipped rest centres were set up. Councils also began establishing emergency feeding programmes, and a Special Commissioner for the Homeless was appointed to concentrate on getting damaged houses repaired as quickly as possible. The economic disruption caused by the Blitz was enormous. When war broke out, the Port of London was the busiest in the world, and London's biggest employer. By the end of 1940, a third of its warehouses had been destroyed and the port had been reduced to a quarter of its pre-war capacity.

From November 1940 onwards, London suddenly found the pressure eased, as the Luftwaffe began to turn its attentions to provincial cities, but for another six months, the bombers returned on many occasions to attack the capital. One of the raids for which they returned was, architecturally speaking, among the most devastating of the war. It came on the night of 29 December 1940, a Sunday between Christmas and New Year, and became known as 'the great fire raid'. Offices, warehouses and churches in the City were locked up and deserted, fire-watchers were at home, and the raid was timed to coincide with low water in the Thames. When bombs shattered the water mains, firemen had to struggle knee-deep through mud to try to draw water from the narrow, shallow stream in the centre of the river's bed.

The Luftwaffe started 1,500 separate fires, which merged into two huge conflagrations. One ravaged half a square mile between Moorgate, Aldersgate, Cannon Street and Old Street. The Guildhall was badly damaged, and eight Wren churches were destroyed, as were the company halls of the Haberdashers, Saddlers and Parish Clerks. Throughout the Blitz, St Paul's had become a symbol of Britain's defiance, its dome standing aloof above the fire and smoke. That night, twenty-eight incendiaries hit the Cathedral. It was protected by the St Paul's Watch, a group of volunteers that included John Betjeman, who got to know every nook and cranny of the building.

As the bombs rained down, they ran around seeking out fire in every corner, requesting expert help from the fire brigade only when they needed it. The Cathedral survived the raid, but sadly 163 people, including 16 firemen, did not. Another 250 firemen were injured.

Meanwhile, public shelters grew less inhospitable. Bethnal Green provided a library of 4,000 books. The Tilbury had singing, though it was only allowed until ten o'clock in the main section, and in some Tube shelters the LCC ran evening classes. The Chislehurst Caves were also a popular refuge. They were regarded as safer than the Tube stations, and were certainly more spacious. Electric lights were fitted and lavatories and bunk beds installed. There was a canteen, and an old piano for sing-songs. Special trains were laid on and, at one point, more than five thousand people were making the journey every night. Others took to the basements of West End stores.

Most people, though, sheltered at home. Even at the height of the Blitz, only one in seven went to the public shelters. As the authorities had feared, some families did stay below ground for weeks on end, but most people continued to show the patience, resourcefulness and dogged determination that were needed just to get to work each day. Railway lines were blocked and stations damaged. Everywhere streets were closed, meaning the bus services that ran became mystery tours, but workers would climb aboard or take lorries, carts or anything else that could move. People even tried to go out for the night. *Gone With The Wind* ran for four years in Leicester Square, and cinemagoers would queue to get in while fire engines raced around, and fires burned a few hundred yards away.

Each day's bombing brought at least seventy breaks in London's water mains. This was quite a problem as 375 million gallons of water a day were needed for fire-fighting, so the authorities built a huge underground network of emergency water mains with diesel pumps to force water from the Thames to the areas most at risk. They also erected 1,400 steel tanks that could each hold 5,000 gallons, though they soon also held fish and chip wrappers, drowned cats and other debris. In winter, they froze over, and firemen had to use their axes to break the ice while flames raged around them. In addition, there were portable canvas tanks, and lorries that could carry 500 gallons of water. Breweries, laundries or other businesses that had their own artesian wells had to make them available.

A network of psychiatric clinics was set up to deal with an expected rash of neuroses caused by the bombing, but after the first two weeks, only one case had been reported, and in ten weeks, there were just twenty-three. Astonishingly, in spite of the fact that one Londoner in three was getting less than four hours sleep a night, mental health actually seemed to improve. There were fewer suicides, and drunkenness was halved. The left-wing intellectual Harold Laski remarked: 'The people are simply superb.'

Sporadic raids continued during the early part of 1941. On 13 February a single aircraft attacked Hendon, destroying 100 houses and killing 60 people. Four days later, a bomb fell on a public shelter near London Bridge station. It fractured a water main, and 63 people died. The Café de Paris in Coventry Street, which was 20 feet below ground, had been promoted as a very safe night spot. On 8 March, the band leader 'Snake Hips' Johnson was performing when a bomb went straight through the ceiling. Johnson was killed, as were more than thirty staff and guests. After the blast, looters prowled the club, ripping open handbags, and tearing rings from the fingers of the dead and unconscious. In fact, looting became such a problem that Scotland Yard had to set up a special squad. Nearly half the arrests it made were of civil defence workers.

In April, German bombers killed more than 1,000 people on the 16th and the 19th. Among them was a 101-year-old Chelsea pensioner, killed when the Royal Hospital was hit, but the pensioners scornfully dismissed any idea of evacuating the place. Three weeks later, with the moon full and the Thames very low, came the worst raid of the war, as bombers pounded the capital for five hours. The British Museum was hit and a quarter of a million books were burned. As fire crews fought the blaze there, and other fires in Bethnal Green and the Royal Albert Dock, at five to two in the morning, three bombs hit the Houses of Parliament. The House of Commons was gutted and Westminster Hall was set on fire. Firemen had no key, but a veteran MP picked up an axe and hacked at the door, enabling them to get in and save the ancient building.

Big Ben's face was scarred, though it struck two o'clock right on time, while Westminster Abbey was badly damaged, and Lambeth Palace, the Law Courts, the Tower of London and the Mint were all hit. Every main line station except Marylebone was closed. Seven hundred gas mains were fractured and, in East London, Beckton gasworks was blown up. In the south, fierce fires around the Elephant and Castle blazed till daybreak. Firemen soon ran out of water and it had to be pumped through 9 miles of hosepipe from the Thames and Surrey Canal.

The raid left 1,436 people dead; the heaviest toll of the war in a single night. One American observer noted that things must be getting serious – he could see City gents going to their offices in the mornings unshaven. But although Londoners did not know it at the time, the Blitz was over. The cost for Germany had been getting higher as radar transformed air defence. During the first ten days of May 1941, seventy German aircraft were shot down, the same number as in the first four months of the Blitz, but, more importantly, the *Führer* had other things on his mind. In June, he invaded Russia and, for two and a half years, London was relatively free from air attack.

With the bombers out of the way, at least for most of the time, the government tried to make London less depressing. A Special Commissioner was appointed with a brief to clear away debris and get roads and railways reopened. The unemployed were drafted in, as were soldiers, including Indians from the Punjab who specialised in railway construction. Derelict buildings were dynamited and the rubble carted off, leaving only the foundations, some of which served as emergency reservoirs. The housing repair programme was stepped up by bringing in building workers from the rest of Britain and Ireland and, by August 1941, more than a million homes had been made weatherproof.

There were still occasional attacks. In January 1943, two raids each killed more than 100 people in Shoreditch, Deptford, and St John's Wood, and a bomb on a school at Catford killed 38 children and 6 teachers, but the thing that struck many observers about London during the middle years of the war was its apparent normality.

'Business as usual' was the favourite slogan. Blackout regulations were relaxed; traffic lights could shine through a half moon instead of just a cross, pedestrians were allowed to carry undimmed torches and 8,000 evacuated children were returning to London every month. 'Double summer time' meant the clocks were shifted forward not one hour, but two, providing very long summer evenings to enjoy or to use 'digging for victory' in allotments.

One of the worst incidents of 1943 was a tragic accident. On 3 March, the BBC reported a 300 bomber raid on Berlin, and London braced itself for massive retaliation. As sirens sounded in the early evening, people headed for the shelters. Five hundred yards from Bethnal Green Tube station, a new battery of anti-aircraft rocket launchers opened up. People mistook the sound for falling bombs and there was a rush for the steps leading down to the station, where over-zealous shelterers had removed lamp bulbs so they would not help enemy bombers. Close to the bottom, a woman stumbled. Others fell over her and were crushed against the wall. In the panic, 27 men, 84 women and 62 children were suffocated or crushed to death, and another 60 seriously injured. No bombs fell anywhere in the East End that night.

On the whole, though, London enjoyed its respite, and the New Year of 1944 was seen in by huge crowds in Piccadilly Circus. Three weeks later, to almost universal surprise, nearly 450 German bombers struck. The 'Little Blitz' had begun. These were shorter attacks, hit-and-run raids more likely to last 15 minutes than several hours. On 28 January, the bombers were back again, and started 300 fires. A series of raids in February killed 1,000 people and, by mid-April, there had been 14 major attacks. Shelters that had been closed during the long spell of relative calm had to be reopened, and the trek to the Chislehurst Caves resumed. Attempts were once more made to get people to leave the capital, with the government offering travel vouchers to those prepared to go and find their own accommodation. Eight thousand children were evacuated, but, in spite of growing war-weariness, most stayed.

On 6 June 1944, the D-Day invasion began the liberation of occupied Europe, but rumours had been circulating that the

Germans had a secret weapon up their sleeves, a form of supersonic beam that could shrivel up whole acres of London in seconds. A week after the landings, a big explosion destroyed a railway bridge at Bow, cutting the London to Chelmsford line. The official story was that it was a German bomber that had crashed, but it was actually a V-1. The V stood for *Vergeltungswaffe*, weapon of vengeance. The '1' was meant to give the impression that this was the first of a whole series. Ten were launched on 13 June but five crashed on take-off and one disappeared into the Channel.

They were pilotless aircraft, flying bombs each carrying a 2,000-lb warhead, fired from sites in northern France, forerunners of the cruise missile. When they landed, they could damage houses and shatter glass up to quarter of a mile away. Because the V-1 sounded like a clapped-out car that might give up at any moment, it got the nickname 'doodlebug'. Londoners soon learned that after the engine cut out, you had 12 seconds to find whatever shelter you could, or just fling yourself to the ground, before the explosion. When bus drivers heard the dreaded moment of silence, they would pull over so that passengers could dive under the seats. For all the horrors Londoners had seen, there was something particularly chilling about this new kind of warfare. 'No enemy was risking his life up there,' said Evelyn Waugh, 'it was as impersonal as a plague.' There were desperate demands for action. Tottenham Council urged the government to destroy German cities one by one until the attacks were halted.

Two nights after the first attack, 244 V-1s were launched. Again, many exploded on take-off, often destroying the launch site, but 73 hit Greater London. The government was extremely reticent about revealing what it knew of this new weapon, and a deception plan seems to have been mounted to make the Germans believe the V-1s were landing 2 or 3 miles beyond the point where they actually exploded. The result was that most fell short of central London and landed south of the river, which was unfortunate for places like Croydon, which was hit by about 140 V-1s, or Wandsworth, hit by 124. Some, though, did reach central London. One fell in the garden of Buckingham Palace, where it demolished a summer house.

Another hit the Guards' Chapel in Birdcage Walk during a service on the morning of Sunday 18 June; 119 people were killed and 102 seriously injured, some of whom later died.

Londoners had got out of the habit of being bombed by day, and the doodlebugs could arrive at any time. For the first fortnight, more people were injured in Greater London than in September 1940, though fewer were killed, and destruction was more widespread, with 20,000 houses damaged each day. The worst day was 3 August, when 97 exploded. The V-1s brought horrifying new sights. Trees had their leaves blown off, but were left with shreds of human flesh hanging from them. After one explosion, a man stepped out from the doorway where he had been sheltering, only to be promptly cut in half by a sheet of plate glass falling from above.

The V-1 often ripped the roof off a house, but left the interior intact. So the authorities faced a major new problem – finding storage space for the furniture and possessions left exposed to the elements in roofless houses. In Croydon, 300 shops and 54,000 houses were damaged. In Sutton and Cheam, 18,000 houses were damaged out of a total of 22,000. Those whose homes were still habitable were urged to share them with those made homeless, but the results were disappointing, and it was hard to find accommodation for the hundreds of building workers drafted in to do repairs.

The government had built a number of deep shelters below the level of existing Tube stations, each with 8,000 bunks. When the V-1s arrived, some people virtually lived in them. Others got out of London altogether. By the end of August, a million people had left. V-1s were not actually that difficult to bring down. They flew at a constant speed and altitude in a straight line, but, at first, the anti-aircraft guns blazed away at them when they got close to their targets, so that they often fell where they could do most damage. Then guns were moved to the south coast to try to intercept the flying bombs. The new Meteor jet fighters could also shoot them down, and air crews learned how to tip a V-1's wing to send it off course. Each week, increasing numbers were shot down, so that, overall, more than half of the 6,725 fired at Britain were destroyed and, by the end, only one in six was reaching central London. As the attacks diminished, 20,000 evacuees a day started to return to the capital, often encouraged by their hosts in the country. On 5 September, after eighty days of relentless attacks, Montgomery's troops overran the last of the launch sites. The V-1s had killed nearly 5,500 people and injured 15,000 others.

Two days later, Duncan Sandys, the junior minister responsible for coordinating defences against the V-1s, announced the Allied success and declared that 'except possibly for a few last shots', London's ordeal was over. The last shots proved to be the loudest. At a quarter to seven the following evening, two thunderous explosions were heard at each end of London, one at Chiswick and one at Epping. Once again, the rumour mill got to work, given an extra turn by the blood-curdling warnings emanating from German broadcasts about a dreadful new weapon. The first official explanation was that gas mains had blown up. Once again the government wanted to maintain a news blackout, not letting the Germans know where their weapons were landing, but as more explosions followed, it became impossible to sustain the story. Some believed that London was under shellfire; others that this was a new kind of flying bomb with an engine that cut out later.

Whatever the weapon was, the explosions kept happening, and the effects were terrifying. A man who lived close to where one landed in Islington said: 'I thought the end of the world had come. The earth trembled, the very air seemed to vibrate.' When he went outside to investigate, he was astonished at the devastation. An area about 200 yards square had been flattened, with at least fifty houses swept clean away.

In fact, these were V-2s, ballistic missiles 45 feet long, weighing 14 tons, carrying a 1-ton warhead. They were launched from mobile sites in Holland, travelled at twice the speed of sound, and could reach London in four minutes. When they landed they could knock down a whole row of houses. Radar could pick them up, but there was no way of intercepting them, and no useful warning could be given. Most V-2s landed in the East End or in the suburbs to the east and north. The place worst hit was Ilford, struck by thirty-five of them, but West Ham, Barking, Dagenham and Walthamstow also suffered badly.

During the battle of Arnhem in late September, not a single rocket landed on London or the suburbs, but the British Army could not consolidate its position along the Lower Rhine, and the attacks started again. By the end of October, four V-2s a day were landing. It was only a month later that Churchill admitted that London was under attack from a new weapon. January 1945 was the worst month, and the worst day was 26 January, when thirteen landed.

The most devastating individual strike happened just before Christmas 1945, when a V-2 struck Woolworth's in the New Cross Road, while it was packed with shoppers. One hundred and sixty-eight people were killed; 1,000 men worked for 48 hours to release survivors, but 11 bodies were never found, including those of two babies. Almost as destructive was the V-2 that exploded at Smithfield while women were queuing for their weekly meat ration – 115 were killed. Other places struck included Selfridge's and the Chelsea Royal Hospital. Some found the V-2s less terrifying than the V-1s, because the rockets came without warning, and they did not fear they would have to spend the last few seconds of life in a frantic, undignified scramble for safety, but the government was alarmed. Having made no new Morrison shelters for a year, it now ordered 10,000, and raided supplies in other parts of the country to bring relief to London. At one point, it considered evacuating 85,000 civil servants, and hospitals were emptied as 25,000 beds were prepared for the expected casualties.

Finally in March, the launch sites in Holland were captured. One of the last V-2s to land on the capital hit a block of flats in Bethnal Green on 23 March, killing 134 people and seriously injuring 40 more. More than 500 had fallen on London, killing more than 2,700 people. Together the V-1s and V-2s had destroyed nearly 30,000 houses in the London area, and damaged more than a million. Meanwhile, the last serious attack by manned aircraft had come twenty days earlier when a dozen fighter-bombers managed to drop bombs on the capital at a cost of six shot down.

On 30 April, the face of Big Ben was lit up for the first time in more than five years, and just over a week later came V-E Day. American sailors and their girlfriends formed a conga line down the middle of

Piccadilly, the teenage princesses Elizabeth and Margaret slipped out of the Palace to join the celebrations and there were bonfires in Oxford Street and Green Park, but, perhaps because the war with Japan had still to be won, the festivities did not have the wild abandon of those that had greeted the end of the First World War.

The Second World War had caused a greater volume of destruction than any other disaster in London's history. It had been a sustained ordeal over six years, with the alert sounding in the capital more than 1,200 times, on average once every 40 hours over the whole duration of the war. London had suffered more than 350 raids, nearly three times as many as any other city in Britain. Nearly 30,000 Londoners were killed and 50,000 seriously injured, more than half of the total for the whole of Britain. Houses in London were three times as likely to have been damaged as those in the rest of the country. Greater London lost 116,000 houses, and was left with another 280,000 in need of major repairs. Another 1 million – half of the total housing stock – needed more minor attention. To take one example, the Borough of Acton said its 400 builders would have to work flat out until 1947 to complete even minimal repairs, and, because of the V weapon attacks, the number of homeless in London had doubled over the last year of the war.

To try to deal with the problem, the Minister of Labour, Ernest Bevin, toured the north, recruiting 45,000 workers, who had to be lodged in rest centres or requisitioned hotels, or even the Chinese Section of the Victoria and Albert Museum. The government also manufactured 125,000 prefabricated buildings for quick assembly on bombsites, with US servicemen often helping to put them up. People became angry at the number of large, dilapidated but habitable buildings that were empty in central London, particularly in areas like Paddington and Kensington and Chelsea, and activists began installing the homeless in them, especially if they were servicemen returning from the war.

One hundred and sixty-four of the City's 460 acres had been devastated. Of its churches, 18 were destroyed, including 14 by Wren; 17 Company livery halls were virtually destroyed, and 6 more were badly damaged. The halls and libraries of Gray's Inn and the Inner Temple were destroyed along with Staple Inn Hall. Stepney, Poplar, Bethnal Green, Bermondsey and Southwark all lost 15 per cent or more of their built-up area. Greenwich, Lambeth, Camberwell, Deptford, Hackney, Woolwich and Lewisham lost about 10 per cent. West London was less badly hit, but both Holland House and Chelsea Old Church were destroyed.

Just as after the Great Fire, London recovered. The bombsites were built on, the public buildings replaced. The City livery halls, such as the Brewers and the Butchers, were rebuilt, the churches, such as St Bride in Fleet Street and St Dustan in the East, were restored. In 1950, the reconstructed Chamber of the House of Commons was reopened, while the new, grander John Lewis store appeared in 1960, though one of the last sites to be built on, Ludgate Hill, was not developed until the 1990s. The war reinforced the flight of industry from the City, which lost half its factories and warehouses between 1938 and 1949, while the drift of population away from the East End also accelerated. After the war, between a third and a half of the population of East London moved away to new housing estates around places such as Hainault and Epping. However, what the war did not do was to reverse trends, so it produced only a pause in the growth of office building in the City and the West End.

The destruction also, of course, offered an unrepeatable opportunity for comprehensive redevelopment of the capital. It had been discussed as early as 1941, with the LCC commissioning Professor Patrick Abercrombie to come up with a plan. His ideas were bold, envisaging demolition of slums, the creation of big new parks and better roads. Unfortunately, the war was followed by painful austerity, and the plan never had a chance as immediate need quickly took precedence over the more visionary approach. In some areas, improved housing was built, but even in 1951, more than one in three East End homes had to share a toilet, and it was only in the 1960s that the slums really began to be swept away.

The Second World War may have been the disaster that brought the most widespread destruction, but it was also, surely, London's finest hour, earning its people a worldwide reputation for dogged, understated heroism. According to one of the official histories of the war, 'London, that is the people of London, symbolised to many onlookers the spirit and strength of resistance.' When the BBC broadcast defiantly to occupied Europe, the opening words would be 'This is London'. At the height of the Blitz, three New York City firemen were sent over by Mayor Fiorello La Guardia to see how their London colleagues were coping. One described riding through the wrecked streets of the blacked-out city on a fire engine – 'a jolting journey through a deep, dark tunnel. Bad enough while going but worse when one got there.' He could see what London was going through, but his assessment was unambiguous: 'The British will see the crisis through because they have got the guts.' Noël Coward immortalised Londoners' indomitable resilience in song:

> Every Blitz your resistance toughening,
> From the Ritz to the Anchor and Crown.
> Nothing ever could override
> The pride of London Town.'

FOUR

Terrorism

The first enemy bombings of the Second World War were inflicted on London not by the Germans but by the IRA. On 22 February 1940, under cover of the blackout, they planted devices at Marble Arch and in Oxford Street. Both caused injuries; the one in Oxford Street had been put in a waste bin close to a bus stop and, as it exploded, a piece of flying metal tore off a woman's leg. The following month, bombs went off outside Whiteley's and the Grosvenor House Hotel. While the war with Germany had been going for only a few months, these bombs were the latest episode in a struggle that had continued for centuries, and had first scarred London's streets more than seventy years before.

Back in 1867, two members of the Fenians, a group dedicated to the liberation of Ireland from British rule, were being held in Clerkenwell House of Detention awaiting trial. One was the armaments organiser, Richard O'Sullivan Burke. To try to forestall any attempt to free him, he was constantly moved from cell to cell, but he was allowed visitors, and they smuggled in invisible ink enabling him to communicate with his friends outside. The prison walls were 25 feet high and 3 feet thick at their base, but Burke spotted a section he believed had been weakened by building work. He pointed it out on a diagram that was smuggled out to a Fenian group in London. They agreed a plan. On 12 December they would explode a barrel of gunpowder against the weak spot while the prisoners were having their afternoon exercise, after throwing a white ball over the wall to signal to Burke and his comrade, Theobald Casey, that this was the moment to make their dash for freedom.

The Fenians had been heavily infiltrated by the security services and news of the plan soon reached the Home Office, but warnings of this kind were not rare and, when he was told about it, the prison governor was sceptical. Still, extra police and prison officers were drafted in. In spite of that, at the appointed time, three Fenians managed to trundle a beer barrel packed with gunpowder to the wall, and then throw a small white ball into the prison while the prisoners were walking around the yard. Things were always being thrown over the wall, so a prison officer simply picked up the ball to take it home to his children. Burke left the exercise line and stood by the wall, taking off his shoe as though he had a stone in it. Then he knocked it against the wall, but outside, the Fenians were having trouble. Three times they lit the fuse. Three times they ran for cover. Three times nothing happened. After the third attempt, the fuse was dangerously short, and, although the police did not seem to have noticed anything, a number of local people were beginning to take interest, so the conspirators gave up and rolled the barrel away again.

That night, they met and decided to have another try the next day. Burke and Casey's visitors went to the prison as usual, and presumably passed on the news, but the next day, the governor took the precaution of changing the exercise session from the afternoon to the morning, and it was noted how agitated this made Burke. Still, when afternoon came, no one stopped the Fenians from once again wheeling the barrel up against the wall, but at first they had no more luck than before getting the fuse to light. Meanwhile, passers-by were growing suspicious, and a woman went to alert a policeman. Just as he was about to investigate, there was a fearful explosion that rocked the whole area. The gunpowder had finally gone off, but it had done a lot more than knock the wall down.

When the dust settled, a hole 20 feet wide was revealed, and so was a scene of utter devastation. Most of the houses in Corporation Lane, opposite the prison, lay in ruins, and fourteen other streets were damaged. The main prison building had been hit by flying debris, and the exercise yard looked like a battlefield. It was littered with fallen bricks, masonry and shattered glass, though an explosives expert testified that if a prisoner had crouched where Burke had the day before, he would have escaped injury. Some cell doors had burst open, but rather than escaping, prisoners were wandering around bewildered. Others still locked in their cells banged on their doors in terror, while Casey shouted offers of money to anyone who would help free him. Sightseers were soon wandering into the prison through the breach in the wall, and the governor had to order blanks to be fired over their heads to disperse them. Firemen had a dreadful task trying to free people from their wrecked homes. One woman had been killed instantly, and three more people died as they reached hospital. Over the next few days, the death toll reached fifteen, with forty seriously hurt.

The police arrested three men they had seen loitering suspiciously outside the prison, one of whom turned out to be a police informer specifically posted there, and the authorities swore in more than 20,000 special constables. Eventually, six men were charged, including a 27-year-old stevedore named Michael Barrett, arrested in Glasgow a month after the explosion, who was alleged to have lit the fuse. His counsel produced six witnesses to testify that he had been in Glasgow at the time, getting his boots repaired, but the Lord Chief Justice dismissed the evidence, though he pointed out weaknesses in the cases against the other defendants, all of whom were acquitted.

Barrett was found guilty, and though he made an eloquent speech from the dock attacking the case against him, he was sentenced to death. On 26 May 1868, he became the last man to be hanged publicly in Britain, meeting his fate outside the gates of Newgate Prison. Burke was sentenced to fifteen years for treason, but was released under an amnesty in 1872 and allowed to go to the United States, where he became Assistant City Engineer of Chicago.

The Fenian attacks went on. In 1881, they were believed to have started a huge fire at the Royal Victoria Dock that caused £500,000 worth of damage. Two years later, they brought chaos to the Underground by setting off two bombs during the morning rush hour. In 1884, they exploded four bombs simultaneously in central London, including one at Scotland Yard, but, like most Fenian devices, they resulted in few serious injuries. In 1885, they bombed the Tower of London, the House of Commons, and Westminster Hall, but again caused little damage. The following year, the first

Irish Home Rule Bill was introduced, but rejected by Parliament, and over the next quarter of a century the debate over the island's status continued to rage. Ireland secured its independence in 1922, but only part of Ireland. The fact that Ulster remained British meant for some that Ireland was only 'half-free', and, in the bitter civil war that followed, the Irish Republican Army opposed the settlement.

Once again, just as the Easter rebels had risen during the First World War, with the Second World War looming, the IRA wanted once again to turn England's difficulty into Ireland's opportunity. On 12 January 1939, they sent an ultimatum to the Foreign Secretary, Lord Halifax, demanding British withdrawal from Ireland. Five days later, at six o'clock in the morning, eight bombs went off simultaneously in London and other cities. The biggest was at the Central Electricity Board's premises in Southwark. No one was injured, but the bomb caused extensive damage and the explosion was heard 2 miles away.

On the day of the explosions, posters appeared in London announcing the IRA's plans to bomb English cities. In February, Republicans planted time bombs in left-luggage offices at Tottenham Court Road and Leicester Square Underground stations. This time, two people were seriously injured. There were also explosions at St Pancras goods depot, and a coal store at King's Cross station.

In June, the IRA set off numerous incendiary devices in pillar boxes, and also attacked Madame Tussaud's and a number of banks, sometimes simply pushing a bomb through the letter box. Thirteen people were injured, including two young boys who suffered severe eye damage. By now, there was a massive police hunt for the bombers, and on 24 July 1939, the House of Commons debated the Prevention of Terrorism Bill which would allow the authorities special powers to detain and deport suspects. While they were discussing the new law, two bombs went off. One at Victoria station injured seven people, and another at King's Cross killed a man waiting to get on a train; fifteen others were injured. When the news reached the House, the bill was rushed through in five minutes.

The attacks continued into 1940, but a number of the bombers were caught and gaoled, and two who had been involved in a bombing at Coventry that killed five people were sentenced to death. By then, though, the Irish President, Eamon de Valera, was getting more and more worried about the extreme Republicans, and alarmed that their flirtation with the Nazis might jeopardise Ireland's neutrality during the war. He brought in a series of measures against them, culminating in internment without trial, and the IRA's campaign in England petered out – for the moment.

In the late 1960s, Roman Catholics in Northern Ireland began a determined struggle for civil rights, which was followed by inter-communal violence, the arrival of large numbers of British troops, and the appearance of the Provisional IRA in 1970. The following year, terrorism returned to London, with an explosion at the Post Office Tower that severely damaged three floors, and resulted in the permanent closure, for security reasons, of the revolving restaurant at the top.

There was a strong feeling in the IRA that the British took little notice of bombs in Northern Ireland. Dolours Price, for example, said: 'an incursion into the mainland would be more effective than 20 car bombs in any part of the North'. She and her sister Marian joined the Provisionals in 1970 and Dolours was put in charge of a new campaign planned for 1973. The idea was to plant a series of car bombs in central London that would be timed to explode only when the IRA team was already flying back to Ireland. The day selected was 8 March. Four cars were hijacked in Belfast and the owners were told they would be shot if they reported the loss. The cars were then resprayed, fitted with false English number plates, and packed with gelignite and home-made explosives. The Price sisters had been in London the year before the bombing, and had even been photographed standing with the policeman on duty outside 10 Downing Street. Another member of the team knew the city because he had worked in a restaurant in Jermyn Street.

On 5 March, two of the cars were brought over on the ferry to Liverpool and then driven down to London. The other two followed the next day. A customs officer stopped one of the vehicles when he saw it did not have a tax disc. He asked to see the log book, which the driver could not produce, but eventually he let them go.

The next day, the sisters went to the Royal Court Theatre to see a play about Bloody Sunday. At breakfast time the following morning, the cars were taken to their selected positions. One was driven to the Army Central Recruiting Depot in Whitehall; another went to British Forces Broadcasting in Dean Stanley Street, Westminster; a third was taken to the Old Bailey, where a policeman saw it being parked; and the fourth went to New Scotland Yard where it was left in a space vacated by a detective who had just come off night duty.

The timers were set for three o'clock in the afternoon and, by a quarter past ten, all of the team were at Heathrow. Meanwhile, at Scotland Yard police noticed that the car carrying the bomb was showing a 1970 registration number even though it was a 1968 model. When an inspector looked inside, he saw wires under the front passenger seat. Explosives experts defused the bomb, and the Anti-Terrorist Squad warned all air and sea ports that the bombers might be trying to leave the country. The Price sisters and eight others were captured at Heathrow. Detectives pleaded with them to say if there were any other bombs primed, but they were met with a wall of silence.

Just before two o'clock, *The Times* received a call using a recognised code, saying that four bombs had been planted, but only the one at British Forces Broadcasting was discovered and defused. The remaining two exploded just before three o'clock. Each car was flung across the road. One man was killed and 180 people injured, and there was serious damage to property. Although police had captured the bombing team, it did not stop the IRA. In September 1973, there were explosions at two London stations and at Chelsea Barracks. The following year saw a sustained onslaught, beginning with bombs in January at the Boat Show at Earls Court and at Madame Tussaud's. In April, fourteen bombs went off in London stores and shops. In June, there was an explosion at Westminster Hall, then the following month a woman was killed at the Tower of London. In November, a pub in Woolwich popular with soldiers was the target. Two people were killed. In December, as Christmas shoppers crowded the stores, there was a whole series of bombings, including attacks on Selfridge's and Harrod's.

For much of the early part of 1975, the IRA observed a ceasefire, but when the political concessions they had been hoping for did not materialise, they returned to the bomb and the bullet. The Army Council called off the ceasefire in August, and an active service unit in London planted five bombs in ten days. One in Kensington Church Street killed an army bomb disposal expert, and injured many other people. Then in September, a bomb at the Hilton Hotel killed two people. The IRA's target list also included upmarket restaurants, like Scott's in Mayfair, where they killed a customer. A second attack on Scott's resulted in four IRA men being captured after a six-day siege at a flat in Balcombe Street, Marylebone. For some time afterwards, the IRA leadership seems to have regarded London as too hot, but the capital was getting only a temporary respite.

Another IRA tactic was assassination. Among their victims was Ross McWhirter, co-editor of *The Guinness Book of Records*, who had offered a £50,000 reward for information leading to the arrest of IRA bombers, and Professor Gordon Hamilton-Fairley, one of the world's leading cancer specialists, blown up while out walking his dog by a bomb intended to kill a Conservative MP. Just over a month before Margaret Thatcher's election victory in May 1979, another Irish Republican group struck. The victim was Mrs Thatcher's close associate, Airey Neave, a war hero who had escaped from Colditz, and a determined opponent of the terrorists. The Irish National Liberation Army had attached a bomb to the underneath of his car and it blew up as he was leaving the underground car park of the House of Commons. Neave died of his injuries.

In the 1980s, the IRA turned their attention to military targets. An attack on Chelsea Barracks in 1981 killed two people. Then came the most devastating terrorist explosions in London for more than a century. At a quarter to eleven on the morning of 20 July 1982, the Blues and Royals were riding through Hyde Park on their way to the Changing of the Guard at Buckingham Palace. As they passed a parked car, a remote-controlled nail bomb was detonated. Flames burst high into the air and nails shot out like bullets. Windows were shattered for blocks around and bodies were flung across the street. Two guardsmen were killed and seventeen civilians injured. Horses hobbled through the haze of dust and debris, or lay on the ground in a writhing mass. Two hours later, musicians from the band of the Royal Green Jackets were performing at Regent's Park. As they played a medley from the musical *Oliver!* a bomb exploded under the bandstand, killing six soldiers and injuring four others, plus more than twenty civilians.

The following year, it was back to 'economic' targets as Harrod's was attacked again in the run-up to Christmas. This time, 6 people were killed, including 3 police, and 90 injured. During the IRA campaigns of the 1970s and '80s in London, altogether there were 252 bombings and 19 shootings, and 56 Londoners died.

On 7 February 1991, the official minute records 'a brief interruption to the war committee of the Cabinet'. The first Gulf War had just got under way and the committee was discussing the important question of how other countries might be persuaded to contribute to the cost. During the 1970s, the IRA had twice tried to kill former Prime Minister Edward Heath and, in 1984, they had come very close to killing Margaret Thatcher with a bomb at the Grand Hotel in Brighton during the Conservative party conference. In 1990, they began planning another attempt. This time, they were going to use a home-made mortar that would fire over the rooftops of Whitehall and hit 10 Downing Street.

In the autumn, they began making mortar shells from gas cylinders packed with home-made and industrial explosives, which they fitted into steel tubes fixed to a frame. The mortar's range was between 200 and 400 yards. They also bought a Ford Transit van and cut a hole in its roof. Then in the middle of the preparations, in November 1990, Mrs Thatcher was suddenly ousted from power and John Major took over as Prime Minister. But the IRA carried on regardless.

On the morning of 7 February, London had been surprised by a heavy fall of snow. At ten o'clock in the Cabinet Office, John Major, Douglas Hurd, the Chief of the Defence Staff and other ministers and senior officials were listening to a presentation by David Mellor, Chief Secretary to the Treasury. Meanwhile, an IRA man drove the van to the junction of Whitehall and Horse Guards Avenue, within sight of the Ministry of Defence, while an accomplice followed on a motorcycle. After parking about 200 yards from the target, the driver removed the makeshift cover from the top of the van, exposing the three mortar tubes. Then he set the timing device, leapt onto the back of the motorcycle and sped away. About eight minutes later, a policeman walked over to check the vehicle, which was parked illegally, but, as he approached it, the mortars went off with a huge roar and the van burst into flames as the pre-set incendiary inside went off. One mortar shell smashed into a cherry tree in the garden of Number 10, and exploded with a huge blast, spraying metal and wood about the garden. The Cabinet Room shuddered and flakes of paint drifted down from the ceiling, but the bombproof netting on the windows did its work, saving the War Cabinet from being showered with lethal glass splinters. No one was injured, and the meeting resumed in an underground bunker. Outside, in Whitehall, four people were slightly hurt. Eleven days later, the IRA struck again, when a bomb in a litter bin killed a commuter at Victoria station.

Next began a systematic attack on the economy. On 10 April 1992, a bomb weighing several hundred pounds went off in the City, destroying the Baltic Exchange and blowing the windows out of numerous office blocks, including the Natwest Tower. The tall buildings around the Exchange had confined the blast and funnelled it along the narrow City streets, spreading devastation. Three people were killed, and ninety-one injured; damage to property was estimated at £700 million, more than the compensation paid out for all the damage caused by thousands of bombs in Northern Ireland in the twenty-three years since 1969. The next day, another huge bomb at Staples Corner closed the crucial road interchange at the start of the M1 for months.

Just over a year after the Baltic Exchange bomb, on 24 April 1993 two IRA men left a tipper truck filled with a ton of homemade explosives in Bishopsgate. The bomb killed a freelance photographer and left the area deep in rubble, with damage estimated at £800 million. This latest attack revived fears that key financial institutions might move abroad to safer cities. To try to foil further attempts, the police had to put a 'ring of steel' around the Square Mile with vehicle checkpoints. From late 1994, the IRA observed a ceasefire for seventeen months. Then, at about half past five on the evening of

9 February 1996, warnings were telephoned to the media. An hour and a half later, a huge bomb exploded in Docklands. Half a ton of explosives had been left in a lorry close to South Quay station. Two newsagents were killed and dozens of people were injured, mainly by flying glass. A six-storey building collapsed, and the total damage was estimated at £85 million. A 29-year-old bricklayer from County Armagh was convicted of conspiracy to cause explosions and gaoled for twenty-five years. After spending two years in prison, he was released under the Good Friday Agreement in 2000.

That agreement stopped IRA bombings in London, but dissident Irish Republicans from groups such as the Real IRA continued to target the capital. In 2001, they planted bombs at postal sorting offices, at Hammersmith Bridge and at BBC Television Centre. They also attempted a rocket attack on MI6's headquarters. Potentially the most devastating attack was a car bomb in August in Ealing Broadway which exploded at midnight when the area was crowded with people leaving pubs and clubs, flinging debris 200 yards. Only seven people were injured, but many could easily have been killed. Still, Londoners might reflect with cautious relief that after nearly a century and a half of Irish terrorism, the first outrage remained the most serious.

Others imitated IRA tactics. On 17 April 1999, a nail bomb exploded in Brixton injuring fifty people. A week later, six people were hurt by a similar device planted in Brick Lane, and then on 30 April, the most lethal bomb was planted at the Admiral Duncan pub in Old Compton Street. This one killed three people and injured sixty more. What did all these places have in common? They were the haunts of minorities – black people in Brixton, Bangladeshis and Sudanese in Brick Lane, and gays at the Admiral Duncan, though, in fact, the three people who were killed were a pregnant woman, the best man at her wedding and his friend. Her husband was seriously injured. They had been on their way to see the Abba musical *Mamma Mia!* at the nearby Prince Edward Theatre. A 23-year-old man was sentenced to life imprisonment for the attacks, which were a chilling demonstration of how vulnerable a crowded city can be to the malice of the terrorist.

PART TWO

Fires

FIVE

Great Fires of London

After its destruction by Boudicca in AD 61 (see Chapter 1), the rebuilding of Londinium had proceeded quite slowly, but by the time Emperor Hadrian visited Britain in 122, it was once again one of the leading cities of the province – a bustling place of merchants, shopkeepers and manufacturers. There was a forum, a governor's palace, a fort, an amphitheatre, public bathhouses and a wooden bridge across the Thames.

During the eight years after Hadrian's visit, though, there was a serious fire, or perhaps a number of fires, that visited terrible destruction on Londinium. Over 100 acres were devastated from Newgate Street in the west almost as far as the present-day site of the Tower of London in the east. Some major stone buildings like the fort at Cripplegate, the basilica, the forum and the baths at Huggin Hill seem to have survived, but the close-packed timber-framed wattle and daub buildings, many of which probably had thatched roofs, appear to have suffered very serious damage. At some sites, excavations showed no sign of renewed occupation until the end of the second century. Others look to have been abandoned completely, and at others still, buildings that had been reconstructed soon fell into disuse. Within eighty years of the fire, much of Southwark seems to have been deserted, as well as significant parts of Londinium, and the big public baths at Cheapside and Huggin Hill were demolished.

According to some estimates, the population fell by two-thirds after 150. This decline was not caused by the fire alone. Another factor may have been the Plague of Galen, a disease brought back by soldiers who had been fighting in the east, which swept across Europe in 166–7. Some believe it was bubonic plague; if so, this was

53

the first of its many disastrous visits to London (see Chapter 13). The increasingly turbulent political climate may also have contributed. At the end of the second century, construction began on a great defensive wall around the city, but it would not be enough to save Roman London. During the centuries that followed, old Roman London would be completely deserted for a time, while the Saxon invaders established new settlements around it (see Chapter 1).

Between the time of Hadrian and the Norman Conquest there seem to have been at least half a dozen serious fires in London. During the seventh century, the first St Paul's Cathedral, built of wood, was destroyed, and with its houses of timber, pitch and thatch, with upper floors that almost met across the street creating a fearful wind tunnel effect at ground level, for centuries London was a fire waiting to happen. William the Conqueror did his best, bringing in a tough new law, the '*couvre feu*', or curfew. When a bell rang at eight o'clock at night, fires and lights had to be put out. Basic fire-fighting equipment was also provided – like buckets of water and hooks to pull burning thatch from a building so it could be put out on the ground. There may also have been grappling irons and chains to demolish houses and create a firebreak.

It is not clear whether the curfew was honoured more in the observance or the breach. After all, putting a fire out at night would mean having to get it started again on a cold winter morning; besides, Londoners might also have been tempted to defy the new regulation as a badge of resistance to the Norman occupation. What is certain is that it did not stop fires. Eleven years into William's reign, in 1077, there was another major blaze.

Ten years later, in the Conqueror's last year, fire struck again. The Anglo-Saxon Chronicle recorded that 'the holy church of St Paul . . . was burnt down, as well as many other churches and the largest and fairest part of the whole city'. London was burning yet again in 1093 and 1132, and then, in 1135, came a particularly big fire. It started the day after the Christmas festival in a house near Cannon Street and swept east to Aldgate and west to St Paul's, as well as burning down London Bridge, which was still made of wood. London Bridge, incidentally, was damaged by fire on ten occasions.

At this time, most people regarded fire as an act of God. The only way to avoid it was to pray. According to Thomas à Becket's twelfth-century biographer, William Fitzstephen, the capital in the 1170s was perfect apart from a couple of inconveniences, one of which was 'frequent fires'. (The other was 'the immoderate drinking of fools'.) In 1189, London's first Mayor, a goldsmith named Henry Fitzailwyn, tried to do something about it by insisting that houses should be built only of stone, that party walls should be of a minimum thickness, and that roofs should not be made of thatch.

Even if the new regulations were observed, which they probably were not, they did not stop the Great Fire of London. The Great Fire of 1212, that is, as many called it until 1666 (though some historians put the date at 1213). The fire broke out on 11 July in Southwark. It spread rapidly, destroying much of Borough High Street and the church of St Mary Overie, which stood on the site of the present Southwark Cathedral. Crowds poured onto London Bridge as it reached the houses at the southern end, some to try to rescue victims and put out the flames, others just to watch. Then the wind fanned the flames so that houses at the north end caught fire too, and the crowds were trapped. Boats appeared below to try to rescue them, but a saying of the time held that London Bridge was for wise men to go over and fools to go under, and many of the people who clambered down the piers to try to reach safety lost their lives in the treacherous rapids and currents produced by the narrow arches of the bridge. Writing in the late sixteenth century, the historian John Stow put the death toll at 3,000. It is very hard to accept that figure, but the loss of life was probably considerable and certainly far greater than during the Great Fire of 1666. On the bridge, many houses were destroyed and the chapel dedicated to St Thomas à Becket was severely damaged.

Further major fires followed in 1220, 1227, 1299 and 1428, the last destroying Castle Baynard, which had been built on the banks of the Thames at Blackfriars by a Norman who had come over with William the Conqueror. Then in 1497, it was the turn of a royal palace. On the evening of 21 December, Henry VII and his relatives had settled in for Christmas at Sheen Palace at Richmond when fire almost completely destroyed it. The flames spread quickly, leaving little time for possessions to be salvaged, though a £20 reward was handed out for saving the King's jewels.

After the Dissolution of the Monasteries under Henry's son, Henry VIII, a huge amount of land was released for building, and London became more and more crowded. By now, the better off were beginning to fit chimneys in their houses, but these were often made from hollowed-out tree trunks and caused so many fires that the Lord Mayor tried to ban them. 'Burned in his bed' became a regular description of the cause of death, especially when tobacco smoking became popular. Other risks arose from the many potentially dangerous trades to be found in residential areas like those of the bakers, potters and blacksmiths, all of whom needed ovens and furnaces, and often kept stocks of fuel, while inns had hay and straw. Warehouses would be thatched or roofed with timber, while shipyards would be stacked with planking, masts, hemp, rigging, sails, tar and turpentine.

In 1582, a waterwheel was built under London Bridge to supply enough power to work a pump that raised water from the Thames and drove it through pipes in the streets and, by 1600, the first fire engines were beginning to appear. These were simple machines consisting of a wooden cask or two attached to a handcart, with a squirt like a gun barrel to shoot water at the flames. Some needed a team of three to operate them, but they could propel no more than a gallon or two of water at a time.

In the early years of the seventeenth century, James I made another vain attempt to turn London into a stone-built city, but just eight years after his death it was caught up in another conflagration. St Magnus's Corner, by the Church of St Magnus the Martyr at the north end of London Bridge, had been an important spot in medieval London, a place where notices were read and wrongdoers punished. Close by in 1633 was the home and workshop of a needle-maker named John Briggs. The night of 11 February was cold, and his maidservant wanted to be sure she would be able to get the fire going without any trouble the next morning, so she left a tub full of hot ashes under the stairs.

It was something she often did but, on this particular night, it had disastrous consequences. Briggs's house and the one next door both burned down, and the fire spread southwards along the bridge, setting many more alight. Fortunately, there was little wind, but there was not much water either. The Thames was low and frozen. People had to cut open pipes in the streets and use brooms to sweep the water down towards the fire. At the Southwark end of the bridge, brewers used their drays to carry water to the flames. In spite of their efforts, the blaze burned fiercely all through the night and for part of the next day, and the new-fangled fire engines did not seem to make much impression. Around a third of the houses on the bridge were destroyed as well as fifty more around St Magnus. A number of people were killed, and the ruins were said to be still smouldering a week later. In addition to John Briggs the needle-maker's, those premises burned out included seven haberdashers, four hatters, four mercers, two grocers, a curate, a glover and a distiller of 'strong waters'. The flames were finally halted by a natural firebreak, the Square by the Chapel, an open space about halfway across the bridge.

After the fire, a commission was set up to investigate whether the houses that had been destroyed should be rebuilt or whether all the houses on the bridge should be demolished. King Charles I resisted the proposal to rebuild, but by 1647 he had been defeated in the Civil War and was in no position to resist any longer, so rebuilding began.

The rule of the Puritans that followed Charles's defeat positively buzzed with apocalyptic prophecies, with many believing that the Second Coming of Christ was literally at hand. Sinful Londoners were warned of the terrible judgement they faced. One preacher predicted 'a consuming fire', while another foresaw 'kindling sparks that will set all in a flame from one end of the city to the other'. What actually happened was that in 1660, King Charles I's son, Charles II, was restored to the throne at the head of one of the most spectacularly immoral courts in English history. Its ungodly antics gave the millenarian mood fresh stimulus. A Quaker foresaw a blaze that could not be put out: 'all the tall buildings fell, and it consumed all the lofty things therein.' Another walked naked through Bartholomew Fair with a pan of fire and brimstone on his head as a terrible warning. The year often chosen for the capital's reduction to ashes was 1666, because, in the Book of Revelation, 666 is the number of the Beast, who, among other things, can bring fire from heaven.

The previous year, London had suffered the terrible scourge of the Great Plague (see Chapter 13). The disease had struck during a parched summer, and had been followed by a long drought stretching right through to September 1666, by which time wooden buildings were tinder-dry.

1 September was a typically busy Saturday in London and Pudding Lane, just to the north-east of London Bridge, was, no doubt, as smelly as ever. This was where the 'puddings', in other words, the guts and entrails of animals, were brought down from the butchers' shops in Eastcheap to the dung barges on the Thames. A man named Thomas Farriner had a bakehouse there, in which he made ship's biscuit for the Royal Navy. He said that at about midnight he had wanted to light a candle and had gone downstairs to see if there were any red embers in his oven. There were none because the fire was completely out, so he had gone back to bed. An hour or so later, he was awoken by smoke. The downstairs rooms were already blazing as Farriner roused his wife, his son and daughter, and the maid.

When questioned later by the commission investigating the cause of the fire, Farriner would say that he just had time to notice that the flames were nowhere near his oven before he realised he and his family were trapped. The only escape was through the window and across the roof to a neighbour's house. Choking, they crawled to safety, but the maid was too frightened; she stayed in the house, so becoming the first victim of the Great Fire of London. At first the fire spread slowly and the next-door neighbour had time to remove his goods, but, unfortunately, Pudding Lane was in an area of narrow streets and alleys, packed with wooden houses; with few people around at that time of the morning to fight them, the flames gradually took hold.

At three o'clock, Samuel Pepys, who lived more than a quarter of a mile away in Seething Lane, was roused by his cook, Jane, to see the fire. 'I rose', he wrote, 'and slipped on my nightgown and went to her window. . . . I thought it far enough off, and so went to bed again and to sleep.'

About this time, the Lord Mayor, Sir Thomas Bludworth, had been called out. He took a look at the fire, and, in one of history's great misjudgements, declared: 'a woman could piss it out', whereupon he too went back to bed. It may also have been at this time that he was asked to authorise the pulling down of a shop and four houses to create a firebreak. The Mayor said he could not do so because of the uncertainty over who would pay for rebuilding. For those living near the fire, though, the danger soon became all too evident. Some ran out to throw buckets of water on the flames, and people living on London Bridge were awoken by the bells of St Clement, Eastcheap (which was to be destroyed in the fire), and shouts for help.

A strong wind was blowing the fire westwards through an area dominated by tradesmen's premises selling to the shipping industry, well stocked with inflammable goods such as timber, pitch, tar, hemp and flax. The flames were already threatening wharves along the Thames that were packed with timber and coal, and the odds against getting them under control were lengthening by the minute.

When Pepys got up at about seven o'clock, he records that he 'looked out at the window and saw the fire not so much as it was, and further off', but his relief was to be short-lived. 'By and by Jane comes and tells me that she hears that above 300 houses have been burned down.' Pepys walked to high ground by the Tower and saw 'all the houses at that end of the bridge all on fire, and an infinite great fire on this and the other side of the bridge'.

St Margaret's Church, by Pudding Lane, was already ablaze, and crowds had gathered on the bridge to watch the fire cross Thames Street and set light to St Magnus the Martyr. On the bridge itself, the fire had already taken hold of a much admired multi-storey block, put up after the fire of 1633, and built in wood instead of stone because of worries over its weight. Burning beams fell onto the wooden waterwheels below the bridge turning them into charred ruins before anyone could think of using them to pump up emergency supplies, and on the bridge debris from collapsing houses prevented any help arriving from Southwark.

Soon a third of the buildings on London Bridge were gone, but at this point, the capital had a stroke of good fortune. Rebuilding never had been completed after the 1633 fire, and the gap that was left, in addition to the 30-feet long open space at the Square by the Chapel, created enough of a firebreak to save the rest of the bridge, and with sparks carried on the wind spreading the fire to Southwark, the authorities pulled down enough houses to halt it.

North of the river, the intense heat was making it difficult to get close enough to fight the fire, while the wind continued to fan the flames. As one witness put it, 'now the fire gets mastery and burns dreadfully; and God with his great bellows blows upon it!' At about half past eight, Pepys hired a boat and went on the river. Already, people were trying desperately to get their possessions to safety: 'Everybody endeavouring to remove their goods, and flinging them into the river or bringing them into lighters that lay off.' Pepys watched with alarm as the wind drove the flames into the City, 'everything, after so long a drought, proving combustible, even the very stones of the churches'. What he found most disturbing was the absence of any coordinated effort to halt the blaze, 'having stayed and in an hour's time seen the fire rage every way, and nobody to my sight endeavouring to quench it'. So Pepys raced off to the Palace of Whitehall, where the King and his brother, the Duke of York (the future King James II), were praying in the chapel. 'People came about me and I did give them an account dismayed them all; and word was carried in to the King, so I was called for and did tell the King and Duke of York what I saw, and that unless his Majesty did command houses to be pulled down, nothing could stop the fire.' The King then sent Pepys with instructions to the Lord Mayor 'to spare no houses but to pull down before the fire every way'.

After his first dismissive assessment of the fire, Bludworth had soon been roused again. Pepys went off to find him; 'walked along Watling Street as well as I could, every creature coming away loaden with goods to save – and here and there sick people carried away in beds'.

Eventually, Pepys found his quarry 'like a man spent, with a handkercher about his neck. To the King's message, he cried like a fainting woman, "Lord, what can I do? I am spent. People will not obey me. I have been pulling down houses. But the fire overtakes us faster than we can do it."' That was the end of the encounter and Pepys went home, 'seeing people all almost distracted and no manner of means used to quench the fire'.

Fortunately, the King happened to be interested in firefighting, and would often row along the Thames looking for a good blaze at which he could direct operations. By the afternoon, he and the Duke of York had themselves come to give orders for houses to be pulled down, though some thought it might be too late. In the close-packed streets, it took an enormous amount of effort to pull down enough buildings to make a firebreak. They had to be dragged down by men with fire hooks, but the strong wind quickly blew the flames across narrow gaps, and there were no carts and no time to move out of harm's way the fallen timber and thatch or the inflammable materials with which many of the buildings were packed. It was beginning to look as though the only real hope would be to try to stop the fire at a major thoroughfare like Cornhill or Cheapside.

Not only were the water pumps out of action, but the level of the river was very low. Firefighters cut pipes to provide a supply where they needed it at that moment, but that meant there would be no water further off if the flames spread. Burning debris carried on the wind was now spreading the fire at an alarming speed, with, it was said, a hundred houses an hour being consumed. Queen Christina of Sweden's principal confidential secretary, who was on a visit to London, had lunch at Covent Garden with a 'fine company', some of whom were to get back home only to find 'their houses gone up in fire and smoke'.

The Nonconformist minister the Revd Thomas Vincent lamented that 'London, so famous for wisdom and dexterity, can now find neither brains nor hands to prevent its ruin.' Even when firefighters managed to lay their hands on the few engines that were available in the City, it was impossible to manoeuvre them along the narrow alleyways where the flames had taken hold, in the face of the crowds trying to escape with their belongings. Pepys was in a gloomy mood, seeing little hope of the flames being halted, with the houses 'so very thick thereabouts, and full of matter for burning, as pitch and tar, in Thames Street – and warehouses of oil and wines and brandy and other things'.

People were still trying to get their goods into lighters on the river, but with no quay along the north bank of the Thames, access was difficult, so other places had to be found. Pepys saw 'the churches all filling with goods, by people who themselves should have been quietly there at this time . . . the streets full of nothing but people and horses and carts loaden with goods, ready to run over one another, and removing goods from one burned house to another'. The belief that churches would be resistant to the flames proved a miscalculation.

On Sunday evening, Pepys crossed the river to escape to the cool of an alehouse at Bankside. He could see people's worldly possessions on lighters, or sometimes just floating in the river. Facing the wind, 'you were almost burned with a shower of firedrops', and, as darkness fell, the fire 'appeared more and more, and in corners and upon steeples and between churches and houses, as far as we could see up the hill of the City, in a most horrid malicious bloody flame, not like the fine flame of an ordinary fire'. The north bank was framed in an arch of fire. 'It made me weep to see it', wrote Pepys. 'The churches, houses, and all on fire and flaming at once, and a horrid noise the flames made, and the cracking of houses at their ruin.' By the end of that first day, the fire had burned half a mile of the riverfront. The halls of the Fishmongers', Dyers' and Watermen's Companies had been destroyed and at least four churches had been gutted, including St Magnus the Martyr.

Pepys returned home 'with a sad heart'. By now, the threat to his own house was clear and imminent – 'the noise coming every moment of the growth of the fire, so we were forced to pack up our own goods and prepare for their removal'. He spent the night shifting furniture into the garden and preparing to save what he could. At four o'clock in the morning, a cart appeared to take away

Pepys's treasured possessions, money, plate and his famous diary, to a friend's house in Bethnal Green, 'riding myself in my nightgown in the cart; and Lord, to see how the streets and highways are crowded with people, running and riding and getting of carts at any rate to fetch away things'. Many cart-owners were charging astonishing sums of up to £30 to carry people's goods to the fields of Bethnal Green or Soho.

The fire blazed on through the night, but by dawn on Monday it had still destroyed only a relatively small part of the area within the City walls. During the following day, however, it made considerable progress. Still driven by the wind, it spread westwards, destroying some twenty churches. An attempt was made to stop it with a firebreak at Queenhithe market place on the river, but the flames marched on. Then there were hopes that the stone walls of Castle Baynard might be the place to check it, but the castle met the same fate as 200 years before, and only one turret was left standing.

The fire also advanced northwards, moving through the area beyond Thames Street and crossing Cannon Street. For some time, more drastic measures to halt it had been suggested, like blowing up houses with gunpowder, but powerful men whose property would have been destroyed were not keen on the idea. As the fire approached Cornhill, houses on the south side were pulled down, but timber that had been left in the street caught fire and the flames continued unchecked. By now, the fire was so strong it was also able to advance against the wind, and went up Gracechurch Street and Fenchurch Street. It was starting to destroy the areas where the better off lived, and they were desperate to get their money out, though that did not always make them generous. One alderman who had £10,000 in a chest was said to have given a £4 reward to those who helped him save it.

To stop the firefighters being hampered, attempts were now being made to stop carts coming near the fire to remove people's goods, but in vain. Pepys managed to find a lighter by Tower Dock in which to put the rest of his possessions, 'and we did carry them (myself some) over Tower Hill, which was by this time full of people's goods'. The authorities were alarmed at the creation of this potential looters' paradise with people's possessions lying invitingly in open spaces around the City walls, and the City's trained bands, the militia, were assigned to guard it, while the militias from three neighbouring counties were ordered to assemble near London to be prepared to relieve them.

There was widespread suspicion that the fire was the result of arson. England was at war with Protestant Holland and it was feared it might be a reprisal for an English attack on a Dutch town. In Westminster, a Dutch baker heating his oven to make bread was accused of trying to set the city on fire, dragged out and beaten within an inch of his life. On the other hand, Londoners always felt they were a target for Papists, and with the French now fighting on the side of the Dutch, suspicions grew more feverish. One Frenchman was felled by a blow from an iron bar, while tennis balls found in another Frenchman's chest were assumed to be fireballs. But paranoia showed little discrimination and all foreigners were at risk. The servant of the Portuguese ambassador was seized by a mob. He had been clearly seen putting a fireball on the windowledge of a house – except that it turned out to be pieces of bread he had picked up in the street. A member of the Swedish ambassador's retinue was only saved from being hanged from a house sign by the timely chance appearance of a troop of the Duke of York's bodyguard. Anyone with a foreign accent was liable to be taken into custody for their own protection.

By early Monday evening, moving against the wind, the flames had reached Billingsgate, and were only just over 300 yards from the Tower. A desperate call went out for volunteers to defend it, and the naval dockyards at Woolwich and Deptford were asked to send all their fire engines. To the west, the fire had now reached Blackfriars, and there was precious little water to be had from anywhere to fight it. By the end of the day, the halls of the Cutlers', Vintners' and Salters' Companies had all been gutted, and among the churches destroyed were St Mary-at-Hill and St Michael Paternoster Royal, where Dick Whittington was buried.

The Royal Exchange, built by Sir Thomas Gresham almost a century earlier, was also burned to the ground. The East India

Company had leased the cellars for storing pepper, and a heady aroma of roasted spices filled the air. Sir Thomas's statue toppled over, but remained intact. By now, the King had put the Duke of York in charge of fighting the fire, and the firefighters did achieve one notable success, when, with the flames struggling against the wind, they managed to stop the blaze at the high stone walls of Leadenhall.

Tuesday was to prove the most destructive day. One of the criticisms made of the firefighting so far had been that firebreaks had been created too near the flames, and that if they had been made further away, it would have given the firefighters more time to organise. So the Duke of York ordered houses to be demolished along the line of the Fleet River, present-day Farringdon Street, from Holborn Bridge to the Thames, but again hopes were disappointed.

The flames raced down Ludgate Hill and by midday they were across the Fleet. In Fleet Street, the fire raged so fiercely that the firefighters had to withdraw. The Duke of York's strategy might not have worked, but he could not be faulted for effort. Once he had to run for his life as flames nearly reached him. He and the King could be seen up to their ankles in water, carrying buckets and using fire engines to play water on the flames for hours on end, or climbing onto the roof of a building to assess the situation. The King's fine costume was soaked and clogged with mud, and now and then he would pause to toss gold coins to reward the efforts of those fighting the fire.

These were dark hours, with firefighters growing increasingly exhausted, water in short supply and the wind still blowing strongly. The flames had reached Cheapside, one of the City's grandest streets, and were threatening to engulf the Guildhall. By six o'clock in the evening, they were at the Temple. With fears that the fire might even reach Whitehall Palace, the King's main London residence, his treasures were already being shipped away by river to Hampton Court, and preparations were being made to remove the Exchequer from London. Pepys, meanwhile, was digging a pit in his garden to bury his wine and a Parmesan cheese.

The City wall to the north of Ludgate failed to halt the fire and it ran right up to Holborn Bridge, destroying Christ Church, one of the most impressive City churches. Now, though, an even greater church was under threat, St Paul's Cathedral, once the biggest in Europe. Flames were spreading towards the wooden scaffolding that surrounded the building during restoration work. Then, at about eight o'clock at night, burning debris fell onto the roof and set it alight. Many people had carried their goods into the building, believing it to be a safe haven, but now it was doomed. The church burned for hours, the famous choir roof fell in and crashed through the floor destroying a huge stock of books. The diarist John Evelyn wrote of stones flying from the building like grenades, molten lead running down the streets and the pavements glowing red.

As things grew ever more desperate, the King issued a proclamation calling for churches, chapels, schools and other public buildings in Middlesex, Essex and Surrey to be opened to receive goods that Londoners were having to remove from their houses. Meanwhile, it was beginning to look as though the next major task might be to save the Tower of London. If the flames were to reach the gunpowder store in the White Tower, the consequences could be catastrophic. Pepys walked to Tower Street, 'and there saw it all on fire at the Trinity House on that side and the Dolphin tavern on this side, which was very near us – and the fire with extraordinary vehemence'. Buildings near the Tower were blown up or, in some cases, shot down by cannons, and, fortunately, the wind was still blowing to the west.

At about two o'clock on Wednesday morning, Pepys was once again woken. 'My wife calls me up and tells us of new cries of "Fire" – it being come to Barking Church, which is the bottom of our lane.' He took his wife, his maid and his gold by boat to Woolwich, getting back home at about seven o'clock, and finding to his surprise that his house was not on fire, and that the church had been saved too. He took the opportunity to climb to the top of the steeple, 'and there saw the saddest sight of desolation that I ever saw. Everywhere great fires. Oil cellars and brimstone and other things burning . . . I walked into the town and find Fenchurch Street, Gracious St all in dust.'

In fact, there had been a crucial development. The wind had dropped and the firefighters had begun to get the upper hand, halting the flames at Fetter Lane and Shoe Lane, and then dousing them. They were halted too almost at the gates of the Tower. By midday, the fire had been put out at Holborn Bridge, and by evening nearly all the fires to the west of the City had been extinguished. The firefighters were now able to close in on the remaining flames and, although there was a further outbreak at the Temple, by Thursday morning the worst was over, and the militia was able to begin clearing the streets and damping down the ruins. Pepys could now savour some of the spectacle of the firefighting. 'It was pretty', he wrote, 'to see how hard the women did work in the canals sweeping of the water, but then they would scold for drink, and be as drunk as devils.'

Even when the flames seemed to have been extinguished, for weeks after there were worries they might be blown into life if the wind got up again. Pepys talked of how hot the ground was, and Evelyn reported climbing over great mounds of smoking rubbish. It was only when October brought ten days of rain that the embers were finally doused, but for months fires smouldered in cellars and tallow and oil would burst into flames when they were exposed to the air. It was unsafe to go out at night because of scavengers sifting through the ruins, and Pepys got into the habit of keeping his sword drawn.

In five days, the Great Fire destroyed more of the City than the Blitz. More than 436 acres were stricken, and only 75 acres inside the walls escaped. More than 13,000 houses – one in every three – burned down, as well as 87 churches, 52 livery halls and other notable buildings such as the Royal Exchange, the Custom House and Newgate Prison. The Guildhall was gutted. So much had been destroyed that you could see from one end of the City to the other and to the river from Cheapside. Burned papers from the fire were found as far away as Cranbourne and Eton. Some 70,000 people were made homeless. Astonishingly, the death toll was only half a dozen.

Evelyn said it was like a city 'laid waste by a cruel enemy', and much of the rest of Europe was convinced that London was finished as a great centre of trade and commerce. The clergy presented the fire as a severe judgement, but also as a sign of God's mercy on the grounds that it could have been much worse, and a national fast day was held on 10 October.

For months afterwards many Londoners had to camp in the fields at Lincoln's Inn or Gray's Inn, or on Covent Garden's piazza, or yet further afield at Highgate and Islington, often in tents made from canvas they had been given by the Navy yards. With so many markets destroyed by the fire, the King had to make special arrangements to ensure food was delivered to them and, in the winter that followed, far more died from the hardships of living outside than had perished in the fire.

Often those who had lost their homes were left virtually destitute. 'I met with many people undone,' wrote Pepys, 'and more that have extraordinary great losses.' A favourite topic of conversation was the meanness of the rich towards those who had helped them. Pepys told the story of a very rich alderman, who, 'after our men had saved his house, did give 2s 6d among thirty of them, and did quarrel with some that would remove the rubbish out of the way of the fire, saying that they came to steal'.

Pepys complained that he could not find anywhere to buy a shirt or a pair of gloves and so many premises had been destroyed that business was in chaos, with customers and suppliers unable to find each other, but not for the first time London showed a remarkable resilience. On London Bridge, shopkeepers quickly set up in the ruins, and markets reopened within a week. Workmen were soon at Pepys's house repairing and refurbishing it, and within two weeks he and his wife were back at home. On the very day the flames were finally extinguished, Charles II was informed that some people were already preparing to start rebuilding, but within three days he had issued a proclamation that no work should be done before new regulations had been drawn up. Some believed that the rebuilding should be carried out according to a comprehensive grand plan and, by 11 September, Sir Christopher Wren had submitted one, but there was neither the administrative machinery nor the money to implement it.

The government tried to control reconstruction. Buildings were to be of brick, and major thoroughfares such as Fleet Street and

Cheapside would have to be wide enough to stop flames spreading across them. There was also an attempt to get rid of courts and alleys, but the rules were greatly watered down before rebuilding began in earnest in the spring of 1667. A special tax on coal was levied to raise money for the rebuilding of fifty-two churches, including St Paul's Cathedral, all designed by Sir Christopher Wren.

Before the fire, St Paul's had been in a poor state, and a plan to rebuild it with a lofty dome had been agreed just days before. The fire put everything back into the melting pot, and it was only in 1675 that the design was finally agreed and the foundation stone laid, although the new church did not come into use until 1697. The Guildhall was restored by 1674, and nearly all of the livery halls that had been destroyed were rebuilt, as were the Royal Exchange, the Custom House and Newgate Prison.

House building, by contrast, was relatively slow, and even by the 1690s, not enough had been put up to replace those lost in the fire, though some of the new houses were bigger. It was estimated that about 20,000 people, many of them small tradesmen and craftsmen, never returned to the City. Shops selling luxury goods were especially likely to move to the Strand and the West End.

The smoke may have dispersed, but the air was still thick with conspiracy theories. The King, who did not have much time for them, ordered an inquiry by the Privy Council. The effect, though, was not to dampen down speculation over the fire, but to stoke it up. The fact that a pile of daggers was found in a house where Frenchmen had allegedly been staying was enough to set the rumour mill turning at frantic speed. Thomas Farriner, in whose house the fire appeared to have started, was understandably anxious to persuade the inquiry that he was not to blame. To support his case, he claimed that faggots that had been put in his oven to dry were recovered intact afterwards.

Some members of the inquiry were openly sceptical, like the Earl of Clarendon who could not help smiling at the tales to which he was obliged to listen. The inquiry decided that the fire had been caused by 'the hand of God, a great wind and a dry season'. This conclusion, though, came three months too late to save the life of a watchmaker from Rouen, one Robert Hubert, who was arrested at Romford, apparently trying to flee the country. In his original story, the Frenchman said he had thrown a fireball near Whitehall Palace, but later changed his account, claiming that he and another Frenchman had pushed fireballs into the windows of Farriner's house early on the morning of 2 September. Farriner said that there was no window in the place he described, but Hubert found the ruins of the house easily, and described its appearance before the fire. This was considered adequate evidence on which to hang him, and the sentence was carried out on 29 October. Hubert was described as 'a poor, distracted wretch, weary of this life', and scarcely anyone in authority believed he was guilty.

The Monument to the fire was built close to the site of Thomas Farriner's house. It was 202 feet high, and the inscription on it read: 'This pillar was set up in perpetual remembrance of the most dreadful burning of this Protestant City began and carried on by treachery and malice of the Popish faction.' A similar message was put on the outside of Farriner's house. Seven years after the fire, the Duke of York converted to Roman Catholicism, and thereafter his heroic efforts to fight it were forgotten, and the popular imagination put him down as one of the Papist conspirators who had started the Great Fire of London.

SIX

Enter the Firemen

After the Great Fire of 1666, there was a major shake-up in London's fire regulations. The City was divided into four districts, each of which had to provide 800 buckets and 50 ladders, as well as shovels, pick-axes and hand-held squirts. Each of the twelve main livery companies had to supply a fire engine, and aldermen were required to have firefighting equipment at their homes. Better advice was also given to householders. To quell a chimney fire, for example, rather than firing a gun up it, the new recommendation was to hold a wet sheet across the hearth. The fact that housing in the City was now less dense and that more fire-resistant materials were being used also helped to reduce the risk.

In the meantime, many businessmen bankrupted by the fire languished in the debtors' prison. This spectacle helped spawn a whole new business, fire insurance. Its unlikely father had been christened 'Christ Came Into the World To Save' or 'If Christ Had Not Died Thou Hast Been Damned' Barbon (he was one of two twins thus christened, and no one seemed to know which of them he was), but had understandably taken the first name Nicholas instead. His father was 'Praise God' Barbon, a pious Puritan after whom Cromwell's Barebones Parliament was named.

The son became a property speculator and, in 1680, began offering insurance policies which promised clients the services of watermen as firefighters, or the rebuilding of their premises if these efforts failed to save them. This was the beginning of professional firefighting in London and soon Barbon's company had many imitators. Policyholders were given signs to put up to show which company insured them and initially firemen would not fight fires at premises covered by other insurers.

Meanwhile, the city continued to burn. Less than ten years after the Great Fire, in the early hours of 26 May 1676, letter carriers spotted flames in the basement of an oil shop in Borough High Street, but before they could break the door down, the oil had exploded and the fire spread to neighbouring buildings. Once again, the King himself appeared to direct operations, and was said to have been very interested to watch a new fire engine that was able to squirt great quantities of water with enormous force. Showing the kind of decisiveness that might have made quite a difference in the early stages of the Great Fire, the authorities blew up densely packed houses in the path of the flames, as well as the old courthouse and the gaol, and managed to save Southwark Cathedral and St Thomas's Hospital. Unfortunately, several people were killed in the blast, and the number of buildings destroyed by fire still reached about 500, including several brothels and historic taverns, among them the Tabard, where Chaucer had his pilgrims meet in *The Canterbury Tales.*

One legacy of King Charles II's interest in firefighting was a set of strict fire regulations for Whitehall Palace. The Palace, acquired by Henry VIII from Cardinal Wolsey and then extended, became the greatest in Europe eventually covering 23 acres between St James's Palace and the Thames. There was good reason for the King's concern. In 1619, two workmen accidentally set fire to some clothes in the Banqueting House. The flames spread to the roof, and they were unable to put them out. Afraid of getting the blame, they had shut the doors and made a run for it. They were caught and sent to prison, but the Banqueting House was burned down, and there had been fears for the whole Palace. In spite of Charles's new precautions, six years after his death, in 1691, a 'sudden and terrible' fire began in what had been the apartments of his mistress, the Duchess of Portsmouth. The eight-hour blaze destroyed them and much of the south part of the palace which housed, in Evelyn's words, 'lodgings of such lewd creatures who debauched King Charles'.

The fire of 1691 should have acted as a terrible warning, but it did not. Just seven years later, on the evening of 4 January 1698, a servant put out some linen to dry by a fire in an upper room of the palace, and then left it unattended. The linen caught fire and soon ignited the whole room. By the time the alarm was raised, it had taken such a hold that the fire engines were unable to put it out. It raged for sixteen hours, and the only complete buildings left standing were the Holbein Gate and the rebuilt Banqueting House, with its magnificent Rubens ceiling. A contemporary remarked: 'It is a dismal sight to behold such a glorious, famous, and much renowned palace reduced to a heap of rubbish and ashes, which the day before might justly contend with any palace in the world for riches, nobility, honour and grandeur.' The fire also destroyed 150 houses nearby, mostly homes of the nobility. The king of the time, William III, disliked Whitehall, because he thought it aggravated his asthma, so the palace was never rebuilt, and virtually all that is left today is the Banqueting House.

In the eighteenth century, insurance companies began to realise that it was not necessarily in their interest for their firemen to leave a building burning if it was not insured by them. The fire might soon spread to one that was! So a new system was brought in, with rewards for the first firemen on the scene. The trouble was that fights sometimes broke out between competing firemen while the fire still burned, with some even resorting to sabotaging their rivals' equipment. Gradually, though, the companies began to cooperate more and more closely and, in 1833, a number of them got together to form the LFEE, the London Fire Engine Establishment, which comprised nineteen stations and eighty firemen.

The LFEE's first chief was the redoubtable James Braidwood who had headed the Edinburgh Fire Brigade, the first municipal brigade in the country. The year after he arrived in London the Houses of Parliament caught fire. For centuries the nation's financial records had been kept on tally sticks of notched and split wood, until in 1828, the practice was finally abolished, and on 16 October 1834, a clerk was instructed to burn the old tallies in the central heating furnaces of the Palace of Westminster. He shovelled them in, and went off home.

At about half past six in the evening, flames were spotted near the entrances to the House of Commons and the House of Lords. The burning tallies had set fire to the chimney and the blaze had then spread with alarming speed. Braidwood was called at about seven o'clock, by which time the interior of the House of Lords was already alight. Twelve engines and sixty-four firemen turned out. In the name of parliamentary privilege, the Palace was exempt from most safety regulations, and the firemen knew nothing of its layout. In fact, it was a rambling rabbit warren, largely built of timber. There was a stiff wind fanning the blaze, and a low tide in the river meant water was in short supply. MPs had to break down doors so that books and other treasures could be rescued and carried across the road to St Margaret's Church. The Foreign Secretary, Lord Palmerston, other peers, MPs, staff and passers-by all joined in the salvage effort. The Deputy Serjeant-at-Arms entered a burning room on a ladder to rescue the Mace, but among the many important documents destroyed was an original warrant for the execution of Charles I.

Everywhere sightseers were gathering. Westminster Bridge was so full it became dangerous. Some climbed onto the roof of the Abbey, some waded into the Thames mud, others hired boats at extortionate prices. So many looters and pickpockets appeared that the Guards had to be called out to help the police. Fortunately, one of the sightseers was J.M.W. Turner who had spotted the blaze on his way back from the country and left some extraordinary pictures of the scene.

Meanwhile, the fire had spread to the Lords Chamber, the Painted Chamber and the House of Commons. Braidwood decided to abandon most of the complex in order to try to save Westminster Hall, the only surviving part of the original eleventh-century Palace of Westminster. His men dragged their pumps into the building and cut away part of the roof where it was joined to the Speaker's House, which was burning fiercely. Braidwood achieved his objective and, as dawn broke, with the Prime Minister, Lord Melbourne, looking on, it was clear that the flames were under control, but the Painted Chamber, the Library of the House of Lords and the Speaker's House were reduced to ashes. There was some criticism later of Braidwood for his decision to concentrate his efforts on Westminster Hall. This seems particularly churlish in view of the fact that one fireman had been killed and several more seriously injured at a fire they had no obligation whatsoever to attend as the buildings were not insured.

The LFEE later wrote to the government to point out that if they had been needed at a fire at an insured property, they would have had to leave Parliament to burn. In those circumstances, the only fire engines obliged to go to the fire would have been the parish pump at St Margaret's and any others in the neighbourhood. The LFEE warned that parish engines were neither prompt nor powerful enough to deal with big fires. The government was dismissive. Many politicians shared the view of the Duke of Wellington that using public money to fund a fire service was likely to undermine people's vigilance.

Another man who had spotted the fire on his way back from the country was Sir Charles Barry; he had seen the glow in the sky as he reached the top of the South Downs. When he realised it was the Houses of Parliament that burned, he is supposed to have said: 'What an opportunity for an architect', and told the coachman to take him there at once. After the fire, a competition was held to find a design for the new building. Barry won, and created the Gothic masterpiece that has since become a world-famous landmark.

The fire at the Houses of Parliament was just one of a series in famous buildings that Braidwood's men were called upon to fight. After its destruction in the Great Fire, the Royal Exchange had been rebuilt, and it opened again just three years later. The Exchange did not have its own nightwatchman, so it was the ones at the Bank of England who spotted flames bursting out of its windows at about half past ten on the very cold night of 10 January 1838. The LFEE's Watling Street headquarters was only a stone's throw away, but when the firemen arrived, the first thing they had to do was to force open the gates. Then they found that the plugs in the water mains had frozen solid and had to be chipped free so stand pipes could be put in. The delays meant that before any serious firefighting could start, the fire, which had probably begun in an over-heated stove in Lloyd's Coffee House, had taken complete hold. Soon the whole of the front of the building was ablaze. Porters had to heave furniture and records out of the windows to the cheering of the crowds who had gathered in spite of the weather. They cheered even louder when a bag containing twenty sovereigns came out, and the lucky ones helped themselves.

Inside, the firemen attempted to halt the flames, but eventually the heat and smoke became so intense, they were forced to retire. Once again they had been handicapped by having to fight a blaze in a building with numerous staircases and passageways. Now, it became a battle to prevent fire spreading to neighbouring houses, from which the inhabitants had to be evacuated, and, despite the firemen's efforts, some houses in neighbouring Sweeting's Alley were destroyed. At the centre of the Exchange stood a great clock tower containing eight huge bells, which played a tune four times a day. When they struck up the traditional Scottish air, 'There's Nae Luck Aboot the Hoose', the tower collapsed and the bells came crashing down. Some of the statues were saved, but the Exchange was virtually destroyed. Once again, though, after the flames had been put out, the Exchange was rebuilt, and reopened in 1844.

Three years after the Royal Exchange, it was the turn of the Tower of London. Again the alarm was raised at about half past ten at night, this time on 30 October 1841. A sentry on duty near the Jewel Tower noticed a light in the Round Tower, near the Armoury. He fired his musket, and an entire battalion of Guards turned out, but by the time their commanding officer appeared on the scene, flames were bursting out of the windows. The good news was that the Tower had its own fire brigade; the bad news was that its firefighters were inexperienced and their equipment amounted to nine old and decrepit hand pumps.

Not surprisingly, they were unable to save the Round Tower, nor to stop the flames spreading to the roof of the Armoury, which was 345 feet long and contained a magnificent collection of historic weapons. The Tower firemen tried to save the building from inside, but the fire spread very quickly, and they had to settle for carrying outside as much of the collection as they could, as the building itself was destroyed. The losses were severe. Two thousand eight hundred historic items were destroyed, including that instrument of torture on which so many hapless prisoners had suffered, the rack, as well as fifteenth-century cannon, arms used in an assassination attempt on King William III, and carbines seized from the Jacobite rebels of 1715.

Now the fire brigade was sent for, but James Braidwood's men were already fighting another fire in the Strand, and further time was lost because, when they arrived, the Guards at first would not let them in. Once again, police had to be called out to control thousands of spectators. It was said that even several hundred yards from the fire, the light was so bright you could read newsprint. From the Armoury, flames spread to the Clock Tower, which fell at one o'clock in the morning with a resounding crash, and it began to look as though they might engulf William the Conqueror's White Tower, the ancient church of St Peter ad Vincula, and the Crown Jewels in the Jewel Tower.

The only keys to the Jewel Tower were held by the Lord Chamberlain, and no one knew where he kept them. Fortunately, the police arrived, and a superintendent took it upon himself to use an axe and a crowbar to break open the bars behind which the jewels were kept, and removed them to the Governor's residence in the nick of time. The firefighters were hampered by the poor water supply, which gave them only about a fifth of what they needed, and soldiers began removing the stocks of gunpowder held in the building. When the crowd realised what they were doing, many suddenly remembered pressing engagements elsewhere! The firemen kept three engines playing water onto the outside of the White Tower, while soldiers covered the inside of the windows with wet blankets. Eventually the fire was brought under control, but not before one fireman had been killed by bricks falling from the walls. During the weeks after, tables were set up in the roofless shell of the Armoury and damaged items were sold off for a few shillings each.

Another famous building that Braidwood was called out to save was Windsor Castle. On 19 March 1853, a young cook living in the Prince of Wales Tower raised the alarm after finding his room filled with smoke when he went to bed. At the time Queen Victoria was heavily pregnant (her eighth child was born just three weeks later), but she watched from a window as her husband Prince Albert directed operations. The Castle's own fire brigade had been joined by local volunteers from Windsor and Eton, and 700 soldiers were also summoned from their barracks to lend a hand, but as midnight approached, a message was sent via Buckingham Palace to the LFEE requesting its help.

Braidwood rushed off to Waterloo station, but there was no train available. So he went to Nine Elms where he did find one, and loaded aboard engines, horses and ten men. They arrived at Windsor at half past one in the morning and helped to put the fire out by four o'clock. Most of the damage was confined to the ceiling of the dining room and two floors of bedrooms in the Prince of Wales Tower, mainly occupied by servants. Prince Albert investigated the cause and came to the conclusion it was probably a furnace overheating. The Queen sent a 'gratuity' of £50 to Braidwood and the firemen who had come with him.

Meanwhile, many of the places in which poor Londoners lived were death traps. In 1858, fire broke out in a building in Gilbert Place, Bloomsbury, which had eight upstairs rooms let to three families, who had a total of fourteen children. A policeman on his beat saw smoke pouring from the front of the house, and banged on the door to try to wake the occupants, but their only means of escape was a narrow wooden staircase that was already ablaze. The eldest of the children, a seventeen-year-old boy, jumped from a top window, but died from his injuries.

There were two parish fire engines just one minute away, but no one knew who had the keys to the fire station or where they were kept. A local painter managed to get a ladder to one of the windows, and rescued a family of four, but the message to call the LFEE was delayed, and the firemen did not arrive for half an hour, by which time the building was an inferno. Within minutes it collapsed, and all the firemen could do was to prevent the blaze spreading. A total of fifteen people were killed, including one whole family of mother, father and ten children. An investigation revealed that the building was in flagrant breach of regulations and should have been condemned.

The scene of the most formidable fires James Braidwood had to fight was the south bank of the Thames. The Southwark shoreline was like a wall of warehouses flush to the water, divided by small alleys with Tooley Street running at the back. The first fire he fought here was in 1833, when a granary was totally destroyed and there was severe damage to Davis Wharf. Altogether, he would be called here five more times. The fifth occasion was on Saturday, 22 June 1861.

Braidwood had been fiercely critical of the safety standards in many of the warehouses, but the one to which he would be called this time, Scovell's, was actually one of the better equipped. Great iron fire-proof doors divided different bays into which were packed a whole variety of goods, many of them highly inflammable – hemp, cotton, sugar, tallow, jute, tea, spices and oil. The day's work was over, and the doors should have been shut tight, but it was hot and one had been left open a crack. The sun warmed up bales of cotton and, once they had begun to smoulder, the breeze fanned the flames into life. Smoke was spotted by a delivery foreman, and he sent a runner to Tooley Street Fire Station. Then the foreman and a colleague managed to turn two water jets onto the fire, but it was not enough and, by the time the first engines arrived at a quarter to five, huge flames were leaping from the building.

At ten to five, news of the fire was passed to Braidwood at Watling Street, and he galloped off towards London Bridge. By the time he arrived just before five o'clock he could see it was already spreading to neighbouring warehouses, where there was oil, paint, sulphur, cheese, flour, rum and brandy. To make things worse, the tide in the river was going out fast. The next high tide was not due until one o'clock the next morning. In fact, within an hour the river itself was ablaze, as burning rum floated on the surface with molten tallow. Ships had to cast off to escape the flames, but an estimated 30,000 sightseers once again raced to see a 'good fire'. Some of those who had jumped into small boats to get a better view were drowned, as were people who tried to snatch liquor barrels from the water.

Nearly every fire engine the LFEE commanded was rushed to the blaze, though some were delayed by the crowds, and a new floating platform with steam-powered pumps was also drafted in. Braidwood believed in the importance of getting to the heart of a fire rather than tackling it from a distance, a risky philosophy when firemen had to rely on hand-held jets. So, as always, he was to be found in the hottest spot when, at about seven o'clock, two firemen ran up to tell him that the fire floats on the river were being scorched by the heat and asked what they should do. Braidwood set off down one of the narrow alleys that ran from Tooley Street to the river.

A young fireman said he heard a wall begin to groan and Braidwood shout to his men to run for their lives. At sixty-one the chief was still fit and agile, and he too started to run, but then seemed to pause to check that his men were all right. Before he could reach safety, a 40-feet high warehouse wall bulged, cracked and, with a great roar, collapsed on Braidwood and the officer with him. It took three days to recover his body from the rubble. For his funeral London came to a standstill. It was the biggest the city had seen since the Duke of Wellington's. The procession was over a mile long, with more than 1,700 police and soldiers in the cortège. Queen Victoria sent her condolences, poems were written, handbills were sold in the street and commemorative china figures were produced. A memorial to Braidwood was put up in Tooley Street, and visitors to the Museum of London today can see commodities burned in the fire and shapes made from the molten glass that flowed in the gutters.

The fire burned out of control for two days from London Bridge to where Tower Bridge now stands. The flames leapt so high they could be seen from 30 miles away, and it was a whole month before they were put out completely. It was London's most devastating fire since the Great Fire, but it also effectively gave birth to the London Fire Brigade. The insurance companies faced £2 million worth of claims. They wrote to the government, pointing out that no other major European city relied on private funding for firefighting, nor did Edinburgh, Cardiff, Manchester or Liverpool. They said that for thirty years they had put out fires regardless of whether the buildings were insured or not, but they were not prepared to do so any longer. After many arguments over what it would cost, a publicly funded Metropolitan Fire Brigade was born on New Year's Day 1866.

The first Chief Officer of the Metropolitan Fire Brigade was Captain (later Sir) Eyre Massey Shaw, a close friend of the Prince of Wales, the future King Edward VII, a monarch who numbered his paramours in hundreds. Sir Eyre used to go out for nights on the town with the heir to the throne, and there were hints in the press that he too had an eye for the ladies. He was a handsome man with striking steely blue eyes. On the first night of *Iolanthe*, W.S. Gilbert spotted him in the stalls, and quickly amended the libretto, getting the Fairy Queen to step down from the stage and sing to him: 'Could thy brigade / With cold cascade / Quench my great love, I wonder?' Shaw loved the theatre, which was just as well, as he had plenty of involvement with it in his professional capacity.

There had always been fires in London theatres. In 1613, the Globe at Bankside had burned down when a cannon fired during a performance of *Henry VIII* set the roof thatch alight. Everyone managed to get out unscathed apart from one man whose breeches caught fire. A bottle of ale sufficed to put them out. The first Theatre Royal, Drury Lane, was burned down in 1672. The second was declared unsafe and closed, while the third lasted just fifteen years before it too caught fire, and in 1809 men of the Phoenix insurance company were called. The great actor-manager John Philip Kemble warned them that the building was packed with inflammable materials, but, in the words of the *Courier* newspaper, 'These brave and bold fellows answered: "Where danger is, there is our duty", and rushed forward.' Several paid for their courage with their lives, others suffered horrific injuries, and the building was still destroyed. The playwright R.B. Sheridan, who had invested in the theatre, was seen dejectedly watching the blaze. When attempts were made to move him away, he asked: 'Cannot a man warm his hands at his own fireside?' Four years later, he was arrested for debt, and he died in poverty.

The Covent Garden Theatre also burned down twice, in 1808 and 1856, while Astley's Amphitheatre in Westminster Bridge Road was burned down no less than four times between 1794 and 1841. In the seventeen years from 1863, there were fourteen major fires in London's theatres, and in 1880 Shaw delivered a report on the inadequacy of their safety precautions. Two years later, one theatre fire almost cost the country its future King. We do not know whether the Prince of Wales used to take Shaw with him on his amorous adventures, but we do know that Shaw took the Prince firefighting. Like his ancestor Charles II, the Prince was fascinated by the spectacle of a big fire, and he had an arrangement that Shaw would alert him. The Prince would then dash off to his local fire station at Chandos Street, don a fireman's uniform with a special silver helmet, and hop onto the engine. Sometimes, he would turn up with his friends, the Duke of Sutherland and the Earl of Caithness. Firemen liked having the Prince along because he would always hand out cigars after a 'good' fire. It was thought quite unsuitable, though, for his future subjects to know about his exploits, and the papers observed a news blackout.

At one o'clock in the morning of 8 December 1882, the theatre fireman at the Alhambra in Leicester Square was making his regular inspection when he found a fire in the balcony stalls. At about the same time, an off-duty detective in the street saw smoke coming out of the windows. He hailed a cab and raced round to Chandos Street Fire Station to raise the alarm, but by the time the engines got there, the Alhambra was blazing 'like a Christmas tree'. The firemen quickly had jets playing onto the building from all sides, and the Prince joined in, climbing onto a wall in the thick of the smoke and flames, hosepipe in hand.

With flames spreading in all directions, cracks began to appear in the front of the building. Shaw looked around desperately for the Prince, and sent one of his men to search for him. Fortunately, by then he had climbed back down to the ground, because just as Shaw's man found him, a shout of 'Run for your life' went up, and the wall on which the Prince had been standing collapsed, sending a vicious shower of hot bricks, masonry and wooden beams down on two firemen who had been just a few feet from him. The Prince helped to dig them out, burning and lacerating his hands, but the two men were dead. The façade of the Alhambra was saved, but the rest of the building had to be completely rebuilt. It went on to become one of London's most famous music halls until it was knocked down and replaced by the Odeon cinema in 1936.

London's department stores have also suffered disastrous fires. One of the worst happened at Whiteley's in Bayswater on 6 August 1887.

In 1863, William Whiteley had opened a ribbons and fancy goods store in what was then the comparatively rural area of Westbourne Grove. The neighbourhood was known as 'Bankruptcy Avenue' because of the number of shops that had failed there, but Whiteley did so well that within nine years he had bought up shops all along the street and was selling such a wide variety of goods that he styled himself 'the Universal Provider', which did not endear him to his remaining competitors. Certainly, Whiteley was not short of enemies. He was said routinely to take advantage of pretty shop assistants, and he would eventually be shot dead in his office by a young man claiming to be his illegitimate son. This was the fifth fire at the store in five years; the four previous ones had been arson.

When this latest fire broke out, the store's own brigade soon realised that they could not deal with it, and just before half past seven in the evening, they called the Metropolitan Fire Brigade. The officer in charge knew the store well because he had attended the previous four fires. This time, his men had just got to work when the whole front wall collapsed and the interior of the building fell in. A fire engine outside was buried, and passers-by rushed to try to free firemen trapped in the rubble, but found that four had been killed. Another twelve were injured and had to be sent to nearby St Mary's Hospital in cabs. Two policemen were also seriously hurt.

As soon as Shaw heard that Whiteley's was ablaze again, he rushed to the scene to find that other large buildings were now threatened. Nearly a third of the MFB's total strength of 578 men turned out to the fire in a building that was riddled with gas pipes. In the heat, they melted and the gas burst into hissing fires, which gave way to roaring masses of blue flames against which the water from dozens of hoses seemed to have no effect. As the fire blazed on and on, the MFB sprayed more water onto the fire than on any other they ever fought. The big clock at the front of the building managed to keep going till twenty to midnight, when it stopped, but the fire did not. It continued well into the early hours of the morning, and the store was destroyed along with fifteen adjoining buildings.

Whiteley's total losses amounted to more than £½ million, but, because of the store's previous history, he had only been able to buy insurance cover for £16,000. Nonetheless, it was rebuilt and reopened in nine months. There was widespread suspicion that the blaze was arson, with suggestions that dynamite had been concealed in, or thrown into, the building. Scientific evidence showed that dynamite had not been used, but the inquest jury decided arson was the probable cause.

Four years before the Whiteley's fire, another store owner, Charles Harrod, had found his premises in Brompton Road ablaze on 8 December 1883 at a time when his staff were working flat out to deal with Christmas orders. Bizarrely, the fire broke out while it was snowing heavily, but it still beat the best efforts of the fire brigade, and the building was reduced to a ruin. Harrod, though, was a resourceful man. He salvaged as many orders as he could and went to the nearest pub, where he wrote to customers: 'I greatly regret to inform you that in consequence of the above premises being burnt down, your order will be delayed in the execution a day or two', but he made sure that everyone got what they wanted by Christmas and created such a good impression that he was soon able to open a bigger store.

Another department store that was burned down in the run-up to Christmas was Arding & Hobbs at Clapham. On 20 December 1909, one of the staff had gone into a window to get a necklace for a customer when he heard an explosion from a fairy-light bulb, and flames burst out all around him. The display of celluloid dolls, toys, tinsel decorations and cotton wool immediately caught fire. He did his best to put it out but it was hopeless.

Although the first fire engine was on the scene within four minutes, and eventually thirty joined in the fight, they could not prevent nine people being killed, mainly women shop assistants. One man died when the floor collapsed beneath him as he was helping a woman escape through a window. The heat was so intense, it was said to have cooked the turkeys in a poulterer's across the road. The store was a ruin, and it took three months to clear the rubble, but Arding & Hobbs was open again in time for the next Christmas. Five shop assistants were killed in another big department store fire at John Barkers of Kensington in 1912, while the Civil Service Stores had three major fires – in the Haymarket in 1881 and 1903, and in the Strand in 1982, when the store was gutted.

The 'fancy goods' that proved to be such a hazard at Arding & Hobbs's store could also cause disastrous fires in the factories where they were made. Around the end of the nineteenth century, most of the workers were women and most of the factories were in an area of close-packed buildings and narrow streets around Cripplegate, which had acquired the ominous nickname 'fire island'. On 19 November 1897, just as City workers were streaming out for lunch, they saw a major part of London's fire brigade arriving. By this time, the capital had a new fire chief, Captain Sir Lionel de Latour Wells, an ex-naval officer, one of whose ancestors had been executed during the French Revolution.

The fire had started in a factory specialising in ostrich feathers, but it soon swept through the tall neighbouring buildings. Fifty engines and more than 220 firemen fought the blaze, and the new fire chief had a narrow escape when a plate-glass door fell on his helmet, but, for all the fire brigade's efforts, by the end of the day more than a hundred buildings had been reduced to a blackened patch of ruins. Total losses were estimated at more than £1 million, and about 4,000 people were thrown out of work.

Within five years and just a few streets away, there was another disastrous fire, this time at General Electric's factory in Queen Victoria Street. It was a five-storey building, with the top three floors used as offices, while the lower part was given over to making decorative lamp holders from celluloid. Nearly all the workers were young women. The building had its own hydrant and fire service, and the workers were supposed to put out the fire themselves rather than call the fire brigade. On 9 June 1902, a blaze started in a wastepaper basket, and the brigade was called by a member of the public who had seen the flames, but by then the fire had had ten minutes' start.

The office staff on the top floors shouted for help from the windows, and spectators who had gathered watched in horror as they saw that the ladder brought by the firemen was 6 to 10 feet too short. A special 70-foot ladder was galloped across from Southwark and arrived in time to rescue several office girls, but eight young women and one young man who had tried to rescue them were all killed. The agony of the trapped women for whom the ladder was too short made headlines all over the world. Since 1894, buildings more than 60 feet high had been required by law to have fire escapes, but the regulations did not apply to those like General Electric's factory that had been built before that date. After the fire, the remains of the building were demolished and Cannon Street Fire Station was erected on the site.

Ten years later, the City was the site of yet another devastating industrial fire, in a Christmas card factory in Moor Lane. A consignment of 1,500 lb of celluloid was being stored on the premises and a youth who had been given the job of parcelling it up dropped some hot sealing wax. The celluloid burned so fiercely that within minutes the fire was out of control. The only means the staff had to fight the fire were buckets of water. There had been no fire-drills and no one knew what to do. Once again, the death toll was nine.

One of the capital's most disastrous fires of the nineteenth century in terms of loss of life happened in the early hours of New Year's Day 1890 at Forest Gate Residential School in East London. The building housed 542 children, aged from three to sixteen, who were either orphans, illegitimate, abandoned or paupers whose parents could not afford to keep them. Fun of any description was not on the curriculum so there had been no celebrations at the school. By midnight, the boys had long been in bed, the gas had been turned off for hours and the school was in pitch darkness. At about twenty past, one of the teachers thought she could smell smoke. She managed to grope her way to the needlework room and peer inside to see a fire close to the wooden partition that divided it from the wardrobe room. The rooms were full of clothes and linen and, by the time she had managed to raise the alarm, smoke was already seeping into the two dormitories above. Boys were beginning to wake coughing and choking and, knowing the dormitory doors were locked, running to the windows and screaming for help.

The master who should have slept in one of the dormitories was away on leave and the school had seen no reason to replace him, so a twelve-year-old monitor had to take charge. He managed to get down the stairs, but, sure enough, found the door that would have led outside to safety was locked. Because it was New Year, some local people were still in the vicinity, and they helped to bring ladders up to the windows, enabling some of the boys to escape. Several of the younger boys, though, were too terrified even to try to get out. They just crouched in corners and died where they crouched. There was a member of staff in the other dormitory, but he was a notoriously heavy sleeper and it took a long time to wake him. Once he was roused, he managed to lead some of the boys out, but others were overwhelmed by smoke. Meanwhile, the monitor told the boys from his dormitory to hold hands, and led the line downstairs, where another member of staff had managed to force open the door so they could get out. It was not until half an hour after the fire started that the fire brigade was sent for. In the darkness, it was hard to know how many boys had got out. There should have been eighty-two, but a count revealed that only fifty-six had escaped.

Police, staff, volunteers and firemen tried to reach those still in the dormitories, but it was hopeless. All they could do was drag out dead bodies. It took the fire brigade forty minutes to put out the fire, and it was even longer before the dense, choking smoke had cleared. The dead were all aged between six and twelve. One pupil lost his two brothers aged nine and ten; they had all been put into the school when their father died. The twenty-six victims were all buried at West Ham Cemetery in five graves. Several thousand people lined the route of the funeral and Queen Victoria sent condolences. The local church launched an appeal to raise money for a stained-glass memorial window, which the school's managers refused to support, though they did contribute £36 for a headstone for the boys' graves.

One of London's most spectacular fires of the twentieth century engulfed the Crystal Palace, perhaps the most famous exhibition centre in the world. It was not the first exhibition centre in the capital to fall prey to the flames. Alexandra Palace twice burned down, in 1873 and 1980; on the first occasion, it lasted only two weeks from its opening, and in 1925, £200,000 worth of wax figures and Napoleon's bullet-proof coach were destroyed at Madame Tussaud's.

The Crystal Palace was originally built in Hyde Park for the Great Exhibition of 1851, and was then moved in a modified form to Sydenham Hill. The building stretched over a quarter of a mile. It was 168 feet at its highest point, contained 1½ million square feet of glass and nearly 10,000 tons of iron. It was flanked by two huge water towers, each more than 100 feet taller than Nelson's Column.

The Palace became a home for exhibitions, circuses, spectacular firework displays and a museum of wonders from all over the world. The interior housed works of art, plants, fountains and statues. There was a concert hall, a theatre and an auditorium that could seat 20,000. There had been a number of fires at the Palace and, in 1866, part of the building was severely damaged, never to be rebuilt, but in the 1930s, when John Logie Baird took his pioneer television studios there, it was still world famous.

The night of 30 November 1936 was cold and windy. By half past seven in the evening, the building was virtually empty apart from about thirty musicians from the Crystal Palace Orchestra who were rehearsing. One of the two night watchmen had just started his regular check around the building, while Sir Henry Buckland, the General Manager, was out walking the dog with his daughter Chrystal. When the watchman reached the entrance to the Egyptian Court, he noticed a faint smell of smoke, but he could not find where it was coming from, so he continued his walk and went down to bank up the office boiler. Climbing back up from the boiler room, he noticed a stronger smell of smoke coming from the general offices. He pushed open a few doors, and when he looked in the ladies' lavatory, he saw flames reaching to the top of a wooden wall at the back of the room, and rushed to find his colleague. Outside, Sir Henry and Chrystal had spotted a strange red glow in the central transept.

The two watchmen turned a hose on the flames, but they soon realised the fire was too big for them, so at ten to eight they asked for the fire brigade to be called. When Sir Henry and his daughter reached the Palace, parts of the building were already filling with smoke, but it was so vast that the first the musicians knew that anything was wrong was when Chrystal Buckland came rushing in and told them to run for their lives. They obeyed, carrying their instruments under their arms.

Penge fire brigade arrived just after eight o'clock, but all they had was one jet of water. One fireman described the scene: 'It was a terrific sight – flames shooting into the sky, and so much molten glass that it looked like a waterfall. We soon realised we would never be able to beat it.' They sent out a desperate call for help. In the end, there would be 88 fire engines, every available one in London, manned by more than 430 firemen, and the whole area around the Palace would be ankle-deep in inter-woven fire hoses, but it was an uphill struggle. The building was long and narrow with no firebreaks. It was a perfect natural tunnel, and the wooden floorboards were tinder-dry after seventy years of under-floor heating. Close to the area where the fire had started were a paint store, a stock of inflammable black pitch and a stack of 2,000 wooden chairs. To make things worse, the flames were being fanned by a strong wind.

Within half an hour, the whole Palace was on fire. An estimated 100,000 people rushed to the scene to watch, and police had to be called to help fire engines get through the crowds. Houses were damaged and fencing broken down as people clambered onto roofs for a better view. Others climbed trees or jumped on top of cars, some of which gave way under the weight. With the flames leaping hundreds of feet in the air, every hill for miles around was packed with spectators. In Streatham, field glasses were being hired out at 2*d* a look. From Biggin Hill, 8 miles away, 'it was like a huge scarlet bonfire'. At Vincent Square in Westminster, every balcony was packed. As far away as Hampstead Heath, they turned out. Those with enough money could charter aeroplanes from Croydon Aerodrome. A *Daily Mirror* photographer who flew over the flames remarked that it looked like 'the blazing crater of a volcano', and it was said that the red glow could be seen in Brighton. The youngest brother of King Edward VIII, the Duke of Kent, came hotfoot to the scene in full evening dress. Did he know that in twelve days time, the King would have abdicated?

The Palace's ornamental lake provided a useful addition to the inadequate water supply for the firemen, and at one point they did manage to get inside the building, but were beaten back by the molten glass raining down on them. Six had to be taken to hospital. Section by section, the building fell apart with creaks and moans. One of the musicians said she heard 'the most ghastly groans rather like a giant in great pain'. She realised later that it was the heat making the bellows of the organ contract and expand and, when the transept collapsed, the explosion echoed across London like thunder.

Molten glass and metal flowed down roads near the park, but the biggest fear was that the great water towers might fall, particularly the South Tower which contained 12,000 gallons and was close to densely populated streets. Many local residents were told to leave their homes. As the flames raged, the firemen's efforts were now concentrated on trying to stop this disaster. They fought on until midnight, and the blaze was finally checked just 15 feet from the tower.

The next morning, many spectators returned. They saw the two towers still standing, though blackened by smoke, but of the Crystal Palace all that remained was a great, broken skeleton on a pile of smouldering ashes, with molten glass starting to harden on the surrounding earth. In the ornamental fountain, there were still a few goldfish, though their scales had turned completely black, and the grounds were full of birds that had been released from the aviary to let them escape the flames. Firemen stayed at the Palace for days damping down, and being approached by people who wanted pieces of misshapen glass as souvenirs. Among the treasures destroyed were original manuscripts by Handel and other famous composers. Some of the statues were salvaged, and a number were sold off to Bing Crosby.

The twin towers that had been saved with so much effort were demolished in 1940, when it was thought they were too helpful as a landmark for the Luftwaffe. As for what caused the fire, no one was ever certain. Was it a spark from a faulty piece of wiring under the floor, or had debris fallen between gaps in the floorboards, causing a layer of inflammable material to build up, and could a discarded match or cigarette then have fallen through? Whatever it was,

Sir Henry Buckland was understandably distraught. 'I am heartbroken, my Crystal Palace is finished,' he lamented; 'there will never be another.' Local people were also deeply upset. A woman from South Norwood said: 'Everybody was crying. It didn't matter who it was. It meant so much to everyone. We couldn't believe that it was never going to be there any more.'

SEVEN

London's Still Burning

For the fire brigade, the end of the Second World War (see Chapter 3) meant a return to more routine disasters, like a fire in 1958 at the Smithfield wholesale meat market, an underground labyrinth of railway lines, passages, stairways and cold storage cellars. It took two days to contain and two firemen were killed.

The worst post-war fire in terms of loss of life happened just off Charing Cross Road in the summer of 1980. The area had long been a favourite location for illegal drinking clubs and gambling dens, and on the upper floors of a three-storey building in Denmark Place were a South American club named *Rodo's* and a Spanish nightclub called *El Hueco*, the hole. Neither was licensed, and many of the patrons were illegal immigrants. The ground floor was made of concrete and rented out as a garage, while the other floors were of timber. The drinking clubs had been closed down on a number of occasions, but they always seemed to reopen under new management. Now, the police were due to close them down again on Monday 18 August.

The only way into the clubs was by the building's front door. There was no doorman. When someone rang the bell, one of the staff would open an upstairs window and ask for the caller's name and membership number. If they got the right answer, they would throw down the door key. Inside was a flight of wooden stairs leading up to a landing off which was the entrance to the club on the first floor, and a wrought-iron fire escape enclosed with plywood that led to the club on the second floor. Members were allowed to move between the two clubs. The fire brigade did not know of the clubs' existence, and the last time the place had been visited by a fire prevention officer was when a music shop in Denmark Street, onto which the building backed, had taken it over as a hostel for budding musicians. At that time, the LFB had insisted that a fire escape to the ground floor was fitted, but then the music shop had given up the hostel, and the fire escape had fallen into disrepair, while the door into Denmark Street to which it led was bolted and barred.

The upstairs windows had wooden shutters, and the front door was of double thickness, lined with steel and secured with concealed locks on the inside. The Friday night before the clubs were due to be closed, 15 August, was warm and humid, and both clubs were beginning to fill up. Because of the heat, the doors onto the fire escape were open; by the early hours of Saturday morning there were about 150 people inside.

Soho Fire Station, just a few hundred yards away, got a call to say the building was on fire just after half past three on Saturday morning. As the firemen arrived, a breathless, injured man told them that many people were trapped. Once they had got alongside the clubs, they could see smoke starting to seep from the shuttered windows. As they tried to force the front door, sparks and embers showered down on them, and they could not budge it. Meanwhile, they could see injured people desperate to struggle off into the night, plainly not wanting to wait for treatment, and giving highly evasive answers when they were asked where they had come from.

One of the firemen went into Denmark Street, where he found the music shop that backed onto the clubs. Inside were people trapped behind security grilles as the building filled up with smoke. He managed to break in and rescue six, most of whom were badly cut or burned. Then he and some colleagues started to attack the fire in the clubs from the back windows of the shop. At the front of the building, it took firemen nearly four minutes to break down the door, then they had to battle against fierce flames on the staircase. Fortunately, the fireball had been so fierce it had burned the roof away, and much of the heat had escaped. Once the firemen began to get the flames under control, they started to find bodies. One fire officer said: 'People seem to have died on the spot without even having time to move an inch.' Some were slumped at tables. Seven were at the bar and appeared to have fallen as they stood, with

93

drinks still in their hands. Thirty people were treated in hospital, but many others had simply melted away into the night. The last body was not removed until four o'clock on Saturday afternoon, and the final death toll was thirty-seven.

When fire had spread at this speed, it was hard to believe it could have been an accident, and the firemen had smelled petrol around the foot of the stairs. A few moments before the blaze began, a man had been seen leaning against the door of the club. The streets were quiet, and the few people who saw him assumed he was urinating. In fact, he was a customer who had been thrown out about fifty minutes before, after getting involved in a fight. He had found a 2-gallon plastic container outside and gone to fill it with petrol. At about twenty past three, he had returned and poured the petrol through the letter box. When he lit a scrap of paper and pushed it in, the flames shot straight up the wooden staircase.

The whole building was on fire within a couple of seconds. Some people had ripped shutters from the windows and broken the glass with their bare hands, then jumped to the ground with their clothes on fire, smashing bones. Survivors spoke of the screaming, the skin peeling off faces, of trying to get out by the back door but finding it locked. Those who had broken through the rear windows of the shop, cut themselves terribly, then found the front windows fastened with metal grilles, and waited agonisingly as the shop filled up with smoke until the fire brigade freed them. Some managed to climb a high wall and escaped to neighbouring premises. Others could not remember how they got out. It had been a dreadful disaster, and it was to have an eerie echo fourteen years later.

In the 1980s, the authorities launched a big clean-up in Soho, and one of the results was that dubious enterprises tended to open up elsewhere. In 1994, a four-storey building in St John Street to the north of Smithfield Market housed an unlicensed cinema club, known as Dream City. Seven days a week, up to 120 men paid £10 each to watch hardcore pornographic films on two screens. The cinema had been prosecuted three times, but the local council complained that fines imposed by the courts were not high enough to deter clubs from operating illegally.

Just after five-thirty on the evening of Saturday 26 February, 1994, firemen were called by someone in the building opposite the club who had seen flames coming from it. By the time they arrived, people were trying to escape by climbing out of windows. One man jumped from the second floor trying to reach the firemen's ladder, but missed and fell to the ground, sustaining fatal injuries. Three other men who jumped with him were seriously hurt. Firemen managed to rescue twelve men from the second floor and seven from the first, as well as one who had jumped 30 feet on to the top of a lorry parked outside, and another who had managed to get onto a flat roof at the back of the building.

The total death toll was eleven, with fifteen injured. It was soon clear that the fire had not started accidentally. Again, petrol had been poured through the letter box, and fire had spread very quickly up the main stairwell cutting off the escape route. Three days afterwards, a 34-year-old man walked into Walthamstow Police Station and gave himself up. He had had a drunken, violent argument with the club's doorman about the price of admission, been thrown out, and then returned to take his revenge. He was gaoled for life for manslaughter.

Sandwiched in time between these two fires in unlicensed clubs was the most serious blaze ever on the London Underground. Not that fires were uncommon on the system. Between 1956 and 1987, there were about 400. More than 40 happened on escalators, and 32 were caused by cigarettes or matches. There was also a history of rubbish catching fire, as had happened at Goodge Street in 1981 in a blaze in which 1 man died and 16 people were injured. Then in 1984, 14 people were taken to hospital suffering from smoke inhalation after a cigarette end set fire to rubbish on one of the platforms at Oxford Circus. Smoke in the tunnels caused trains on three lines to stall, and more than 700 passengers had to walk along the tracks to safety. After the fire, the Victoria Line was closed for a month.

The fire brigade had complained repeatedly to London Underground about the risk caused by litter, but what was also disturbing about the Oxford Circus fire was the lack of communication between stations. While smoke was pouring onto the platforms at Piccadilly Circus, one station from Oxford Circus on the Bakerloo Line, staff in the booking hall were still selling tickets and allowing passengers to go down the escalators. After the fire, the fire brigade demanded a top-level meeting with London Underground to discuss an incident it believed might easily have turned into a disaster. It pressed for a number of improvements such as the installation of alarm bells, smoke detectors and sprinkler systems in booking halls and passageways, but without success. One thing that did happen, though, was that smoking was banned in all areas beyond the ticket barrier in all Underground stations wholly or partly below ground.

Bizarrely, the underground system was not required to have fire certificates, unlike less potentially lethal buildings above ground, and the London Transport rule book said staff had to deal with any outbreak of fire themselves if possible, and only call the fire brigade if they felt it might be beyond their ability to control. Indeed, staff were not supposed to talk about 'fires' at all. London Underground insisted they should instead refer to 'smoulderings'. In the months and years that followed the incident at Oxford Circus, there were a number of 'smoulderings' on escalators – in 1984 on the Piccadilly Line at Leicester Square, when three people had to be taken to hospital, then in January 1985 on the Piccadilly Line at Green Park. An internal inquiry noted that, in spite of the smoking ban, 'it was common to see people lighting up as they travelled up the escalator'.

There were two more fires on Piccadilly Line escalators in 1985, at Manor House and at Holborn. Two years later, there was an escalator fire at Bank and another at Green Park on the same Piccadilly Line escalator that had caught fire in 1985. Before they called the fire brigade, staff had tried to fight the fire and failed. At Bank, it was believed that a lighted cigarette had set fire to accumulated grease and debris on the escalator's running track. A senior LFB officer had written to London Underground: 'I cannot urge too strongly that . . . clear instructions be given that on any suspicion of fire, the Fire Brigade be called without delay. This could save lives.' In October 1987, Assistant Chief Officer Mike Doherty, an international expert on tunnel disasters, also expressed his concern, saying that 'ever since Oxford Circus, the Brigade has been terrified that another fire will come and that next time it will bring fatalities'.

King's Cross was the busiest station on the Underground, with five lines converging, and more than 30,000 commuters passing through during the evening peak. It was a baffling maze of passageways and tunnels, and the only station on the system that was built at five different levels below the surface. At about half past seven on the evening of 18 November, 1987, a dustman was coming up Piccadilly Line escalator no. 4 when he noticed a small fire underneath it. He reported it immediately to the ticket office, and a member of staff went to investigate, but he had received no fire training and he did not tell the station manager or the line controller. A minute later, a computer programmer coming up the same escalator also saw the glow beneath. When he got to the top, he pressed the emergency stop button, and shouted to people to get off. Meanwhile, another passenger reported the fire to the booking office clerk, but the clerk, who had had no training in evacuation procedures, did not think it looked very serious and did not leave the office. Fortunately, two British Transport Police constables happened to be on the station and they went along with a ticket inspector to investigate. They saw smoke and a flame about 4 inches high. One policeman decided to call his control room and ask for the fire brigade to be alerted, but his radio would not work underground, and he had to go back to the surface.

When British Transport Police headquarters received his call, they informed the fire brigade. A couple of minutes later, the station inspector went to the lower machine room of the escalator, but could not see any sign of fire. By now, though, smoke was clearly coming from escalator 4, and London Underground staff blocked access to it. This time, the inspector went to the upper machine room, and saw smoke and flames underneath the escalator. He tried to use a fire extinguisher but could not get close enough. There was also equipment available to throw a mist of water over the escalator, but, in the confusion, he did not think to use it. It was revealed later that he had never used the equipment, nor had he ever seen it used.

Now the police decided to evacuate the ticket hall. They also stopped the booking clerk selling tickets and allowing people to go down the escalators, which he had been doing quite happily until 19.41. At this point, police ordered the booking office staff to leave, though in the confusion no one alerted people in a bureau de change or in the public lavatories in the subways and, not knowing the geography of the station, police were still sending passengers up the escalators as this was the only escape route of which they were aware. They did not know there was another way out through the Midland City subway.

The nearest fire station to King's Cross was Euston, but, unfortunately, its crew was out on a call, which turned out to be a false alarm, so the first engines available had come from Soho. It took them six minutes to get through the rush-hour traffic. When they arrived at 19.42, all they knew was that an escalator was on fire. They were led by Station Officer Colin Townley, who found himself at London's busiest and most complex Underground station with no idea where the fire was, no prearranged rendezvous point with London Underground staff, and no sign of anyone in authority. Together with Temporary Sub-Officer Roger Bell, who had just arrived with the Clerkenwell engines, he went to investigate. Roger Bell said the fire he saw was about the size of a large cardboard box – 'not a big fire at all' – though flames were licking up the handrail of the wooden escalator. There seemed no cause for panic. He went down to stop passengers coming up the escalators, while Townley organised things on the surface, asking Temporary Leading Fireman David Flanagan to request more fire engines. He met the Manchester Square Fire Station crew who had also arrived, while the Clerkenwell men were already bringing a hose into the booking hall. When he got to the bottom, Bell tried to get people back onto trains, and, looking behind, he saw that the escalator fire that had seemed so small was now raging right up to the top of the shaft. He looked for a hose to fight the flames, but the firefighting equipment was kept in an unmarked cupboard.

Meanwhile, British Transport Policeman Stephen Hanson was telling the people on the Victoria Line escalator to hurry up to safety.

A fireman was seen in the concourse with a torch, urging people to get out. This was probably the last sighting of Station Officer Townley alive. Suddenly, there was a fearful flash and the whole ticket hall was engulfed in intense heat followed by dense, hot, acrid, black smoke. Everything went dark and the air was filled with the sound of people screaming and crying for help. David Flanagan was just on his way to ask for assistance when he and the other firemen in the concourse had to run for their lives towards the St Pancras exit, dragging with them as many people as they could. In the escalator shaft, PC Hanson saw 'a jet of flame that shot up and then collected into a kind of ball', then hit the ceiling of the ticket hall. It knocked him off balance and burned him severely.

He shouted to passengers to bend low and get out of the ticket hall by the nearest exit. Flames were now licking the roof. He vaulted over a barrier, and crawled to where he thought the exit was, managing to escape to the Euston Road, from where he was taken to hospital. One passenger dived under the flames, which had not got down to floor level, and escaped. Another had to roll on the floor to put out his burning jacket. He suffered 40 per cent burns, but survived. This was the flashover, rather like a giant blowtorch – the moment that turned the King's Cross fire into a disaster. It stopped the digital clock at the head of the Piccadilly Line escalators at 19.45, just three minutes after the fire brigade had arrived. Very few of the people who saw the flashover in the ticket office survived, and most of those who did were seriously injured. In the fifteen minutes since the fire had first been reported to London Underground staff, nothing had been done to impede its progress, in spite of the fact that all platforms were equipped with fire hydrants and sand buckets, there were fire extinguishers at the top and bottom of each set of escalators, and the machine room had extinguishers and a hose reel. Right up to the moment of the flashover, trains were still stopping at the station and disgorging passengers into a death trap, and, as late as 20.45, one Northern Line train driver had not received the order to drive through King's Cross, and stopped to let off passengers, who were promptly put back on the train by police.

Below ground, fireman Roger Bell could see that the tops of all three Piccadilly Line escalators were now ablaze. With the help of a police constable, he found the hose and began attacking the flames, tearing off wooden panels, but each time they seemed to have knocked it out, the fire took hold again. The burning escalator shaft acted like a chimney, with draughts of air from the passing trains playing the part of a pair of bellows. One fireman said: 'every time a train came through the station it was like a blast furnace . . . virtually everything was alight, even metal'. Ticket machines exploded, the air was filled with the noise of metal panels banging and buckling in the heat, of tiles cracking and flying off walls, and of hoardings splitting. The conditions for fighting the fire could scarcely have been more difficult. The thick smoke meant firemen had to stumble along, using hoses as guide-lines. The searing heat made them breathe much harder, so the air in their breathing apparatus ran out more quickly, and turned a jet of water to steam a few feet from the nozzle. The only means of communication for London Underground staff was telephone or word of mouth. British Transport Police and the fire brigade had personal radios, but they could not be used to link surface and underground. In practice if you could not see the person you wanted to talk to, you could not communicate.

A London Underground technician had the initiative to flag down a train that was crawling slowly through the station, having been ordered not to stop, and got the driver to evacuate about 150 passengers. By 19.55, all the deep 'Tube' platforms had been cleared. One London Underground staff member did send passengers to the alternative escape route through the Midland City subway exit, but they found it was locked. It was only at 20.15 that the gates were finally opened, by a British Rail cleaner who had heard cries for help. Rescuers had been trying to get a badly burned passenger out that way for twenty minutes.

Up above, firemen were fighting their way back into the ticket hall, using a jet spray. Now they were beginning to find bodies. The first was a passenger. Then they found Station Officer Townley, face down, 6 feet from the bottom of a flight of stairs that would have

100

taken him to safety. He lay next to the body of a woman he had been trying to rescue. Over the next half-hour, more and more bodies were found. Nearly all were flat on their faces in the concourse and the subways around it, having made a desperate dash to escape during the first few seconds after the flashover, though a dead man was found in the bureau de change and two more bodies were discovered in the toilets in the subway. The cause of death was generally asphyxiation, though some of the bodies had later been burned. The fire, funnelled up the escalator shaft, had been highly concentrated, and the wooden panels on the walls of the concourse had hardly been charred at all, while two Underground staff who were rescued from a staff mess room by the St Pancras subway had been saved by nothing more elaborate than a wooden door.

For more than an hour, the only information the firemen had had about the layout of the station was a plan drawn by a British Rail manager. There were two sets of London Underground plans to which they should have had access, but one was in a box behind a builders' hoarding that also concealed a fire hydrant and hose, while the other was in the station's perimeter subway and could not be reached because of the dense smoke. It was not until 1.45 that the fire brigade was able to announce that the fire had been contained. More than 200 firemen had been involved in fighting it; 31 people died, and more than 50 were injured. Fifteen years later, one of the dead had still not been identified. Station Officer Townley was awarded a posthumous George Medal.

The inquiry into the causes of the fire found that grease, dust, fibre and other debris had gathered under the escalator, providing an ideal place for the flames to take hold once a lighted match fell on to it. A maintenance manager said that, as far as he knew, the running tracks of the Piccadilly Line escalators at King's Cross had never been cleaned completely. After the disaster, several matches were found by investigators. It was clear that fires had started on many previous occasions, but then gone out. This time the fire had taken hold, and the treads then carried it to other parts of the escalator where there was more oil and grease, and where wooden balustrades and decking provided more fuel for the fire.

The inquiry chairman, Desmond Fennel QC, agreed that on the whole London Underground operated a safe system, but he added that its management had 'a blind spot – a belief that fires were inevitable, coupled with a belief that any fire on a wooden escalator, and there have been many, would never develop in a way which would endanger passengers'. Much of his report is a scathing indictment of London Underground's unpreparedness. There should have been twenty-three staff on duty, but three were absent, and two others were not at their posts. These two, the ones rescued from the mess room, were taking a meal break of an hour and a half, even though they were only supposed to take half an hour, because it was 'accepted practice'. One effect was that there were only two staff on barrier duty instead of five, but the inquiry concluded it would have made no difference if everyone had been at their posts, because staff were not prepared, commenting that: 'The response of the staff was uncoordinated, haphazard and untrained.'

Only four of those on duty said they had received any training in evacuation or fire drills. It was clear some did not know where to find hydrants or firefighting equipment. The most senior member of staff, the station manager, was a long way from the fire, stuck at the far end of the Metropolitan and Circle Lines platforms where his office had been moved during building works, in spite of his complaints. His only means of communication was by an internal telephone in his office. He was not even told about the fire until twelve minutes after it was first reported, and he had scarcely left his office before the flashover happened. Even then, though, he made no attempt to contact the firemen, and it was another hour before any senior London Underground official offered them help. The public address system at the station was not used at any time during the fire, and the failure to turn on the water fog equipment in the first few minutes meant a vital chance was lost to slow the progress of the flames enough to enable the fire brigade to deal with them. The report concluded that 'there was no effective control of King's Cross station by London Underground supervisors or staff', and that, fortunately, the decision to evacuate passengers and order trains not to stop was taken by British Transport Police 'who effectively assumed responsibility for station control'.

London Underground had not even enforced its smoking ban properly. The relevant by-law said smoking was not allowed where it was 'expressly prohibited by the Executive by a notice exhibited in a conspicuous position'. The areas around the escalators at King's Cross had been included in the ban since 1985, but the inquiry was told there were probably no conspicuous 'No smoking' signs, so smoking was not unlawful, nor was the discarding of the fatal match, dropped by a person whose identity we will probably never know.

PART THREE

Accidents

EIGHT

Crushes, Collapses and Fatal False Alarms

London has been a crowded city from earliest times, and crowds can sometimes bring disaster, as happened on 3 July 1322, when a group of poor people gathered around daybreak at the gate of the Black Friars' Priory to seek alms, and more than fifty men and women were crushed to death. In 1396, the attraction was not money, but the arrival of the new bride of King Richard II, seven-year-old Princess Isabella of France. So many people had come to try to catch a glimpse of her as she came across London Bridge that at least seven were killed in the crush. In 1714, disaster struck another royal event, the coronation of George I, when scaffolding holding spectators in Palace Yard collapsed and several people died.

Entertainment also brought its share of crowd disasters. For many Londoners in the late sixteenth century, there were few things more exciting than bear-baiting. On 13 January 1583, fans had flocked to the sport's home – Southwark, beyond the constricting jurisdiction of the City. When the scaffolding on which they were standing at Paris Garden gave way, eight people were killed and many others injured.

In eighteenth-century London, the theatre was a genuine mass medium attracting huge audiences. On 3 February 1794, patrons were pouring into the Haymarket Theatre, when a man fell as he was going down some steps. Those immediately behind fell over him, but people entering the theatre, not knowing what had happened, kept pushing forward, so that those on the ground were trampled to death. Fifteen people died.

Thirteen years later, in 1807, a false fire alarm at Sadler's Wells Theatre caused a stampede for the exits, which claimed the lives of at least eighteen people. Public executions drew some of the biggest crowds of all, often attracting tens of thousands of spectators, and in the same year, the hanging of two prisoners at Newgate proved such a big attraction that a cart collapsed under the weight of spectators, up to thirty of whom lost their lives. In 1828, the Royal Brunswick Theatre, off Wellclose Square near the Tower, opened with a gala performance. Three days later, at a rehearsal, the manager noticed a chandelier was shaking, and took refuge in a box. A few moments afterwards, the roof fell in and the front façade of the building collapsed. The manager survived along with a young girl he had rescued, but twelve people were killed.

On Boxing Day 1858, another false fire alarm caused a disaster at the Royal Victoria Theatre, now the Old Vic. It was a less salubrious establishment in those days, and the audience was often rowdy. At five o'clock in the evening, the matinée performance of the Christmas pantomime was drawing to a close, and a big crowd had already gathered for the evening show at six. Local residents had been complaining about the unruliness of crowds waiting to get in, so they were allowed to queue up on the stairs inside the theatre.

Smoking was not allowed in the auditorium, but the rule was not universally observed. As a man lit his pipe, his box of matches caught fire. Two women in the front boxes spotted it and shouted 'fire'. In fact, the man threw the matches to the floor and put out the fire at once, but it was too late. About 900 people in the gallery rushed for the exits. Those on the stairs, seeing the doors open, thought the performance had ended, and pressed forward. Then hearing the cry of 'fire', the ones at the top tried to turn back. For fifteen minutes, there was chaos on the packed stairs, with the crowd pushing forwards and back. In the confusion, fifteen boys and young men were killed.

The manager decided the show must go on and the evening performance took place as scheduled. His decision attracted strong criticism in the press, but he defended it on the grounds that it would have caused more chaos and might have been even more dangerous if he had tried to fight his way through the crowd to tell them it was off. He paid the funeral expenses of all those who were killed, and announced that he would hold no more matinée performances to try to avoid any risk of a similar accident.

Public sympathy for the victims was muted because many regarded them as unruly working-class louts. *The Times* commented: 'the rabble refused to listen to reason and remain passive; hence the calamitous consequence that followed'.

In 1878, a new law on entertainment venues laid down rules on exits and firefighting equipment, but they were difficult to enforce, and did not apply to private clubs, like the Hebrew Dramatic Club in Spitalfields. From the front, the club looked like an ordinary house but at the back was a hall that could hold up to 500 people on two floors; the first floor shared the same exit as the ground floor, which would not now be allowed in a licensed theatre.

The club often used to put on 'benefit' performances to raise money for members in distress. The one held on 18 January 1887 attracted about 400 people. As the show was moving to its climax, some of the young men in the gallery wanted to get a better view, and tried to haul themselves up on a gas pipe. The pipe cracked and, as the audience began to smell gas, the cry of 'fire' went up. Almost immediately, the gas was turned off and the hall was plunged into darkness. Terrified people headed for the exits, falling over chairs and each other. By the time the first-floor audience was reaching the way out, it was already crowded with people leaving from the ground floor, and the staircase became packed with a desperately pushing throng. Within five minutes, 16 people, mainly women and children, were crushed to death. A seventy-year-old man died of a heart attack in a vain attempt to rescue his wife.

Religion could draw big crowds too. In the seventeenth century, the right of Roman Catholics to worship was severely limited, and on 26 October 1623, more than 300 Catholics crowded into the French ambassador's house at Blackfriars to hear vespers. The floor collapsed under the weight, and the priest and 94 worshippers were killed. For Protestants, it was a clear sign of God's wrath; Catholics thought it was a Protestant plot.

In 1856, disaster struck at another religious service, this time because of the preacher's star quality. The Surrey Gardens Music Hall had been hired for the 22-year-old Baptist, the Reverend Charles Spurgeon, who was drawing crowds far too big for his church in

Lambeth. An estimated 15,000 people had come to hear him, when someone uttered the fatal shout of 'fire'. The only way of escape was by four spiral staircases. In a now familiar story, in the dash to safety, one person fell, bringing down those immediately behind, then others collapsed on top of them. Six people were trampled to death and more than thirty injured. At the inquest, it was concluded that 'fire' had been shouted in a deliberate attempt to cause panic, perhaps by enemies of the preacher, or perhaps by pickpockets, who sought to profit from the confusion. A reward was offered for information, but the culprit was never found.

When the railways arrived, it gave Londoners the opportunity to get out of town on public holidays and head for 'the country'. Hampstead Heath was very popular and on Easter Monday 1892, an estimated 100,000 people turned out there, but as tea time approached, rain and sleet began to fall and the crowds headed for Hampstead Heath station in a rush to get home. There were twenty-eight steps leading down to the platform and, as the crowd hurried, someone, probably a young child, tripped. In the resulting chaos, those at the bottom were trapped against the ticket barriers. One man arriving on a train described 'a howling wilderness, shrieking, bustling, and cries of women and children . . . a scene of wildest confusion'. Eight people, including six children, were killed.

NINE

Explosions

One of the first major disasters in London caused by an explosion happened near the Tower of London on 4 January 1650, when twenty-seven barrels of gunpowder being stored by a ship's chandler blew up. The blast knocked down the Rose Tavern and fifty houses, killing at least sixty-seven people. Thereafter, explosives grew ever more powerful, but, sadly, expertise in handling them did not keep pace. So the morning of 2 October 1874 saw the steam tug *Ready* hauling a train of five barges along the Regent's Canal at the start of a journey to Nottingham. The cargo included sugar, coffee and nuts, but one of the barges, the 70-foot-long *Tilbury*, was also carrying six barrels of petroleum and 5 tons of gunpowder. It had a crew of three and, as usual, they had a fire going in the cabin. It was still dark as they passed London Zoo, and just before five o'clock, they were about to go under Macclesfield Bridge, which links Avenue Road with the Outer Circle, when there was a burst of blue light on the *Tilbury*.

The barge train stopped so the skipper of the tug could investigate. After a while, he was sufficiently reassured to restart the engines of the *Ready*, and the little convoy moved on, but not for long. Within seconds there was a deafening roar. The *Tilbury*, which was passing under the bridge at that moment, was blown into tiny pieces, while the barge behind sank and the bridge was totally destroyed. Two nearby houses were completely wrecked and others up to a mile away had their windows shattered and their doors blown in. Part of the tug's keel was found embedded in a house 300 yards away. Trees in Regent's Park were blasted or thrown down, railings were torn up and twisted, the canal banks were charred for 100 yards, and from Camden Town to Kilburn, people

111

in their night-clothes ran out into the street in alarm. The animals in the zoo howled and screeched, or huddled together in terror. The cages housing exotic birds were damaged and many escaped. Fearing that this was a Fenian bomb outrage, a detachment of soldiers arrived at the scene from the nearby Albany Barracks.

Fortunately, the canal at this point has high steep-sided banks, so the blast was deflected upwards and was less deadly than it might otherwise have been. The three men on the *Tilbury* were all killed instantly, but the crew of the barge that sank escaped with minor injuries. The only other person injured was a park keeper whose house by the bridge was completely wrecked. A government investigation concluded that the explosion was probably caused by vapour from the petroleum being ignited by the fire in the cabin or by a lamp. The inspector described the decision to carry gunpowder and petroleum in the same barge as being of 'an imprudence which is scarcely credible'. Not surprisingly, there were angry complaints about the transporting of dangerous cargoes like this through the heart of the capital, while Macclesfield Bridge earned the nickname 'Blow Up Bridge'.

Explosives were the business of the Royal Arsenal at Woolwich, and explosions were an occupational hazard. One in 1883 set off streams of rockets, each packed with 24 lb of high explosive. They smashed through nearby houses and fences, and one blasted through the wall of a crowded classroom at Plumstead. Amazingly, the only people killed were two men at the site of the original explosion. The worst disaster at the site came in June 1903, when there was an explosion in a hut where men were making shells. They had to pack high explosive in through a hole, then press it down by using a lead hammer to ram in a wooden plug, an operation in which a stray piece of grit could have catastrophic consequences. Shells were flung across the Arsenal, and many of the eighteen people killed worked some distance away from the scene of the explosion.

Fireworks factories presented similar hazards. In the 1850s, Mrs Coton held the prestigious position of firework artist at the Royal Gardens at Vauxhall, but she was still essentially running a cottage industry from the family home in Westminster. In 1854, the building blew up, killing Mrs Coton's husband and a boy who was helping him to paper the fireworks. But Mrs Coton was not easily discouraged. The house was rebuilt, and soon she was back in business with contracts not just for the Vauxhall but also the Cremorne Pleasure Gardens. Most of the dangerous work was now done at a second house in Peckham, but some filling was still carried out in Westminster, often by boys aged ten to thirteen who were paid 3s a week. On the evening of 12 July 1858, there were two explosions. Spectators gathered even though rockets, roman candles and other fireworks were flying around threatening life and limb. One hit a neighbouring house that was also a firework factory and set off explosions there too.

The known death toll was five, including Mrs Coton who survived for several days before succumbing to severe burns. Two eleven-year-olds were also killed, as was a young woman who was running for her life when she was set on fire by a rocket, then trampled to death by a terrified horse. In the streets around, more than 300 people were injured, many of them seriously. Two years later, Parliament passed a new law which effectively outlawed firework manufacture in the inner city, though many workshops carried on illegally.

The biggest explosion in London's history happened during the First World War, but it was probably nothing to do with the enemy. In the first months of the war, the British Army was being consistently outgunned by the Germans, partly because they had more guns, but also because the British did not have enough shells. In 1915, the commander Sir John French complained to the newspapers that this state of affairs was a 'fatal bar to our success'. Fresh supplies of the high explosive TNT were urgently needed, and the government began looking for a new site where it could be purified, a more hazardous process than the actual manufacturing.

In May 1915, the Ministry of Munitions was created, with the energetic David Lloyd George in charge. For some time, the government had had its eye on a plant at Silvertown, where Brunner Mond, the seed from which ICI grew, had been making caustic soda until it was closed down in 1912. One problem was that TNT and caustic soda added up to a potentially lethal cocktail, but, in the existing desperate state of affairs, this seemed too good an opportunity to miss. At first, Brunner Mond was reluctant to set up a TNT purification plant in such a densely populated area, but the company bowed to the demands of a national emergency and, within weeks of Lloyd George taking over, preparations began. The plant was scrubbed to remove all traces of caustic soda, and new equipment was moved in. Dr Andrea Angel, a forty-year-old Oxford don, was recruited to supervise the process, a team of known and trusted workers was selected and, in September 1915, the Silvertown works began purifying 9 tons of TNT a day.

It was not a great money-spinner for Brunner Mond; the government bore the costs and simply paid it a small royalty. The crude TNT was delivered in sacks and barrels and hoisted to a room above a melt pot. Then about 5 tons were poured into the pot, then the molten TNT was dissolved in warm alcohol. When the solution cooled, the purified TNT was left behind as crystals and the impurities were run off with the alcohol, then the purified TNT was skimmed off and packed into bags.

The rest of the factory still produced soda crystals and the purification plant was separated from it by a fence with barbed wire on top. To the west was the plywood and packing case works of Venesta, and to the east, Silvertown Lubricants' oil depot. Other factories in the area made soap, India rubber, and sugar. Within a quarter of a mile to the north was a residential district of 3,000 people, and even more lived three-quarters of a mile to the east.

On Friday 19 January 1917, the afternoon shift came on as usual at two o'clock. At twenty to seven in the evening, two hoist workers, Hetty Sands and Ada Randall, were due to take a break. First, Hetty went up to the melt pot room to check that the two workers there, Walter Mauger and Catherine Hodge, had enough TNT to keep them going. They saw some spilt TNT on the floor, but no more than usual. Walter and Catherine said they had all they needed, so Hetty and Ada went off to the lavatories, which were about 120 yards away. When they were inside, Hetty heard two sounds 'like an iron door being banged', as she put it later. Ada went outside to investigate, and came back screaming: 'Good God, it's all afire!'

The top of the melt pot room was blazing. The two women ran to the fence at the edge of the works, but could not climb over. It was now nearly ten to seven, and as they debated the best way to get out, a fearful explosion knocked them senseless. While Hetty and Ada had been making their way to the lavatories, beneath the melt pot room a young man named James Arnell had been sweeping up spilt TNT when he saw red drops like molten glass falling from above. He rushed down to the ground floor shouting 'Fire!' The leading hand for the shift, Edgar Wenbourne, was opening casks of crude TNT when he heard Arnell's shout above him. In turn, he yelled to the women workers: 'Run, girls, run', then went to look for Dr Angel. That was the last Arnell ever saw or heard of him.

As Arnell ran for his life, he saw that firemen were already on the premises and spraying water at the top of the building. He climbed over the factory wall and got into North Woolwich Road, where he stood watching for three or four minutes until the explosion knocked him down. The assistant chemist, Frederick Blevins, had been in his cubicle above the works lab when the alarm was raised. When he saw the melt pot room on fire, he too set off to find Dr Angel, telling everyone he passed to run for their lives. Blevins saw two workers connecting a hose to a hydrant. He knew there were 83 tons of TNT in the building and told them to get out because there was going to be a terrible explosion at any moment, but they seemed intent on fighting the fire. He found Dr Angel in his cottage next to the works and shouted to him that the works was ablaze. Dr Angel came out, insisting that he had to go to his office. Blevins begged him not to, but Angel ran off into the plant. A few moments later, Blevins heard a 'terrific rumble', and was thrown over and over.

Silvertown Fire Station stood opposite the factory and firemen had arrived on the scene before many workers realised there was a fire. As some of them entered the factory gate, they passed a worker running for his life, who shouted to them: 'Run for it! We'll be gone in a minute.' One of the firemen later recalled: 'There was a terrific bang and when I came round I was in the London Hospital.' Just four minutes after the fire started, the whole works had been turned into a giant bomb.

Molten metal, stones, bricks and debris rained down on the surrounding neighbourhood. Venesta's works and every other building within 400 yards was flattened, leaving a plain of rubble. Two of Silvertown Lubricants' oil tanks were torn open and set on fire. All that was left of the fire station was the training tower, and several streets of houses were demolished. Two flour mills were set alight, as was a ship in the dock. A gas holder on the other side of the Thames was demolished, sending a spectacular fireball into the night sky, and sparks blowing across the river ignited a tar manufacturer's yard at Greenwich. In North Woolwich Road, a boiler weighing 15 tons was flung into the air. Some said the explosion made the sky flash as bright as noon. The glow of the fire could be seen for 25 miles, and the noise was heard in Cambridge, 50 miles away. One woman said: 'It seemed as though the whole world shook. I've never heard a noise like it.'

The explosion cut electricity lines, so that apart from the fires that seemed to be burning everywhere, Silvertown was plunged into darkness. The explosion also destroyed the telephone lines, and it was half an hour before the first outside help arrived. Fires were to rage for 48 hours and cause almost as much damage as the blast itself, with the flames at the flour mills particularly hard to put out. The Port of London Authority estimated that 17 acres of warehouses and other dock buildings were destroyed or seriously damaged. Altogether, about 70,000 homes were damaged, with windows in houses as far away as Blackheath shattered, as were more than 200 at the London Hospital in Whitechapel. Firemen from all over London were drafted in, while an army of volunteers helped to extricate the dead and injured from the wreckage.

There had been twenty people working on the afternoon shift in the TNT purification plant; ten men and ten women. All ten who were in the building when the explosion happened were killed – nine men (only James Arnell escaped), and Catherine Hodge, the woman who was working in the melt pot room. Dr Angel and five other men in the plant also died, including the workers who had tried to fight the fire, and a 62-year-old watchman who was going to run for his life, but decided to wait for a moment so he could hold the gate open for the firemen.

Two of the firemen who had entered the plant were killed instantly, and three others were seriously injured. Some parts of their fire engine were found a quarter of a mile away. Another fireman was buried in the rubble as the fire station collapsed, but was dug out and survived. Also killed was the local policeman who had been on his beat near the plant at the time, and had stayed to clear as many people from the area as he could. Then there was a young clerk from the sugar refinery who had run to his manager's house to warn him of the impending disaster. As he was knocking at the door, the explosion came, and a wall collapsed and buried him. Another victim was the driver of a train that was passing on the nearby goods line.

Three people were killed in the cottages next to the fire station where the firemen's families lived, including a four-month-old girl. In the streets around, many children were in their beds on the upper floors of their houses and stood little chance of escape as roofs collapsed and debris rained down on them. One man lost his wife and four children aged ten to thirteen. Another family lost four children aged two to nine. One worker escaped from the plant only to find his twenty-year-old daughter lying dead outside his house. Until ambulances got to the scene, local people took the injured to hospital in wheelbarrows, carts, lorries, cars, boats, taxis or whatever they could commandeer. One child of eight walked in carrying a baby in her arms, and leading a four-year-old by the hand, as doctors and nurses raced in from all over London. The fact that many of the injured were treated on the spot saved hospitals from being overwhelmed by the sheer number of casualties. By midnight, most of the injured had been freed, though rescue work continued through the night and by daylight, more than thirty bodies had been recovered and put in temporary mortuaries in nearby halls and schools. Altogether, sixty-nine people were killed and four more died later from their injuries. Ninety-eight were seriously injured. Fortunately, there were relatively few workers in the factory at the time, or casualties would have been even greater. Dr Angel was posthumously awarded the Edward Medal by the King, and a number of firemen were also decorated.

Firefighters were at the scene for ten days and, with devastation so widespread, hundreds were left homeless. In the first fortnight after the explosion, nearly 900 people had to be housed in an emergency centre, and many others were taken into the already overcrowded homes of kindly neighbours. The government drafted in more than 1,700 workers to repair houses. In addition, over 18,000 children had no schools to go to, and other local schools had to operate a shift system so they could have their lessons. The explosion did more damage than any air raid during the war (see Chapter 3) and the government paid out £3 million in compensation, which left the interesting question – what caused it?

Because of the war, the government confined itself to a terse statement that an explosion had occurred in a munitions factory 'in the neighbourhood of London' and that there had been 'considerable loss of life and damage to property'. There would be an official inquiry, though its findings would not be published, because information in it might be of use to the enemy. The official silence, of course, helped to spawn many rumours: the plant had been attacked by invisible Zeppelins; or a German spy had planted a bomb. Soldiers with fixed bayonets sealed off the area. The authorities said it was to stop looting, but the soldiers' presence also fed the mood of paranoia.

The inquiry by Sir Ernley Blackwell looked at various possible causes for an accident. Could it have been started by a match? Unlikely, since none of the staff smoked. Could the TNT have ignited spontaneously? Possibly. Were there traces of caustic soda left from the previous process? If there were, that could have been enough to spark the explosion. The inquiry discovered that a government inspector had visited the plant in December 1916, less than a month before the explosion, and had said the management 'did not pay sufficient attention to the explosion risk attached to the handling of TNT', and that, following his report, some changes had been made. For example, the very night before the explosion, iron tools were replaced by brass ones which were less likely to cause sparks. The inquiry also examined the possibility of enemy involvement. All the workers were thoroughly investigated, and Sir Ernley concluded that 'no suspicion attaches to any one of them'.

It was also 'in the highest degree improbable' that there had been any unauthorised person on the premises. There was a German working at the neighbouring soda crystal plant, but he was a trusted employee of good character, who had been in Britain for forty-seven years, and had three sons in the Army.

Disturbingly, a similar explosion had occurred at a TNT purification plant in Scotland in 1915. After that a report had recommended more stringent conditions for storage, including a provision that only a certain amount of TNT should be held at any one time. These recommendations, though, were never brought to the attention of the people setting up the Silvertown plant, and because the site was so cramped, there was no room for properly protected storage magazines that might have reduced the risk even further. 'The situation of the works in fact was, from the point of view of explosives manufacture, extremely bad,' was Sir Ernley's conclusion, 'and in normal times it is certain that no such work would have been undertaken on these premises.' After his report, things were tightened up at other purification plants, but in spite of that, five months after the Silvertown explosion, another TNT works, this time in Lancashire, blew up at a cost of forty lives, while in February 1918, the government TNT purification plant at Rainham was destroyed in another explosion.

The report on the Silvertown accident concluded that 'the possibility that the disaster was in some way due to enemy agency cannot in the circumstances be overlooked'. If anyone had wanted to sabotage the plant, it would not have been too difficult. Caustic soda could be bought from any ironmonger, and just one stick in a bag of crude TNT would make it burst into flames and trigger an explosion when it was emptied into the melt pot and heated. The crude TNT arrived at Silvertown after a tortuous journey of at least a month. It began in Huddersfield, from where it was taken by rail to Dagenham. From Dagenham, it went by barge to Rainham, then from Rainham by lorry to Silvertown. It was usually packed in barrels, which often arrived at Rainham with the lids broken, but no one examined the contents of the bags before they were emptied into the pot. So, certainly, there was opportunity, though the poor safety record in Britain's TNT factories suggests that a lapse of some kind is a more likely explanation. Sadly, the only people who saw the fire start, the young man and woman who worked in the melt pot room, were killed, and the mystery of what exactly caused London's worst ever explosion seems destined to remain unsolved.

One of the most disastrous explosions in postwar London happened at Dudgeon's Wharf on the Isle of Dogs in 1969, where huge 20,000-gallon tanks that had been used for storing oil were being demolished. There had been several small fires caused by workmen's cutting equipment before the morning of 17 July, when firemen were again called to the site. When they got there, it seemed the workmen had managed to put out the flames, though there were still a few wisps of smoke. One group of firemen had climbed in to flush out the inside, and was removing the inspection hatch when there was a huge explosion that killed five firemen and one worker instantly.

The 1960s was the decade of comprehensive redevelopment, when many Londoners found themselves moving for the first time into homes with all mod cons, often in blocks of flats like Ronan Point in Newham. At six o'clock in the morning on 16 May 1968 a couple in their sixties were suddenly awakened in their seventh-floor flat there. 'Our bedroom wall fell away with a terrible ripping sound. We found ourselves staring out over London,' said James Chambers. 'Our heads were only a matter of 2 feet from the 80 foot drop. The room filled with dust, and showers of debris and furniture were plunging past us.' Mr Chambers, who had lost a leg in an accident at work, had to get himself and his wife out as best he could.

Eighty-year-old Anne Carter was on the fifth floor, half-awake, when she heard a terrible crash, and was thrown out of bed. 'I did what I had been taught to do in the last war,' she said, 'and crouched down.' Neighbours broke the door down and helped her downstairs, then she was wrapped in a blanket and taken to hospital. Up on the eighteenth floor were a young couple. The wife was expecting a baby in a month's time. As the bedroom door shot across the room, and debris began raining down, her husband threw himself across the cot in which their eighteen-month-old toddler was lying. 'I thought our last moments had come,' he said.

Ronan Point was a brand new 23-storey block. The first families had only started moving in two months before. Now the whole of one corner had simply fallen away. Fortunately, it was the corner where people's living rooms were. If it had been bedrooms, casualties would have been much worse. A man passing the flats said he saw a flash and a cloud of black smoke coming from the top. The top floors collapsed, and then the floors below fell – 'You could see yellow doors hanging open in the air.' Some furniture fell, other items – dressing tables, chairs, and sofas – were left perched on the edge of the abyss. With the lifts switched off, standard practice in an emergency, the staircases filled with terrified people, many of them barefoot and in their night-clothes, running down for their lives, though on the nineteenth floor, an elderly man did not realise anything had happened until the firemen reached him. He came out in his pyjamas and asked, 'What the hell is going on?'

The cause of the collapse was believed to have been a gas explosion in a flat on the eighteenth floor, the one where the young couple lived. One resident, 56-year-old Ivy Hodge, had been making a cup of tea. All she remembered was filling the kettle. 'Then,' she recalled, 'I found myself on the floor.' Ronan Point was built with pre-cast concrete sections that were brought to the site ready-made. Some were sceptical about this 'industrialised' building method, but the government had decided it was the only way to provide the schools, hospitals and homes people wanted, and Newham had 8,000 people on its housing waiting list. Four people were killed in the explosion, with eleven injured; Anne Carter died two weeks later in hospital. Twenty-two flats were destroyed, and some local people started a petition asking the council to stop work on other similar blocks in the borough when they discovered that the longest escape ladder the local fire brigade had only extended to 100 feet, while the flats soared to more than 200 feet.

A government inquiry concluded that the explosion had been caused by a leak from a substandard brass nut connecting Ivy Hodge's cooker to the gas supply. When she lit a match to boil her kettle, the lethal mixture of gas and air exploded. It was not a particularly fierce explosion, but it blew out the load-bearing flank walls of the flat and a progressive collapse brought every living room crashing down on top of the one below. Disturbingly, the report concluded that although Ronan Point complied with existing building regulations and codes of practice, there was considerable danger of a similar collapse in other buildings constructed in this way, and it called for the block to be strengthened, adding that, until then, the gas supply should be disconnected. The GLC said that in all blocks of similar design to Ronan Point, the gas had been cut off.

The block was repaired and people moved back in, but the prestige of the system-built tower block was fatally damaged. People had long made criticisms – that children had nowhere to play in sight and sound of their parents, that residents had no private open space, and that public spaces soon deteriorated – but now they resurfaced with renewed vigour. By the beginning of the 1980s, tower blocks were being demolished and Ronan Point itself was knocked down in 1986.

The year before Ronan Point was demolished, residents of Newnham House, a low-rise block in Putney had been complaining there was a gas leak, but no one could find it. On the morning of 10 January, the paper boy had just arrived at the block when he saw a big blue flash, and was thrown against a wall. 'The flats simply crumbled down,' he said. In a scene reminiscent of the Blitz (see Chapter 3), for three hours firemen burrowed in the rubble searching for survivors, though now they had thermal imaging and special listening equipment. Eventually, they heard a tapping sound and began tunnelling carefully towards it from above and below, shoring up the rubble with bits of wood as they went.

A 35-year-old woman had been in the bathroom at the time the explosion happened. Various items of debris, including a towel rail, had fallen on top of her, but, fortunately, they had created a tent-like hollow in which she was trapped, and she had managed to tap on the side of the bath to let the rescuers know she was alive. She had serious leg and back injuries, but firemen got her out and she survived. Lying beside her, dead, was her sister. Seven other people in the block were also killed.

TEN

Death by Water

Prosperous Victorians loved skating and the winter of 1886/7 offered plenty of opportunities. It was one of the coldest of the Queen's reign and London's lakes and ponds were frequently covered with thick layers of ice. Helpfully, the newspapers carried daily ice bulletins and at the weekends thousands would turn out at the lakes in St James's Park, Hyde Park and Regent's Park. Injuries from spills and collisions among the slashing skate blades were not uncommon; nor was falling through the ice and drowning.

In an attempt to make skating safer, the Royal Humane Society established emergency first-aid stations with rescue equipment and hot baths, manned by 'icemen', beside London's rivers and lakes. The Society would also post warning notices when it thought ice was too thin, but these were often ignored. During five weeks of the winter of 1860/61, an estimated 160 people were rescued after falling into the water in the royal parks. On 15 January 1867, the Society had posted several notices warning skaters to keep off the ice at Regent's Park, reinforced by direct appeals from the icemen, but to little effect.

At half past three in the afternoon, there were about 300 skaters on the lake, watched by 2,000 to 3,000 spectators, when the ice around the edge began to break away from the shore. Skaters who were close enough rushed for dry land and, seconds later, there was a great crack as the surface shattered. About 200 people were flung into the water. Some clung to lumps of ice to stay afloat, but many were trapped underneath. Spectators watched horrified and helpless as skaters were dragged down by their winter clothing, and, before long, women were rushing around the bank screaming, and boys and girls were weeping hysterically. The icemen were equipped to deal with individuals falling in, not with hundreds at a time. All they had were two wicker boats. Some spectators tried to save people with branches from trees. Others strung together pieces of rope and flung the line across the lake. A few people did manage to grab hold of it, but it proved impossible to drag them to safety.

One skater managed to get to the island in the middle of the lake and save a couple of others from the freezing water, and a boat builder was able to launch his boat and rescue seven people. Local residents sent blankets and sheets for those who had been pulled out, and doctors, police and more icemen rushed to the scene, but by the time they arrived, most of those who could be rescued had been, and it was a matter of recovering bodies. Nine were found by the time darkness fell. Marylebone Workhouse was turned into a temporary mortuary, as well as a hospital for those who needed treatment, and a vast crowd gathered outside, waiting for news. The next morning, scarves, hats, gloves and other items belonging to the victims had begun to float sadly up to the surface of the lake, but finding the bodies of the dead proved almost as hard as rescuing the living.

As the water froze again, channels had to be cut through the ice. In the following three days, another thirty-one bodies were fished out, but as no one knew how many had drowned, the search went on. Divers went down, but found no one, so the many distraught spectators surrounding the lake raised enough money to pay 180 men to clear it. By nightfall, more than 100 tons of ice had been removed, but it was only the following week, when the water grew warmer and the lake was drained, that it became clear there were no other bodies to find. Most of the dead were well-off young men, aged between ten and forty.

The inquest jury called for the depth of the water, which in some places reached 12 feet, to be reduced. Fortunately this recommendation was heeded, because in 1886 skaters once again ignored the warnings of the icemen and swarmed onto the lake. Once again there was a sudden crack, a section of ice broke away and 100 people fell into the water, but by then it was only 3 to 4 feet deep, and no one died.

An eighteenth-century view of Boudicca burning down London – the only time in its history that the city has been completely destroyed. (*Mary Evans Picture Library*)

A highly stylised interpretation of the death of Wat Tyler, the event that virtually ended the Peasants' Revolt, which had seen the destruction of the Savoy Palace and many other buildings. The young King Richard II looks on from his horse. (*Hulton Archive*)

In 1450, Jack Cade declared himself master of London at the London Stone, while his followers looted and raped. Within days his head was impaled on London Bridge. (*Guildhall Library, Corporation of London*)

It is said that more damage was done in London during the Gordon Riots of 1780 than in Paris after the fall of the Bastille. Here rioters burn down the gates of Newgate Prison to free the inmates. (*Guildhall Library, Corporation of London*)

When bomb damage was still a novelty. A crater left by one of the 39 air raids on London during the First World War, which killed a total of 670 people. (*Guildhall Library, Corporation of London*)

The Second World War was London's most sustained ordeal, with more than 100,000 houses destroyed as well as countless other buildings, and nearly 30,000 people killed. (*Guildhall Library, Corporation of London*)

The devastation left when Irish Fenians blew up the wall of Clerkenwell House of Detention in 1867 in an effort to free two of their comrades. Fifteen people were killed in the surrounding houses. (*Guildhall Library, Corporation of London*)

Flowers are left at the spot in Hyde Park where two guardsmen were killed by an IRA bomb in July 1982. (*Observer/Hulton Archive*)

Two hours after the first explosion a bomb planted under the bandstand at Regent's Park killed another six soldiers. (*PA Photos*)

The disaster that wasn't. The IRA set fire to the van from which they tried to kill Prime Minister John Major by a mortar attack on 10 Downing Street in 1991. (*PA Photos*)

One of the IRA's most destructive attacks. In 1993 a bomb driven into Bishopsgate in a tipper truck caused £800 million worth of damage. (*London Fire Brigade*)

The Great Fire of London in 1665 has reached Ludgate, and St Paul's Cathedral is about to be engulfed. Altogether 87 churches were destroyed as well as 52 livery halls and 13,000 houses. (*Guildhall Library, Corporation of London*)

London's first fire chief, James Braidwood, had been in his job for only a year when he had to fight a blaze that destroyed much of the Palace of Westminster in 1834. (*Guildhall Library, Corporation of London*)

Four years after the fire at the Palace of Westminster, Braidwood's men were locked in a vain struggle to save the Royal Exchange from burning down for the second time. (*Guildhall Library, Corporation of London*)

The third famous London landmark at which Braidwood had to fight a major fire was the Tower of London, where the Armoury, with its magnificent collection of historic weapons, was destroyed in 1841. (*Guildhall Library, Corporation of London*).

The last fire James Braidwood fought was in warehouses by the Thames in Tooley Street in 1861. It was London's worst since the Great Fire, and the chief was killed when a wall collapsed on him. (*Guildhall Library, Corporation of London*)

The fire at the Alhambra Theatre in Leicester Square in 1882 that almost cost a future king his life. Edward VII, while Prince of Wales, loved to help the fire brigade at a major blaze. On this occasion, he was nearly killed by a falling wall that buried two firemen. (*Guildhall Library, Corporation of London*)

One of the most spectacular fires in London's history destroyed the Crystal Palace in 1936. People watched the flames from Hampstead Heath, and the glow could be seen as far away as Brighton. (*London Metropolitan Archives*)

The tops of the escalators devastated by the fire at King's Cross underground station in 1987, the worst ever on the tube system, in which thirty-one people died. (*London Fire Brigade*)

At a rehearsal three days after its opening in 1828, a chandelier began to shake at the Royal Brunswick Theatre near the Tower of London. Moments later the whole building collapsed killing twelve people. (*London Metropolitan Archives*)

In 1874, a barge train carrying petroleum and gunpowder blew up under Macclesfield Bridge on the Regent's Canal. The bridge was destroyed, and three men on the barge train were killed. (*London Metropolitan Archives*)

The devastation left by London's worst ever explosion at the Silvertown TNT purification plant at the height of the First World War in 1917. It killed seventy-three people in the plant and the surrounding area. (*Guildhall Library, Corporation of London*)

In 1968, a relatively minor gas explosion caused the collapse of one whole corner of Ronan Point, a 23-storey block of flats in Newham, killing five people. (*London Fire Brigade*)

For a summer day out, Victorian Londoners loved the pleasure gardens at Rosherville, near Gravesend, with their zoo, maze, shows, theatres and dances. The London Steamboat Company worked from dawn to dusk ferrying passengers there on ships like the *Princess Alice*, one of the biggest pleasure steamers on the Thames, which was licensed to carry more than 900 passengers.

One notorious stretch of the river was at Tripcock Point, on the south bank almost opposite the Barking Creek sewage treatment works. In 1867, a steamboat had collided there with another vessel and been cut in two. Fortunately, the accident had happened close to shore and only four people had died, but the inquest jury commented: 'It appears there are no rules whatever to guide the captains of vessels. All is left to the chance . . . that vessels will somehow or other manage to pass one another without coming into collision.'

Eleven years later, on 3 September 1878, the *Princess Alice* left Rosherville Pier at about a quarter past six on a lovely evening to make her way back to London. She was carrying more than 650 ticket holders, but young children were entitled to travel free of charge, so the total number aboard was probably more like 750. The band played and passengers danced and sang. The captain, William Grinstead, had allowed the helmsman to stay behind at Gravesend, so for the journey back an able seaman among the passengers was hired to take his place, though he had never steered a vessel as long as the *Princess Alice*, and had little experience of the Thames.

The ship approached Tripcock Point at about a quarter to eight. Meanwhile, the *Bywell Castle*, an 890-ton collier, had left Millwall Dock at about half past six on her way home to Newcastle, carrying a cargo of ballast. Her master, Captain Harrison, who was unfamiliar with the Thames, had hired a pilot to steer her to Gravesend. She reached Tripcock Point just as the *Princess Alice* was approaching from the opposite direction. The question of which ship should do what was confused. In 1872, rules had been brought in which said that when steam vessels met head-on, they should pass port to port, but the rules were not widely publicised, and they had no force in law. Many captains were more likely to follow conventions established over many years. One was that pleasure steamers rounding Tripcock Point would hug the southern shoreline, which is exactly what the *Princess Alice* was doing, even though it meant passing the *Bywell Castle* starboard to starboard.

At Tripcock Point, the tide would first carry a vessel out into the centre of the river, then swirl her back towards the shore. Seeing the steamer's initial move, Captain Harrison presumed she had turned to starboard in order to pass him port to port whereas, in fact, she was being pulled by the tide, and would soon turn back to port.

The most senior member of the *Princess Alice*'s crew to survive, the first mate, George Long, was acting as lookout. As the steamer rounded Tripcock Point, he said he saw the *Bywell Castle* approach through the evening haze 'like a great black phantom'. The pleasure steamer carried just two lifeboats and twelve lifebuoys. Long raced to one of the lifeboats and tried to free it, but there was no time before the ships collided. A passenger said he lent his knife to a crewman to release a lifeboat, but, in the panic, it was let down into the water without a single passenger aboard, and drifted away.

Another survivor spoke of the captain shouting at the vessel bearing down on them. He saw her change course, but it was too late. The collier ripped through the pleasure boat, 'just as you would push your fist through a bandbox'. Passengers ran to and fro on the deck in terror and, as the *Bywell Castle* reversed away, water rushed into the breach. Within seconds, the *Princess Alice* broke in two. In four minutes she had sunk. One man said it felt like being flung down a shaft.

As the ship went down, the raw, putrid sewage in that stretch of the Thames was joined by a mass of struggling human beings. Most Victorians could not swim and, even if they could, the women were hampered by their big, cumbersome dresses, and the shore was 300 yards away. The crew of the *Bywell Castle* threw down ropes, but it was hopeless. One man did manage to grab one, and tried to climb up the side of the ship with his wife clinging to his neck. He had almost reached the top, when she said she could not hold on any longer, and fell back into the water. He slid back down the rope, but never saw her again. Members of the crew heard his cries for help and hauled him up.

A number of barge owners lowered small boats. One was struck by the speed with which the steamer disappeared: 'One moment she was there and the next moment – gone.' Another skipper said: 'The whole river seemed alive with heads and hair. It looked like a river full of coconuts.' People on the shore could see arms waving wildly in the water and hear the shrieks and screams of the victims. One man managed to rescue eleven people, but his boat was nearly swamped by others desperately trying to clamber aboard, and he had to use his oars to knock them off its sides. The manager of Beckton Gasworks and his assistant also saved a number of people in their boat.

Those aboard the *Princess Alice*'s sister ship, the *Duke of Teck*, following behind, had seen the collision and arrived just ten minutes after. They managed to haul some people aboard, but time was running out. The *Bywell Castle* launched three of her own boats and brought back about forty people, but when the boats went out a second time, 'all was still,' said Captain Harrison, 'and there was nothing to show how many hundred death struggles had taken place there just before'. Within twenty minutes of the accident, the only things to be seen bobbing about in the water were hats, caps and cloaks. One of the people pulled out was the wife of the superintendent of the London Steamboat Company, but she died before she reached the shore. Four of her children, her sister, mother, cousin and family nursemaid were all drowned. The superintendent had not been on the outing, and the first he heard of the disaster was when the *Duke of Teck* arrived at Woolwich with his wife's body on board. Captain Grinstead went down with his ship, along with his son, his brother and his sister-in-law.

Survivors were taken to a local school where they were given tea and dry clothes, and beds were provided in workmen's cottages nearby. Some of the bodies were laid out in a makeshift mortuary at a chemical manure factory; others were taken to the boardroom at the London Steamboat Company, but there were so many that public houses, warehouses and municipal offices had to be pressed into service. The Steamboat Company's offices were besieged by anxious crowds desperate for news of loved ones. Lists of survivors

127

were posted on the doors and published in the newspapers, but those who could not find the names they were looking for had to begin a heart-rending trek around the temporary mortuaries. There was no record of who was on board, so the final death toll will never be known, but in the weeks that followed about 640 bodies were recovered, though it was rumoured that murder victims who had been dumped in the river were sometimes mistakenly thought to have been passengers on the *Princess Alice*. Just over 100 people were known to have survived.

Many whole families had been wiped out. Fifty members of a Bible class from Smithfield had been on board, and only one survived. In 120 cases, no one came forward to identify bodies, and they had to be buried by the parish, though the authorities tried to perform the ceremonies with a respect and consideration not normally seen on such occasions. The first took place on 9 September at Plumstead Cemetery. A mounted policeman led the procession, with thirteen coffins carried on four military wagons. The route was lined with thousands of spectators, but thanks to meticulous work by the police, all but seventeen of the dead were eventually claimed by friends and relatives, and many of the bodies were exhumed and reburied. Public subscriptions paid for a memorial stone at Plumstead, and the *Princess Alice* had a pub in East London named after her.

Far from putting a damper on the pleasure-boat business, the wreck seemed to stimulate it. When the *Princess Alice*'s other sister ship, the *Albert Edward*, sailed past the scene two days later, she was crammed with passengers, and once the two halves of the wreck were brought ashore at Woolwich Arsenal, interest reached fever pitch. Huge numbers of people came from all over the country to look. Two men were sent to gaol for stealing from the wreck as police tried to fight off souvenir hunters, but it was heavily plundered.

The inquest into the accident was highly critical of the lack of life-saving equipment and of the manning levels on the *Princess Alice*. It had a crew of just fifteen, including four firemen and two engineers. A perfect stranger had been allowed to take the wheel, and lads of eighteen and twenty-one had been posted as lookouts. The jury blamed both ships for the disaster, and added that collisions like it 'might in future be avoided if proper and stringent rules and regulations were laid down for the regulation of steam traffic on the River Thames'. The vessels' respective owners sued each other, but the law put the blame squarely on the *Princess Alice*, saying she should have passed the *Bywell Castle* port to port.

Sadly, collisions and near misses on the Thames were 'of incessant occurrence', as *The Times* put it. 'The wonder indeed is, not that such an accident should have happened, but rather that it should have been so long escaped.' Only days after the *Princess Alice* disaster, another London Steamboat Company paddle steamer, the *Ariel*, collided with a barge on her way to Greenwich, though this time no one was killed. Two years later, rules for navigation on the Thames were given the force of law.

The Lord Mayor set up a relief fund to help the 400 families devastated by the disaster and donations poured in at the rate of £2,000 a day. Queen Victoria gave £100, as did the Australian cricket team who were touring England at the time. After five weeks the fund was closed, having raised £38,246, but it proved not to be enough, and many survivors as well as dependants of those who had died suffered severe long-term hardship. About 240 children lost at least one parent, and some of those, as well as those who had lost both parents, were among the 99 for whom the fund bought places in orphanages.

The *Princess Alice*'s engines were salvaged, but the wreck was broken up at Greenwich, while the *Bywell Castle* sank with all hands in the Bay of Biscay in 1883. In a strange tragic coincidence, Queen Victoria's third daughter, the Princess Alice after whom the steamer was named, died of diphtheria on 6 November 1878, the day an official Board of Trade Inquiry blamed the vessel for the worst disaster ever on the Thames.

The launch of a ship is always a great occasion – cheering crowds, the bottle smashed against the hull, the moment of tension as the vessel seems to stand free but motionless before gliding inexorably into the water. The Thames Ironworks and Shipbuilding Company at Bow Creek was a progressive employer and provided its workers with drama clubs, operatic societies and a football team that became West Ham United. The yard built a total of about 900 ships, and 21 June 1898 was to see the launch of the 6,000-ton cruiser HMS *Albion*. The Admiralty had commissioned her as part of its programme to ensure that Britannia continued to rule the waves in spite of Germany's attempts to catch up in the naval arms race that preceded the First World War.

It was to be the yard's first royal launch. Local schools had been given the day off, and 30,000 East Enders turned out in their best clothes in brilliant sunshine. As the launch time of three o'clock approached, the spectators began to jostle for the best vantage points. Even though it had been marked 'dangerous', a workman's slipway by the side of a newly completed Japanese warship seemed to offer a perfect view. The 70 police on duty did their best to keep people off the slipway, but eventually gave up, and it soon filled up with about 200 people.

The guests of honour were the Duke of York, the future King George V, and the Duchess, later Queen Mary, who hurled the traditional bottle of champagne at the ship's hull. It bounced back unbroken. She tried twice more, but the bottle remained stubbornly intact. So the wooden props were cut away anyway, and the ship plunged into the river, setting off a surge of water like a tidal wave, which crashed against the slipway and smashed it into pieces, throwing the spectators into the water.

It was only about 10 feet deep, and the struggling bodies were just 5 yards from shore, but as debris from the slipway crashed into the water, many were knocked unconscious or trapped in the mêlée as everyone desperately looked for something to cling to. Some of those nearby, who could see what had happened, jumped in to try and pull people out. A soldier leapt in to save a woman and her children, but was hit across the face by a plank and knocked out. His life was saved by another soldier who pulled him out, along with a man and two girls.

Fortunately, the police had seen what had happened, and used their boats to rescue as many people as they could. The Iron Works had its own ambulance corps and some of its members leapt into the

130

water to help, while others resuscitated those who had been hauled out. They were joined by people from the work's swimming team, but the dense crowds anxiously trying to discover what had happened to their loved ones often made it difficult for the rescuers to get to the water. Even good swimmers found themselves in trouble. One got jammed between two pieces of timber. He was strong enough to pull himself above the surface. 'The poor women and children,' he said, 'had no chance.' The cheers for the launch had drowned the screams of those flung into the water, so the yard managers did not realise what had happened for at least ten minutes. When they did, the *Albion* was towed further into the creek, to allow the rescue boats easier access.

For a time it was thought that everyone had been saved, then bodies began to float to the surface. By half past five, twenty-four had been recovered. A temporary mortuary was set up in an old galvanising shed, with bodies laid out on benches. An electrician fitted lights and, when he turned them on, he saw the corpses of his mother and his sister. By half past eleven that night, thirty-two bodies had been found. Half a dozen others died in the weeks and months that followed, including a three-month-old baby boy who was pulled from the water, but never recovered. His father had also drowned.

The Duke and Duchess of York had left the yard oblivious to the disaster, and could scarcely believe the reports. The yard director, Arnold J. Hills, was devastated. He personally visited all the families of the bereaved and promised to meet all their funeral expenses. He commented that he was invariably received without bitterness. Within twenty-four hours of the disaster, he had bought a plot of land in the East London Cemetery for the burial of the victims, and most were interred there, though a few opted for private burial elsewhere. Vast crowds gathered along the funeral route, as the eldest victim, a 64-year-old woman, was the first to be buried.

The shipyard donated £1,000 to the relief fund, which raised nearly £2,300, some given by the wealthy, including the royal family, but much coming from the very poor. One of the things it was used for was to buy mourning clothes for the bereaved who had had their only decent outfits ruined when they were washed into the river.

For a wife to lose the husband who was the breadwinner, or a husband to lose the childminding duties of a wife caused great hardship, but, sadly, the fund was closed prematurely so that many widows and widowers had to allow their children to go into homes. One worker at the shipyard had died trying to save others, and his pregnant widow and their two small children were left in great want, but when she wrote to the fund asking for help, she was told that all the money had been spent.

One hundred and eleven years after the *Princess Alice* disaster came a disturbingly similar tragedy. By 1989, all-night party and disco cruises along the Thames were becoming very popular. The Port of London Authority said the number of pleasure craft had doubled since 1984. On a summer evening, there might be up to 30 cruisers on the river each carrying as many as 150 revellers. Sadly, more traffic on the river had meant more accidents. In particular, there had been a number of collisions between barges and pleasure craft. In 1980, the motorised barge *Pepita* collided with the passenger launch *Westminster* on the approach to the central arch of London Bridge while the barge was overtaking. The following year, the *Bowtrader* had struck the *Hurlingham* while trying to overtake her under Tower Bridge and a number of the *Hurlingham*'s passengers were injured. The *Hurlingham* had had no one keeping a lookout astern, while the *Bowtrader* had had men forward, but the only means of communication with the bridge had been by hand signals. In 1983, the *Bowbelle* had collided head-on with the *Pride of Greenwich* in broad daylight. No one was hurt, but a Department of Transport investigation took the view that the accident could be put down to 'grossly inadequate visibility' from the two vessels. On 14 August 1989 the London Fire Brigade published a report warning of the growing danger.

Six days later, at a quarter past one on the morning of Sunday 20 August 1989, 130 passengers set sail from Charing Cross pier on the pleasure steamer, *Marchioness*, sister ship to the *Hurlingham*, to celebrate the 26th birthday of a Portuguese-born financier, Antonio de Valconcellos. He was clever and ambitious, with dark good looks, and cut a dashing figure in the City. He loved fun and parties, and the guests were mainly young men and women in their twenties from the worlds of photography, journalism and modelling, as well as finance. It was a lovely, clear summer night and the party was due to last till six in the morning.

The 90-ton *Marchioness* was more than sixty years old and had taken part in the evacuation of Dunkirk. It had been acquired in 1978 by Tidal Cruises Ltd, who put on an enclosed upper and lower saloon. After the conversion, there were only two ways of keeping watch aft. One was by getting someone to climb three steps at the back of the wheelhouse and put their head out of the top of the hatch. If the captain were to do this he would have had to let go of the wheel, or there would need to have been a second man in the wheelhouse, but it was not really big enough. The other way was to go onto the steps on either side of the vessel outside the wheelhouse. It was not safe for the man at the wheel to do this, and it was not possible to see directly behind the vehicle from either step, though, by moving from side to side of the vessel, a watch could be kept. What the skipper really needed was someone looking out the whole time. The *Marchioness*'s skipper was thirty-year-old Stephen Faldo. His father had been a waterman, and he had worked on the river since he was seventeen. He was described as 'a first-class and responsible waterman'. The *Marchioness*, going at just over 3 miles an hour against the tide, overtook the *Hurlingham*, and, half an hour into her journey, was coming to the most difficult part of the river where Blackfriars road and railway bridges, Southwark Bridge and Cannon Street railway bridges all come up in quick succession. Meanwhile, down below, the disco had just begun, and the first dancers were on the floor, though some partygoers took advantage of the warm night and went on deck. The mate, 21-year-old Andrew McGowan, was inside the vessel helping the two bar staff, who formed the rest of the crew. The skipper had not asked him to keep a lookout.

At about the same time as the *Marchioness* set sail, the *Bowbelle*, a 1,450-ton dredger, left Nine Elms travelling at about 6 miles an hour. The 25-year-old vessel was 80 yards long, with a big hold and deck area for its dredging equipment. The wheelhouse was placed aft and gave a poor view ahead. The master, Douglas Henderson, was on the bridge, with the second mate at the wheel. There were two men on the forecastle head, and five other crew, including the cook. Henderson had been navigating the upper reaches of the Thames for two years. He first served as master on the *Bowbelle* on 3 May and, at the time of the collision, he had completed nineteen round trips. Each involved going downriver to the dredging grounds, loading a cargo of aggregates by dredging, and then sailing back to Nine Elms. The ship was not showing the normal masthead lights, because the masts had to be lowered to allow it to pass under the bridges.

After slowly overtaking the *Hurlingham*, the *Marchioness* passed through the central arch of Southwark Bridge, intending then to go through the central arch of Cannon Street Railway Bridge, which was only about 150 yards downriver. The manoeuvre would have needed a slight adjustment to port. Meanwhile, the *Bowbelle* passed through the central arches of both bridges at Blackfriars, also heading for the central arch of Southwark Bridge. Skipper Faldo would have known that vessels like the *Bowbelle* would be likely to take this course.

At 01.46, between Southwark and Cannon Street Bridges, the *Bowbelle* hit the *Marchioness* about 3 feet from the stern on the port side. This turned her hard to port; four seconds later, the *Bowbelle* hit her again, this time about 30 feet from the stern, plunging her into complete darkness, tearing away the rear section of the superstructure and rolling her over.

In the disco and bar, there was pandemonium. According to one survivor, who was very close to where the *Marchioness* was struck: 'glass shattered over me from behind and the boat lurched sharply right hand side down. Water flooded in through the windows.' Another remembered: 'Everybody who had been on the dance floor lost their footing and chairs and everything movable went sliding from the left to the right, down into the water which was filling the dance floor area incredibly fast. I went under.' The mate, Andrew McGowan, said: 'I looked over the side and saw the bow of the

Bowbelle, and I shouted to Steve in the wheelhouse: "It's going to hit us. Go full ahead." He tried to get out, but within a few seconds it hit us.' McGowan got on the side of the overturned boat, and held the door open for people to get out. When he was in the water, he saw the skipper shouting for the life rafts to be launched. 'When I turned round, Steve had disappeared and I never saw him again.'

The passengers were terrified. A woman 'turned round and saw this huge black thing looming up. It hit us sideways and turned us over.' She found herself swimming to the surface. 'There were all these orange life rafts floating there and a man grabbed me and pulled me onto one. There was a lot of screaming and sobbing and hysteria from people in the water.' A man recalled: 'I could see people getting sucked underneath the water by the huge currents created by the boat going under.' He came across two people who could not swim, but managed to pull them to a life ring – 'I think there must have been about seven of us attached in the end to one life ring.' 'My head went under water and when I came up the boat had been pushed under,' said another survivor, 'there was no *Marchioness*.' A man who saw the collision from the bank said the barge pushed the *Marchioness* 'under the water like a toy boat. Within a matter of about 20 seconds the pleasure boat had totally disappeared.'

A nineteen-year-old woman remembered: 'the exhaustion was terrible. I asked myself, "Can I carry on with this?" as I fought to try and keep myself afloat.' As she was swept along by the current, she was grabbed by some men who had found a life ring. The organiser of the party, a 26-year-old photographer's agent named Jonathan Phang, had become wedged between some furniture and was in terrible pain but, after swallowing a lot of water, he managed to make it to the surface, where he was carried along by the tide. 'It was very fast. I passed under at least two bridges.' Eventually, he clambered aboard a wooden raft with seven or eight others and they were picked up by a passing disco boat.

Some escaped by climbing through an open window. One man stayed afloat by hanging on to the foam back of a chair; one woman held on to a plastic chair. Other boats in the area threw life rafts into the river and picked up survivors, struggling with one of the highest tides of the year and a vicious undertow. The *Hurlingham* arrived, and passengers threw life jackets overboard. A local pub landlady said that even after about half an hour there were still shouts coming from the water: 'In the end, there were only one or two voices left, but the police couldn't locate them. There were policemen on the river banks and in boats calling "Where are you?" and they were still screaming.' Altogether, fifty-one people were killed, and seventy-nine survivors were rescued. Among those killed were Antonio de Vasconcellos and one of his brothers; leading international model Julie Ibbotson; and Francesca Dallaglio, the nineteen-year-old sister of future England rugby captain, Lawrence Dallaglio.

Two minutes after the collision, Captain Henderson sent a message to the Thames Navigation Service saying 'It's this pleasure boat we didn't see.' The dredger struck Cannon Street Bridge two or three times, then after another two minutes, she restarted her engines to move off. Captain Henderson sent a further message confirming there were people on the pleasure craft: 'the pleasure craft was full, the *Royal Princess*, I believe, and the *Hurlingham* are proceeding to its assistance now.' He then proceeded downriver and anchored a few miles away in Gallions Reach, close to Tripcock Point where the *Princess Alice* had sunk.

In 1991, Captain Henderson was prosecuted for failing to keep a proper lookout, but twice a jury failed to reach a verdict, and he was acquitted. For ten years, the families of the victims fought for a public inquiry, and when they finally got it, Lord Justice Clarke concluded: 'The basic cause of the collision is clear. It was poor lookout on both vessels.' The *Bowbelle* had two men at the front of the ship and they told the inquiry that when they first saw the *Marchioness* on the starboard bow, they thought she was in a safe position, but soon after, she seemed to alter course towards them, and that they shouted, waved and whistled to the other vessel. The chief engineer, who was on the bridge of the *Bowbelle*, said he heard shouting, and saw one man waving, but that by then it was too late to take any action.

The inquiry considered that Captain Henderson should have been able to see the stern light of the *Marchioness* for a minute and a half about ten minutes before the collision, and should also have been able to see it for a briefer time after the *Bowbelle* had passed under Blackfriars Bridge. He should have known that it was dangerous to overtake a small passenger vessel navigating through the centre arches of bridges. He should also have known that it was of the utmost importance for a master to keep a sharp lookout for vessels on the starboard bow before changing course to starboard. If he was not sure where the *Marchioness* was, he should have reduced speed until he had found out, and he should have sounded an overtaking signal and not overtaken until he had heard an appropriate signal from the *Marchioness*. Captain Henderson was criticised for failing to give proper instructions to one of the men at the front of the ship to act as lookout, and for not giving him a portable radio to communicate with the bridge. If he had done this, the disaster would probably not have happened.

Between half past two and six o'clock on the afternoon before the collision, Captain Henderson had drunk six pints of lager. The inquiry said it was not 'responsible behaviour for the master of a vessel to drink six pints of beer before returning to his ship', but it did not believe this was why he did not see the *Marchioness*.

The inquiry also criticised Stephen Faldo, saying that if he had been paying proper attention to his radio, he would have known that the *Bowbelle* was close by, and would either not have overtaken the *Hurlingham*, or would have overtaken her more quickly, and then got out of the way. If he had put his head out of the hatch in the top of the wheelhouse, he would have seen the *Bowbelle* for about eight minutes. If he had taken these precautions, then the disaster would probably have been avoided. Both vessel owners were also criticised. Tidal Cruises had failed to enforce the undertaking they had given to the Department of Transport to detail at least one crew member, in addition to the person at the wheel, to maintain an all-round lookout.

There was considerable anger among the friends and loved ones of those who had died at the way Captain Henderson behaved immediately after the accident. The inquiry understood that he was anxious to get clear of the buttresses of Cannon Street Bridge with which he had collided two or three times; however, it criticised him for failing to send a Mayday call, for failing to alert his crew to the emergency and getting them to throw lifebuoys into the water, and for failing to launch the life raft. Captain Henderson's behaviour 'fell below the standards reasonably to be expected of a master', although the inquiry concluded that even if he had done all these things, it might not have saved any lives. Lord Clarke also considered that the emergency services were not properly equipped to deal with an accident of this kind, remarking: 'that there was no specific contingency plan to deal with a major disaster on the river and that there was a dearth of rescue craft'.

ELEVEN

Train Crashes

All of the sights of the hill and the plain
Fly as thick as driving rain;
And ever again, in the wink of an eye,
Painted stations whistle by.

Thus did Robert Louis Stevenson capture the astonished excitement of the early days of rail travel for a human race that until then had been able to travel no faster on land than the speed of a galloping horse. Now trains could thunder along at up to 80 miles an hour and, within just forty-five years from 1825 to 1870, Britain acquired a 13,000-mile rail network. The trouble was that brakes and signals were inadequate and accidents were frequent. To make things worse, carriages were flimsily constructed and liable to be crushed like matchwood in a crash. Third-class passengers were at particular risk. Their seats were often no more than planks, and their carriages had low sides and no roof. Casualty figures became so alarming that Queen Victoria herself expressed concern.

One of the first serious railway accidents in London happened in June 1857 close to Lewisham station. Sunday evenings on the North Kent branch of the South-eastern Railway were always busy as a series of frequent trains carried day trippers back into London. Station masters were supposed to make sure trains leaving their station had passed through the next before they allowed any following train to depart. Information was passed between stations by an electrical signal.

On 28 June, the 21.15 Strood to London train had passed through Blackheath station about fifteen minutes late, and was then stopped by a signal just before reaching Lewisham station. The guard had got out for a moment to wait by the track when he heard the sound of another train approaching. Alarmed, he grabbed a hand lamp that showed a red 'danger' signal, and ran towards it. As the engine came into sight, he waved frantically. The train passed him at about 20 miles an hour, and, in the dark, he could not tell whether the driver had seen him or not. Then he ran back towards his own train, but before he reached it, he heard the impact of the crash; knowing that yet another train was due, he ran back to Blackheath station to tell the station master to stop it.

Back at the scene of the accident, the following train had smashed into the brake van at the back of the 21.15 with such force that it knocked it off the rails and onto the top of one of the third-class carriages, which promptly disintegrated, so that its passengers were crushed in a tangled wreck of wood and metal. The railway had only the most rudimentary rescue equipment available and it was three hours before the brake van could be lifted off the carriage. Eleven people were killed, and sixty-three injured. The driver and fireman of the following train were taken into police custody, but after the inquest revealed that the signalling system on the line often broke down and gave inaccurate messages, they were both cleared.

Railway companies had to pay small amounts of damages to passengers injured in an accident, but nothing to workers. Four years after the crash at Lewisham, an attempt to raise money for injured staff by employees of the North London Railway Company ended in another tragedy. On 2 September 1861, they organised five special excursion trains to Kew. The passengers went out in the morning and were due to come back after eight o'clock in the evening. By about seven, the station master at Kew grew concerned about the number of people already waiting, so he decided to let one of the excursion trains return early, and it left Kew with passengers packed into each of its twelve carriages. These excursion trains did not appear on the timetable and had to be fitted in around scheduled services, so a scheduled train generally carried a warning notice on its end carriage if it was being followed by an excursion, but the 18.35 Kew to London train had already departed carrying no such notice, and the station master had no way of informing other stations along the line.

Meanwhile, between Kentish Town and Camden stations, 6 miles away, a driver was manoeuvring the nineteen trucks of his ballast train across the lines to and from a siding while a partially deaf nineteen-year-old youth, who worked a 15-hour day for 14s a week, was in charge of the signals. Like excursion specials, ballast trains too had to have their movements fitted in around the regular services, and the driver watched in astonishment as the excursion train came rushing towards him. He tried to accelerate out of the way, but it was too late. The excursion special smashed into one of his trucks, came off the track, and careered down a 30-foot embankment, dragging three carriages behind it into a field below. The engine was left on its side puffing out hot steam, while other carriages hung off the bridge.

The air filled with the screams of those trapped and injured and, as it was getting dark, the remains of one of the brake vans was set on fire to provide light. Police arrived with cabs and wagons to take the injured to hospital and, as word got around, people rushed to the scene desperate for news of their loved ones. Altogether, more than 300 people had been injured and 16 died.

Although the Kew to London train had not showed the correct warning on its back, the inquiry blamed the young relief signalman, because he had taken off the danger signal while the ballast train was shunting across the line. In the fading light, with the track curving, nearing the end of a 15-hour shift, it may simply be that he became confused about which of the two tracks it was on.

Fog was always a hazard on the railways. At Harrow, in November 1870, it was responsible for a collision between the Euston to Liverpool express and a coal train in which eight people were killed. There were accidents at Ilford in 1944, and at Gidea Park in 1947, when trains overran signals, and a total of fourteen lives were lost, while worse was to come on the very foggy morning of 24 October 1947, when visibility was down to 50 yards and trains in the Croydon area were being delayed because drivers could not see signals until they were virtually on top of them.

The signalling system was old-fashioned, but it should have been foolproof. It involved interlocked instruments in each signal-box, which prevented a signalman accepting a train into his section until the previous one had cleared it. In the Purley Oaks signal-box that morning was an inexperienced signalman who had never worked in fog before. The Hayward's Heath to London Bridge train was not scheduled to stop at Purley Oaks, but because the previous train had not cleared the next station ahead, the signalman could not clear his signal for the Hayward's Heath train, and so he held it at the signal at Purley Oaks station. In the fog, he could not see the train, and seems to have forgotten about it. Six minutes later, he was offered the Tattenham Corner to London Bridge train, and saw that his signal was shown as 'Blocked'. He assumed the instrument had failed, and used the special release key to free it, allowing him to change the signal and accept the train. This also allowed the Hayward's Heath train to move off, but the Tattenham Corner train was faster and ran into the back of it in the fog. The front coach of the Tattenham Corner train and the last coach of the Hayward's Heath train were both wrecked, and thirty-two people were killed. But the worst accident involving fog was to come five years later. It would also be the worst rail disaster in London's, and in England's, history.

At a quarter to two on the morning of 8 October 1952, a train driver was called up at home and told to take the Perth express from Crewe on the final leg of its journey to London. Driver Jones, aged forty-three, was in the pool from which men are drawn, often at short notice, to replace others who are absent. On this occasion, he was replacing a driver who was on holiday. He had qualified six years before and was regarded as methodical and reliable. He had finished his last turn at a quarter to three the previous afternoon, had a short nap, then spent some time decorating his house, before going to bed at a quarter to eight. The train he was to drive had eleven carriages, including four sleeping cars, and was being pulled by one of the most powerful engines in the country, the *City of Glasgow*. There were about eighty-five passengers aboard.

It had been slowed down by fog, and by the time Driver Jones left Crewe, it was already running thirty-two minutes late. The fog continued, so that by the time he was getting close to London, he was about eighty minutes late. At the north end of Watford Tunnel, he was

142

stopped briefly at a signal, but from then on it was downhill into London, and the engine should have been able to pick up some speed. The fog was clearing too, and the special precautions, which involved having longer intervals between trains, were lifted at ten past eight. The sun was breaking through and visibility around Harrow and Wealdstone station was about 200 to 300 yards, though it was more restricted in the open country between Watford and Harrow.

Meanwhile, at the station, the local train from Tring to Euston had also been delayed by fog, and had arrived about seven minutes late. By 08.19, it had been waiting at Platform 4 for a minute and a half or so. This was the platform on the fast line to London, but it was usual to transfer the local train to the fast line at this point, and the rule was that it should be given precedence over any night expresses running late. The local train was crowded, with about 800 passengers packed into its nine coaches.

Approaching at the same time from the opposite direction on the adjacent track was the 08.00 Euston to Liverpool and Manchester express. Pulled by two engines, it had left Euston about five minutes late, but its fifteen carriages were now racing along at around 60 miles an hour. It was the signalman who got the first hint of impending disaster when he saw the Perth express come hurtling out of the fog on a collision course with the local train. He immediately sounded the alarm detonators, and threw the signals for the Liverpool train to 'danger'.

In the meantime, the local train had just released its brakes and was waiting for the guard's signal to move off. One passenger, Evelyn Hargood, noticed that it seemed very jerky. 'As the train went forward,' she said, 'I knocked a man's hat off, and I remember saying, "Oh, I am sorry"'. Then the whole train bolted forward, and her carriage was flung onto its side. 'The next thing I realised I had feet in my ear, and knees in my chest.'

The Perth express had ploughed into the local train and then been derailed by the impact. It came to rest more or less upright about 80 yards on, with five carriages behind it, but on the track along which the Liverpool train was at that moment racing. Within two seconds of the first collision, the Liverpool train struck it at 60 miles an hour. Both of its engines were catapulted across one of the platforms, and came to rest 75 yards from the point of impact. The signalman quickly turned off the electric current which halted a local electric train approaching from Watford short of the wreckage.

It was the crowded local train that suffered worst. 'I heard one or two people groaning and with that someone else at the side of me said "Oh dear, that one's dead",' said Evelyn Hargood. She groped in the dark and managed to find her husband's hand. 'It was dark and dusty and there was a tremendous smell of sulphur from one of the other trains.' She noticed the carriage was full of sandwiches and apples from people's packed lunches. When they had been trapped for about half an hour, a man got out a penknife, and managed to cut through a leather strap holding the window shut. He got it open, and people outside shouted to them to climb out.

Three passenger coaches of the local train, three from the Perth express, plus seven of the Liverpool express were now compressed into a heap of wreckage 45 yards long and 30 feet high. One end was jammed under the station footbridge, which had had a steel girder torn away. At the bottom of the heap was the *City of Glasgow*. The wooden coaches at the back of the commuter train had been smashed to pieces, and some of the debris from the crash had been flung onto Platform 4.

The first ambulance and doctor arrived within three minutes of the disaster at the same time as the fire brigade, but, by modern standards, the rescue effort was pretty haphazard. One injured man got out of the wreckage, took the bus to Watford and at about eleven o'clock presented himself at the local hospital, where they still had not heard about the crash. A policeman had to flag down a passing RAF truck to ask for help in keeping out sightseers. Firemen were pulling at the wreckage with their bare hands and cutting with hacksaws. Train doors were used as makeshift stretchers. A fourteen-year-old boy scout, who had stopped on his way to technical college, was lowered into the wreckage because he could clamber to the injured through narrow gaps.

One of the first ambulancemen to arrive was greeted by chaos: 'We were inundated with injured people crying "Help!" We opened the back of the ambulance and it was swamped.' People were grabbing bandages, and loading casualties in on train seats. Someone tried to put in one of the victims on a train door but it would not fit. The ambulancemen had no radio, so when they dropped off injured people at the hospital, they had to telephone their control to say they were available again. They were equipped with only a basic first-aid kit, and the key objective was to get people to hospital as quickly as possible. 'The ambulance crews were just seen as removal men,' said one. 'People would hand us the injured and we would take them to hospital. It was known as "scoop and run".' Experience in the Second World War had shown the value of giving some basic life-saving treatment on the spot, but this approach had not yet found favour in the response to civilian accidents.

Doctors were found by touring the area with a loud-hailer. They too climbed into the wreckage to give morphine injections, but once victims were released, they were often whisked away without proper information accompanying them on what painkillers they had been given, or if they had had anything to drink. An appeal also went to the US Air Force base at Ruislip to send medical teams. At half past ten, they arrived. One of the British rescuers noted in awe: 'The Americans had everything . . . they were performing operations on site.' The USAF team put more stress on immediate care, giving intravenous infusions on the spot, and they labelled each injured person carefully before sending them off to waiting ambulances. Local women had been tearing up sheets to make bandages; the Americans opened a proper dressing station.

It took until half past two to free the 157 injured and get them to hospital, though it was only at half past one the next morning that hope was abandoned of finding anyone else alive. Many of the 102 people killed had to be carried away in furniture vans: 98 were passengers, and 4 were railway workers, including the driver and fireman of the Perth express and the driver of the leading engine of the Liverpool express. The driver of the second engine on the Liverpool train was buried in coal as it overturned but escaped with a badly torn hand. In hospital, 10 more passengers later died of their injuries. Of those killed, 64 were from the local train; 23 were on

145

the Perth express and 7 on the Liverpool train. Of the remainder, it was thought that some might have been hit by the engines of the Liverpool train as they waited on the platform, while others might have been crossing the footbridge. It took more than four days to clear the wreckage and reopen the line. The locomotives from the Liverpool train had to be scrapped, but the *City of Glasgow* was repaired and pulled trains for another decade.

An inquiry had to try to piece together what had gone wrong. The driver of the Perth express should have seen a signal showing yellow and begun slowing down almost a mile and a quarter from the station. Then there were semaphore signals set at 'stop' 600 yards and 200 yards from the station. The guard on the train, who survived the crash, said the brakes had worked normally throughout the journey. He had been sorting out his paperwork when he felt sharp braking, which was followed within two seconds by three violent lurches followed by an equally violent rebound. He said the fog between Watford and Harrow had been 'not dense but patchy'.

Investigations suggested that all the signals were working normally. With visibility at about 100 yards, travelling at 50 miles an hour the driver would have seen one of the crucial signals for only about four seconds. Steam and smoke from a passing goods train might also have restricted his view, and the morning sun was breaking through at an angle that would have been in his eyes as he searched for the signal, but these were the normal hazards a driver had to face. Perhaps there had been some unknown calamity in the cab, except that the brakes were put on at the last minute. The inquiry's conclusion was that 'Driver Jones must have relaxed his concentration on the signals for some unexplained reason'.

The inspector remarked that the death toll on the Liverpool train was surprisingly low considering the severity of the impact, and believed it might be because some of the coaches were built to a new all-steel design and kept their shape much better. He also said the accident could have been prevented if the train had been fitted with an automatic warning system that sounded an alarm in the cab if a signal was not showing green. He noted that British Rail was planning to fit it to a third of the network, and considered that 'no financial considerations should be allowed to stand in the way of an ambitious programme'.

Five years later, fog was to cause another disastrous railway accident in London. On 4 December 1957, a thick 'pea-souper' had been playing havoc with services all day and, as darkness fell, things got worse. The eleven coaches of the 16.56 Cannon Street to Ramsgate express left London 45 minutes late. The train was packed, with about 700 passengers on board.

On the viaduct between Cannon Street and New Cross, visibility was fairly good, but as the train entered the three-quarter mile cutting between New Cross and St Johns, it deteriorated, being reduced in places to 20 yards. The main line through St Johns was one of the busiest in the world. Every day, an average of 990 trains travelled on it, and another 125 took the bridge that carried the Nunhead to Lewisham loop overhead. The signals came thick and fast; on average, one every 490 yards.

As the Ramsgate express approached St Johns, it passed a signal known as L 16. This was showing double yellow to notify the driver that the next signal but one, L 18, just over half a mile away, was at red. Until L 16 the driver had had green signals since leaving Cannon Street. It gave ample warning for a train travelling at 45 to 50 miles an hour to stop at L 18, and the express was going a good deal slower. The problem with these signals, though, was that they were sited to the right of the track, while the engine was driven from the left, and they had to be observed from a distance, because the boiler obscured them from the driver once he came close. So L 16 could be seen from more than 300 yards away, but the driver lost it for the last 80 yards. Similarly L 17 was invisible for the last 95, and L 18 for the last 238 yards. In dense fog, the driver would not see these signals at all. The fireman, on the other side of the footplate, did not see the signals until the engine came close, but then they stayed in sight until it had passed them.

The fireman was used to being asked to look out for signal L 18, but not L 16 and L 17. So once they left New Cross, he had begun firing for the long climb up to the top of the North Downs, until approaching L 18, at about twenty past six, he paused from his shovelling to look at the signal, and shouted to the driver 'You've got a red!' The driver applied the brake, but it was too late. Less than ten seconds later, he ploughed at about 30 miles an hour into the back of the ten-coach Charing Cross to Hayes electric train that was stopped at the next signal. Because of the gradient, the electric train, with 1,500 passengers on board, was standing with its brakes on, making the collision more severe. The last two coaches were of stronger build than the front eight, and the impact made Coach 9 carve right through Coach 8 in front of it.

The crash happened beneath the girder bridge that carried the Nunhead–Lewisham loop. The locomotive of the Ramsgate train was not derailed, but the tender and leading coach were thrown to the left with sufficient force to strike and bring down a stanchion supporting the bridge, and 350 tons of steel girder collapsed on to the train, completely destroying the first coach and crushing the front half of the next. Two minutes later, the Holborn Viaduct to Dartford train was approaching the bridge. Fortunately, the driver was slowing as he came towards a red light, and he spotted the track subsiding in front of him in time to apply the brakes and prevent his train toppling off. Even so, the coaches were left precariously balanced on the tilting track.

Ninety people were killed, including the guard on the electric train, and 109 seriously injured. Most of the victims on the electric train were in the eighth coach, which suffered the worst damage. On the Ramsgate train, the majority of the casualties were in the front three coaches. The alarm was raised by someone living in one of the houses by the line, and the first ambulances and fire engines were on the scene within five minutes. Visibility was so bad that at first rescuers could not even see that the bridge had been brought down, but the last of the injured were removed from the wreckage by half past ten. The rescue services had to shore up the bridge with heavy timbers so the Dartford train could be drawn safely back.

Driver Trew from the Ramsgate train was taken to hospital with severe shock. He was sixty-two, had been a driver for eighteen years, and was regarded as conscientious and reliable. He told the coroner's inquest that he had caught glimpses of yellow signals at L 16 and L 17. When the fireman said he had a red light at L 18, he 'was a bit surprised because we never stop there'. He said that he trusted his fireman, and could not explain why he had not asked him to look out for signals, nor had there been any defects in the engine, such as steam leaks, to divert his attention. The inquiry concluded that he did not see the signals, but must have assumed they were clear. It held him responsible for the accident.

The driver was charged with manslaughter. At his trial, he said that he had not seen either signal in the fog, and that, after seeing a green light at the signal before L 16, he believed he 'was all right up to St Johns'. The fireman said that the driver did not ask him to look out for L 16 and L 17. He was looking out for L 18, but could not see it until they were alongside the platform at St Johns. He knew when he told the driver it was red, there was no chance of stopping, though he saw him put the brake handle down. The guard, travelling in the seventh coach, said 'visibility was nil'. He could only see signals at a coach's length. At the first hearing, the jury could not agree, and at a retrial in August, Driver Trew was acquitted.

As at the inquiry into the Harrow disaster five years earlier, the inspector pointed out that it could have been prevented by an automatic audible warning in the cab. Indeed, the inspector said that over the past forty-five years, a third of the deaths in rail crashes might have been prevented by this device. He was pleased to note that British Rail was planning to phase in its installation on all major routes.

Ten years later, just a couple of miles down the track, came another rail disaster. This time only one train was involved, a packed twelve-coach diesel electric from Hastings to Charing Cross. It was just before a quarter past nine on bonfire night, 1967, and the driver was going at around 70 miles an hour as he passed through Grove Park. When he started to brake for the 60 mile an hour limit beyond Hither Green, he felt the train drag. He heard a 'terrific bang', and then the automatic brakes came on sharply. The guard, who was travelling in the sixth coach, noticed debris flying past the window.

He opened it and looked out, and had his hat knocked off. He threw himself to the floor and shouted to the passengers standing in the passage next to him to do the same. One passenger said it sounded as though the train was running over broken glass, then the coach started to rock with increasing violence until there was a crash, the lights went out, and it turned on its side.

When the front carriage had come to a stop 750 yards from Hither Green station, the driver peered behind into the darkness, and saw that his coach was on its own. The other eleven carriages lay more than 200 yards behind, spreadeagled across two main lines and an adjoining siding. The four coaches immediately behind had flipped over, some onto their right sides, some onto their left, and slid along the tracks crushing people beneath as their sides disintegrated. The remaining seven were upright, but derailed.

The signalman at Hither Green saw the accident and raised the alarm. The emergency services were at the scene within five minutes under a newly developed Major Accident Procedure. Mobile lighting and heavy cutting equipment were rushed in, and more than 120 firemen worked to release those trapped. Twenty ambulances were lined up to take the injured to hospital as they were cut free. It was four hours before the last was removed from the wreckage; 49 people were killed.

It soon became clear what had happened. A triangular piece of rail, about 6 inches long at the top, had broken away at a joint between two lengths, probably as the heavy front coach had passed over it. It had been left poking up above the level of the rail like a trip wire and had derailed the front wheels of the third coach. The remaining coaches had managed to jump the gap, and the derailed wheels then slid along for a quarter of a mile until they came to a crossing. Here the third coach became completely derailed, broke away and overturned. In the process, it flipped over the second, fourth and fifth coaches. The couplings between the first three coaches parted, allowing the front coach to go on without being derailed.

The inquiry into the accident exonerated the driver, who was going at the correct speed, but the inspector was scathing about the state of the track. A similar rail fracture had happened in the area less than two weeks before, and ultrasonic tests at that time had found cracks in five rails. An inspection two days after the accident revealed that some of the track in the area was in a 'deplorable condition'. In many places, there was not enough ballast to support the sleepers which meant that they moved up and down as trains passed over, putting enormous strain on rails and joints, which had caused the break where the derailment occurred. The inspector found that there had not been enough staff to carry out proper inspections or maintenance.

Most fractures occur at rail joints, and this one happened at the joint between two 'closures' – short pieces of rail that are put in to fill gaps between long stretches of continuously welded rail. The use of closures had been abandoned on other parts of the British Rail network, but continued on Southern Region. After the derailment, the speed limit was reduced to 60 miles an hour, more staff were provided for inspecting and maintaining the track, and the use of closures was ended.

The worst disaster in the history of the London Underground happened on 28 February 1975 during the morning rush hour at Moorgate. There were forty-three people killed, and seventy-four seriously injured. The rescue services had to work in nightmarish conditions for fourteen hours to free the last live casualty from the wreckage, and for more than four days to remove the last body. The cause remains a mystery.

On the fateful morning, in a block of flats at New Cross, train driver Leslie Newson had got up at four o'clock, drunk a cup of tea and shaved in the kitchen. He was going to work at Drayton Park, where he had been for five weeks, but he was pleased that, in a month's time, he was going back to the Barking line which he had always preferred. His train, which would be making the journey to Moorgate, had been serviced overnight. On the first trip, another driver took it, and checked the brakes including the back-up Westinghouse brake. They worked perfectly.

That morning, Driver Newson made the journey three times. After one trip, he chatted to his young guard Robert Harris in the

151

signal-box at Moorgate while the signalman made tea. When another driver asked Newson for some sugar, he had replied, 'Go easy with it, I shall want another cup when I come off duty.'

In those days, the 3-mile trip from Drayton Park to Moorgate was part of the London Underground system. Altogether, Newson had done the run nearly 230 times. On his fourth journey, taking the 08.39, Newson left Drayton Park half a minute late. As usual, commuters had packed into the front three coaches, because they were nearest to the exit at Moorgate. The train made just three stops, and, in accordance with his reputation as a conscientious and rather cautious driver, Newson brought it to a careful halt at each one, and at the last, Old Street, he checked the Westinghouse brake. The young guard, in the meantime, had grown rather bored and had left his panel at the front of the last carriage to go to the driving cab at the back to see if there was a newspaper. Finding nothing to read he went back into the carriage and was looking at the advertisements as the train approached Moorgate.

From his signal-box at the end of the platform, the signalman watched the train approach. He expected it to slow down, but realised it was accelerating. It burst out of the tunnel 'like an express train'. He watched helpless as it raced through the platform towards the blind 60-foot tunnel at the end. Two railwaymen sitting on Platform 9 recognised Newson with his hands on the controls, sitting bolt upright and staring straight ahead, his cap on his head, his uniform as neat as ever. Inside the train, some of the 300 passengers shouted out; others gripped the arms of seats and braced themselves for the impact. It skittled a danger signal, ploughed through a 15-yard sand drag at nearly 40 miles an hour and shattered the buffers, thundering into a 5-foot-thick concrete wall at the end of the tunnel. The front coach reared up and hit the tunnel wall close to the top of its 16-foot height. It buckled in two places, with a right-angle bend just behind the driver's cab and a further 30-degree bend towards the back of the car. The second coach had ploughed under the first, crushing it further, and pushing it against the tunnel roof. It too was concertinaed, and the third coach hit its back and rode over it to strike the tunnel roof. The front three coaches were now crushed into little more than the length of a London bus. In one place, the space between the roof and floor of one of the carriages had been compressed into just 2 feet, and the 3 feet depth of the driver's cabin had been squeezed to a single foot. The fourth coach was slightly damaged, while the fifth and sixth escaped. A cloud of black dust flew along the tunnel. The guard picked himself up from the floor and groped for the door release, while the signalman called London Transport control.

The first person from the emergency services on the scene was a City of London Policeman who had been outside the station when a man coming out told him there had been a crash. He found his way down to the dust and soot of Platform 9, where he could see a train in the tunnel without its lights on. Railway workers were helping people out of the carriages, and passengers were sitting dazed on the ground. The first fireman to arrive said the train seemed completely silent. He made sure the current was switched off, lowered himself down from the platform and went into the tunnel. As soon as people saw the beam of his torch, they began to call out for help and scream and groan. The fireman shouted: 'The fire brigade's here. You'll be all right now.' The scene was horrifying. The upended wheels at the back of the first carriage had crashed through the roof of the second, landing on some of the passengers sitting at the front, while the roof of the front section of the second coach had sheared off and curled back like the lid of a sardine tin over the back end of the front coach.

The first medical team came from BP's headquarters in the City; two doctors and two sisters. Once the doctors saw how bad things were, they raced up to a local chemist and cleaned out its supplies of pain-killing drugs. Soon they were joined by a squad of doctors and nurses from St Bartholomew's. Firemen were now beginning to force open the doors of the third carriage and help the walking wounded to get out. The doors of the front carriage were open just enough for a fireman and two police officers to get in. Everywhere there were dead and injured; many of them had fallen into the back section of the carriage. In one place all they could see was a row of people's heads, their bodies trapped in the twisted metal, but they did manage to release a young couple who were sitting together holding hands.

A line of firemen began manhandling the injured back to the platform. Doctors were hauled in the opposite direction to the wreckage at the front of the train; one of them remembered wondering whether he would ever get out again. One of the most horrifying things for the rescuers was having to walk on the dead to reach the living. Firemen could not use hot-cutting equipment to release the injured quickly for fear of starting a fire or harming others who were trapped, so they had to resort to levers and hacksaws. Meanwhile, passengers had to be got off the two following trains, which were now stuck in tunnels, and walked along the track to Moorgate.

Many of the rescue workers had expected their next big emergency to be another IRA bomb outrage (see Chapter 4), but Inspector Brian Fisher, the emergency specialist of the City of London Police, who was coordinating police at the scene, said: 'Never, in our wildest imagination, had we envisaged anything as bad as this.' Just after ten o'clock, a makeshift operating theatre was set up on Platform 11 for those who might not survive a journey to hospital. One man was given an adrenalin injection into the heart; others were put on drips; fractured limbs were placed in splints. Then the injured were fastened to stretchers and carried to the surface by teams of ambulancemen with doctors or nurses holding plasma bottles high above them. Casualties were marked on the forehead. 'X' meant minor injuries; 'XX' meant serious, but some delay before treatment possible; 'XXX' meant serious injuries in need of immediate treatment. A field telephone system was set up by running cables down from the surface, but it could not reach the rescue teams, so messages had to be passed by word of mouth, competing with the constant noise from the cold-cutting equipment, with all the confusion that entailed. So 'The doctor needs Entonox' (a painkiller) became 'The doctor needs an empty box'. Fortunately, the rescuers soon managed to borrow some experimental mobile communications equipment.

Police motorcyclists toured City building sites begging for props to stop the wreckage from collapsing as rescuers cut away at it. With the trains stopped, the ventilation their movement provides to the

Underground was lost, and the temperature at Moorgate rose inexorably, soon reaching 100 degrees Fahrenheit. Industrial fan-blowers had to be set up on the platform to try to keep it down. Firemen were working stripped to the waist, while they talked to the people who were trapped about whatever they could think of – their homes, their families, their jobs, where they were going for their holidays. One fireman had to sit on the head of a young woman who was dead while he cut other people out. A man was found on top of a pile of dead bodies with only 6 inches of breathing space, but the moment firemen lifted him down he dusted off his jacket, and walked off along the platform, apparently uninjured. Perhaps he was late for work.

The first body was removed at ten o'clock. An official photographer described how many of the dead seemed to be sitting quite normally or strap-hanging. He said: 'In one doorway there was a row of businessmen, some still with their brief cases, standing as they would have been waiting for the train to stop, but all dead.' A fireman reported: 'People were standing up, dead, staring at us. We couldn't take that so we pinned up a salvage sheet over them.' A Salvation Army officer, who had done rescue work in coal mines, said it was like a mining disaster – 'the darkness and the terrible dust'.

By mid-afternoon, rescuers knew there were a man and woman still trapped in the front section of the front carriage. A City of London woman police constable and keen amateur athlete, Margaret Liles, had only her head free. She had been going to be sworn in that day as a policewoman at the end of her training. A young man named Jeff Benton had been hurled partly on top of her, and both were pinned beneath steel girders from the chassis of the train.

By half past seven in the evening, rescuers decided they would have to amputate Margaret Liles's left foot at the ankle in order to free them both. The operation was carried out in the tunnel, and within seconds, she was on the way to hospital. Still smiling and thanking rescuers, Jeff Benton was released after being trapped for twelve hours. Margaret Liles went on to marry and have a family. Sadly, Jeff Benton's injuries proved too severe, and he died in hospital a month later. Now that the rescue teams believed they had got out everyone left alive, all the cutting equipment was switched off, a senior officer called for complete silence, and firemen walked the length of the wreckage, calling and listening. Just after ten o'clock, the site medical officer certified that any remaining casualties were dead, and firemen could begin using hot-cutting equipment on the wreckage, while trying not to damage bodies and preserving as much as they could of the driver's cab to help analysis of what had happened. It was dreadful work. Bodies were decomposing fast as the temperature had reached 120 degrees, and the smell was appalling. Everyone not essential below ground was moved back up to the surface, and those working in the tunnel had to be given forty minutes to recover on the surface for every twenty they spent below ground. They all had to wear face masks and gloves, and any scrape however minor had to be reported immediately because of the danger of blood-poisoning. The Army sent mobile shower units, and firemen entering and leaving the scene were put through a full-scale decontamination procedure. By the time the last body, the driver's, had been removed, on Tuesday evening, four and a half days after the accident, more than 1,300 firemen from virtually every station in London had been at Moorgate.

Now the focus turned to what had caused the accident. The controls in the cab were examined and all seemed to have been working properly. So, what of the driver? The first thing that became clear was that Driver Newson was not a reckless man. If anything, he was too careful. The driver who trained him said he was worried that Newson might keep falling behind the timetable because he was so cautious. Guards also testified that he was slower than other drivers, normally approaching the platform at Moorgate, where there was a 15 mile an hour speed limit, at 5 to 10 miles an hour. On the three trips they did that morning, Guard Harris said that Newson had seemed perfectly normal.

On the last journey, he said he had no idea they were at Moorgate until he saw the station lights. It never crossed his mind to take any action to stop the train, though if he had been aware they were coming into the station too fast, he would have applied the

SINKING OF THE PRINCESS ALICE ON HER RETURN FROM SHEERNESS SEP. 3rd 1878

MARKS & SONS PUBLISHERS   AS SKETCHED BY THE ARTIST AN EYE WITNESS.   72 HOUNDSDITCH EC

An eye witness's sketch of the sinking of the paddle steamer *Princess Alice* after its collision with a collier in 1878. A total of 640 people were killed in the worst disaster ever on the Thames. (*Guildhall Library, Corporation of London*)

The wrecked hull of the *Marchioness* pleasure craft, sunk in a collision with a dredger on the Thames in 1989. Fifty-one people drowned. (*PA Photos*)

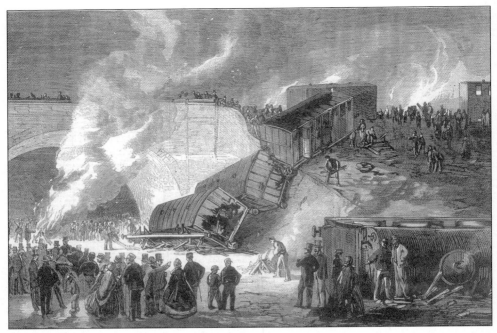

An excursion special crashes off a viaduct at Kentish Town in 1861 after colliding with a ballast train. There were sixteen fatalities in one of London's first major rail accidents. (*London Metropolitan Archives*)

The wreckage from the collision of three trains at Harrow and Wealdstone station in England's worst ever rail disaster in 1952. (*London Borough of Harrow Local History Collection*)

The body of one of the 112 people killed is taken from the scene. (*London Borough of Harrow Local History Collection*)

The rail tracks of the Nunhead to Lewisham loop career drunkenly into the distance. The bridge that carries them has been damaged by the collision beneath of two trains in thick fog. The accident in 1957 cost ninety lives. (*Hulton Archive*)

One of the carriages derailed in the Hither Green train crash of bonfire night, 1967. Forty-nine people died in the accident. (*London Fire Brigade*)

It took firemen four days to remove the last body from the tube train that crashed at Moorgate in 1975, killing forty-three people in the worst ever disaster on the London Underground network. The cause remains a mystery. (*London Fire Brigade*)

Rescue workers struggle to free passengers after a faulty signal causes three trains to collide in a cutting at Clapham in 1988. Thirty-five people were killed and sixty-nine seriously injured. (*London Fire Brigade*)

On the left is the wreckage of the Thames Turbo that collided with a High Speed Train (on the right) after going through a red light at Ladbroke Grove in 1999. The death toll was thirty-one. (*London Fire Brigade*)

The worst disaster in Heathrow's history. In 1972, a BEA Trident came down in a field near Staines shortly after take-off, killing all 118 passengers and crew. (*PA Photos*)

An Edwardian view of the Black Death of 1348–9 that carried off up to 40 per cent of London's population. A man carries his sick child through the streets. (*Mary Evans Picture Library*)

Bodies being buried in a pit during the Great Plague of 1665. It killed an estimated 100,000 Londoners, though the death rate was perhaps half that from the Black Death. (*Guildhall Library, Corporation of London*)

CITY OF LONDON BOARD OF HEALTH

THE City of London Board of Health, anxious to prevent the introduction of the Cholera Morbus into this City, and to arrest its progress, should it unfortunately make its appearance, feel it their duty to direct the attention of their fellow-citizens to the following precautions and observations, and earnestly to recommend that every householder should make them known among the members of his family, and use his influence towards carrying them strictly into effect.

HOUSE.—To guard against accumulations of refuse matter in drains, cess-pools, dust-bins, and dirt-heaps, and to purify such receptacles by solution of Chloride of Lime, to be procured on application at the Medical Stations of each Ward.

To maintain in a cleanly and wholesome condition all reservoirs, cisterns, and sinks, and to allow impurities, where practicable, to be carried away by running water.

To keep inhabited apartments clean, by frequently washing and very carefully drying the floors; and to ventilate them thoroughly, as well by fires as by a free access of fresh air.

To have the windows, especially of bed-rooms, put in good repair, so that the occupants may not be exposed, during sleep, to currents of night-air.

To change bed-linen and furniture frequently, and to clear out those spaces in inhabited rooms which are concealed by beds and other furniture, and which are so often made the depositories of filth and rubbish.

Where persons live in crowded apartments—which should be avoided as far as may be practicable—additional vigilance should be used to preserve a free ventilation; and where offensive exhalations arise, they should be destroyed by the Solution of Chloride of Lime.

PERSON.—To maintain personal cleanliness by frequent washing and change of clothing, and if available, by occasional warm-bathing.

To guard against sudden changes of temperature by wearing flannel next the skin, more especially round the bowels, and to protect the feet and legs by woollen stockings.

To avoid excessive fatigue, profuse perspiration, and exposure to cold and wet, particularly at night, and to change damp clothing without delay.

DIET.—To let the Diet consist of plain meats, bread, and well-boiled vegetables, rejecting as injurious all indigestible kinds of food, such as salads, raw fruits, nuts, rich pastry, and in general such articles as each individual may have found by experience to create acidity, flatulence, and indigestion.

BEVERAGE.—To abstain from undiluted ardent spirits, acid drinks, and stale soups or broths, and to be sparing in the use of sugar, especially if it give rise to a sour fermentation in the stomach.

To maintain regular habits, using moderate exercise, keeping early hours, and taking nourishment at limited intervals, so that fatigue or exposure may never be encountered during an exhausted and empty state of the stomach.

Finally, to preserve a cheerfulness of disposition, a freedom from abject fears, and a full reliance that such measures will be taken by the Government and the local authorities as are best calculated, with Divine assistance, to meet the exigencies of the occasion.

The Board of Health are aware that these precautions cannot all be taken in every case, but they are convinced that the more closely they are followed the greater will be the probability of security; and though they may be thought to be of a general nature, they become more immediately important at a time when the community is threatened with the visitation of a malady which especially affects the stomach and bowels, which usually makes its attack during the night, which falls with the greatest severity on the poor, the ill-fed, and the unhealthy; and which rages most destructively in those districts of towns where the streets are narrow, and the population crowded, and where little attention has been paid to cleanliness and ventilation.

Guildhall, November 6th, 1831.

CHARLES PEARSON, Chairman,
J. F. DE GRAVE, Medical Secretary.

Guildhall, 6th November, 1831.

WE, the undersigned Medical Officers attached by the authority of His Majesty's Privy Council to the City of London Board of Health, approve of the foregoing Precautions and Observations, and earnestly impress upon the Inhabitants of the City the necessity of strictly conforming to them. We have the satisfaction to state that the Metropolis happily continues free from any appearance of the Cholera Morbus.

GEORGE LEITH ROUPELL, M.D.   HENRY FIELD, M.S.A.
B. G. BABINGTON, M.D.   JOHN RIDOUT, M.S.A.

N. B. The Inhabitants are requested carefully to preserve this Paper, and to place it in some conspicuous part of their Houses, for general perusal by their Families and Servants.

Printed by ARTHUR TAYLOR, Printer to the Honourable City of London.

Cholera arrived in England for the first time in 1831, and the City of London Board of Health gave advice on how to avoid the disease. In fact, it reached London in February 1832, and killed 6,500 people. (*Guildhall Library, Corporation of London*)

On 5 December 1952 a London bus tries to pick its way through the enveloping smog, which not only caused traffic chaos for five days, but also killed an estimated 4,000 people through lung and heart disease. (*Hulton Archive*)

One of the estimated 250,000 trees brought down in the Great Storm of October 1987. Mercifully the death toll in the London area was only two. (*Hulton Archive*)

People being rescued from their homes at Rotherhithe during the floods of January 1928. The area worst hit was Pimlico where ten people were drowned. (*Hulton Archive*)

During the floods of 1953, swans swam in the street at Putney, and a man was drowned at Barnes, but London escaped the devastation that brought 300 deaths along the East Coast. (*London Metropolitan Archives*)

emergency brake in his carriage. The inquiry considered Robert Harris had shown himself to be 'idle and undisciplined', but it concluded that he could not have reasonably been expected to realise anything was wrong until the last moment when even an emergency brake application would not have stopped the accident.

There was much discussion as to whether the driver might have been drinking, that perhaps he had put spirits into the milk he was carrying for his tea. One test did find significant quantities of alcohol in his blood, but the alcohol could simply have been produced by the normal process of fermentation in a body that had been lying dead in high temperatures for five days. Newson sometimes had half a pint of brown ale with his evening meal, but he did not like spirits and would drink them only at Christmas. Of the people who had seen Newson that morning, none had seen him take alcohol, none had been aware of the smell of alcohol and another driver who used some of his milk did not smell or taste any alcohol. Indeed, no one had ever seen him drinking on duty. In addition, he appeared to have behaved perfectly normally, going through 270 signals without the slightest suggestion that anything was wrong until he raced through the platform at Moorgate.

The driver had £270 in cash in his pocket, which he and his wife had pooled the previous night to buy their youngest daughter a car. Had he been daydreaming – thinking about which car to buy? Just before Moorgate, trains come out of a narrow unlit tunnel into a more open area where there are lights. They also cross a set of points where there is a change in noise level, and where the red light on the sand drag at the end of the platform comes clearly into view. Even if Newson's attention had wandered, surely these things would have been sufficient to rouse him from his reverie, and simply releasing the so-called deadman's handle in his cab would have been enough to stop the accident. Even if the train had been travelling at maximum speed, he could have stopped it well short of the sand drag when he saw the red lamp, but his injuries suggested that he had been holding the deadman's handle right up to the time of the crash. Newson had never been seriously ill, or complained of giddiness or blackouts, and, even if he had collapsed or lost consciousness, again the deadman's handle should have brought the train safely to a stop.

One of the most baffling things was that the driver had not made the instinctive action of bringing up his hands to protect his face before the final collision, so one of the questions that had to be asked was whether his death might have been suicide, but there was no evidence that he was depressed or facing personal problems. One of his closest friends testified that he loved his work and that on the day before the crash he seemed in good spirits, talking about the car he was buying for his daughter and a trip he was planning to America. Newson had a good relationship with his wife, to whom he had been married for more than thirty years. She had a full-time job and would be in bed when he left at about five o'clock in the morning, but he always came and kissed her on the forehead to say goodbye, just as he did on the day of the disaster. Then there was the comment to the colleague to whom he gave the sugar: 'Go easy, it's got to last me.' The inquest jury dismissed the idea of suicide, and returned a verdict of accidental death.

Sherlock Holmes worked on the principle that once you have eliminated the impossible, whatever explanation is left, however improbable it may seem, must be the answer. At the end of the investigations into Moorgate, there was one theory still standing. Dr Philip Raffle, the Chief Medical Officer of London Transport, mentioned two rare medical conditions, which can each appear suddenly. The first was transient global amnesia, which is caused by a spasm of the blood vessels in the brain. Its result would be to erase all Newson's previous training and experience, without affecting his physical ability to drive a train. There would be no trace left of the condition at the post mortem, but it would not have prevented normal muscular movement. So would he not have raised his hands at the last moment to protect his face?

The second condition was akinesis with mutism, caused by a tiny blood clot in the brain. This could leave him sitting up holding the deadman's handle. He would be immobile, but he would retain the reflex needed to keep him upright in a swaying train. The only evidence would be a lesion so tiny it would need a microscope to detect, and it would not have been possible to find it at the post mortem on Newson because of the damage his head suffered in the crash.

A number of witnesses on the platform had spoken of the driver sitting upright, looking ahead; one saying that he had seemed paralysed or frozen in position, though doubts were raised as to how much they would have been able to discern in the cab of a speeding train. Unfortunately, all this had to remain speculation, because, as Dr Raffle admitted, no evidence could be produced and the post mortem revealed nothing significant. The official inquiry's verdict was that 'the accident was solely due to a lapse on the part of the driver'.

Nothing like it had ever happened before in the history of London Underground. In the five years before Moorgate, there had been half a dozen buffer-stop collisions, but they usually happened because of misjudgement or mismanagement of brakes and were at low speeds. In the most serious, at Tooting Broadway in 1971, the driver had been killed when he drove an empty train at 30 miles an hour into the end wall of a siding, apparently believing he was on the main line. To stop accidents of this kind, London Underground had fitted automatic train-stops in sidings, but it was not thought that these were necessary at terminal stations.

The sand drag was a cheap and effective way of dealing with a low-speed overrun, but it probably slowed train 272 by only about 2 miles an hour. The only way to prevent an accident of the kind that happened at Moorgate might be to fit fully automatic control of a train's approach to a terminus of the kind installed on the Victoria Line. After the accident, trains at Moorgate had to be stopped at the last signal before the platform before being allowed to enter.

By the time the inspector's report was published, the Drayton Park to Moorgate line had been closed and would reopen as part of British Rail, with Moorgate becoming the terminal for suburban services from Welwyn Garden City and Hertford North. Trains would have their brakes applied automatically if they passed signals at danger. They would be automatically slowed down to 12 miles an hour on the approach to Moorgate, and friction buffer stops would be fitted capable of stopping a fully laden train at this speed within the length of the overrun tunnel.

The next thirteen years saw no major disasters on London's railways, and so, paradoxically, the outcry when the next one came was much greater. It happened at about ten past eight on the bright, clear morning of Monday 12 December 1988. The 07.18 Basingstoke to Waterloo train was doing just over 60 miles an hour about a mile south of Clapham Junction station. The next signal, WF 138, was at green, and in the driver's cab a bell rang, confirmation from the Automatic Warning System, now fitted across most of the railway system, that the signal was in his favour, but 30 yards from it, to his astonishment, he saw it turn to red. He brought the train to a stop at the next signal and got out to call the signalman. The signalman said that as far as he could tell, there was nothing wrong with the signal. The driver said he would report it at Waterloo. As he put the phone down, he heard a crash, and saw his train pushed forward. He picked the phone up again, and told the signalman to call the emergency services.

While he was calling the signalman, the 06.14 Poole to Waterloo train had been approaching Clapham Junction station, with all signals clear, when the driver rounded a bend and saw the Basingstoke train stationary in front of him. He braked as hard as he could, but there was no chance of stopping before he ploughed into the back of it. The impact pushed it forward 10 feet. It also derailed the Poole train and knocked it onto the adjoining track.

Approaching along that track, in the opposite direction, was an empty train going from Waterloo to Haslemere. The driver had seen the Basingstoke train stopped, and its driver telephoning the signalman. Just as he was getting near the back of the train, he saw the Poole train on his track. He braked sharply, but could only reduce the force of the collision. His second carriage was hit a glancing blow, separating his coach from the rest of the train.

Another Waterloo-bound train was coming up the main line, and, in spite of the mayhem in front, signal WF 138 was still not showing red, but a single yellow, allowing the driver to proceed to the next signal. Fortunately, he was able to see the back of the Poole train stopped ahead, and bring his train to a standstill just 60 yards from its back. Had he hit the wreckage, the potential disaster 'does not bear contemplating', according to Sir Anthony Hidden QC, who conducted the official inquiry.

All of the thirty-five people killed, and most of the sixty-nine seriously injured, were in the front coaches of the Poole train. The first coach was completely destroyed and the second, the buffet car, was ripped open. The last coach of the Basingstoke train was lifted bodily by the impact, and ended up lying on its side at an angle of 45 degrees on a steep wooded embankment above a 10-foot-high cutting wall where the track goes through Wandsworth Common. The penultimate coach was derailed and came to rest leaning against the embankment. At the top were tall metal railings, and steps had to be cut so the injured could be got out.

Doctors were flown to the scene by police helicopter and a casualty centre was set up at a local pub for those with minor injuries, while teachers and pupils from the nearby Emmanuel School helped the walking wounded from the wreckage and took them to hospital in the school minibus. One passenger in the Basingstoke train was trapped from his chest down in the tangled metal, with one of his legs hanging below, almost amputated. Because of his position, it was impossible to stop the bleeding. So doctors had to pump enough fluids into his arm to make up for what he was losing, while rescuers worked for three hours to free him. He lost the leg, but survived. One ambulanceman spent four hours talking to a man who was hanging upside down by his ankles.

The signal which had behaved so oddly, WF 138, had recently been installed as part of a major overhaul on the approach to Waterloo. Work had been going on at the weekend and it had only been brought back into service at five o'clock that morning. Like most of the signals in the area, it was operated automatically by the movement of trains. While a train is on the section of track the signal protects, it interrupts an electrical signal, and the light automatically turns red until the train has cleared the section of track it controls plus an additional safety 'overlap'. The electrical information that a train is on the section is passed to the signal via a relay room next to Clapham Junction A signal-box, nearly a mile away on a bridge above the tracks near Clapham Junction station.

Here an experienced and well-regarded technician, who had been with British Rail for sixteen years, had been connecting up the new signals on Sunday 27 November, but he had failed to disconnect an old wire, simply pushing it to one side. At that point, Clapham was still a disaster waiting to happen. Then two weeks later, he had to do some more work in the relay room next to the equipment for signal WF 138. That seems to have been enough to dislodge the old wire and allow it to make the fatal contact which meant that when a train was running in part of 138's section, the current would not be cut off, and the signal would not change to red.

It could scarcely have happened at a worse place. Clapham is the busiest junction in Britain. At first, there was enough space between the trains for the signal fault not to matter, but when peak time approached, and they started to go through at two-minute intervals, something was bound to go wrong. The technician accepted responsibility for the accident, and when asked why his lapse had happened, he could only reply: 'It is still beyond me.' The Hidden Inquiry was told that while he was doing the job on the Sunday before the accident, he was constantly being interrupted, and that he never went back to finish it. The inquiry said that the direct cause of the accident was 'undoubtedly' the wiring errors he had made, but its report was a damning indictment of British Rail management. It said that the whole resignalling project was a shambles. There was no individual responsible for running it, its organisation was inefficient, the timetable was unrealistic, and there were not enough people working on it. In the thirteen weeks before the accident, the technician had had only one day off. An independent check should have been done on his work to make sure the wiring was correct. None was. Indeed, the technician said no one ever checked his work.

The reason that WF 138 had suddenly turned to red when the Basingstoke train was almost on top of it was that the train in front had moved from the section where the faulty wiring made it effectively invisible to the next section which also controlled WF 138, but where once again its presence would automatically turn the signal to red. One of the problems exposed was that there was nothing in the signal-box at Clapham to show what the signals beside the track were actually displaying. If there had been, there was a good chance the fault might have been identified before it caused a disaster. Nor was the automatic warning system in the driver's cab any help, because that derived its information from the automatic signalling system.

The inquiry was also concerned about the number of similar signal failures that had occurred through faulty work and a failure to check it. One at East Croydon had resulted in a side-on collision between two passenger trains. The report said that had lessons been learned from these incidents, then the Clapham disaster could have been avoided.

While the inquiry was sitting, on 4 March 1989, there was another train crash at Purley, in which five people were killed and carriages fell into suburban back gardens after a driver had gone through a red light and run into the back of another train. The Clapham inquiry was asked to take into account any factors from that crash that might be relevant. In fact, the Purley crash was caused by a lapse of concentration by the driver, even though his cab was fitted with the Automatic Warning System (AWS) that sounded an alarm whenever he approached a signal that was not at green. The driver was convicted of manslaughter and is believed to be the first train driver in British history to have been sent to gaol for an error he made at work.

All the coaches involved in the Clapham crash had been of the old-fashioned slam-door type, and Sir Anthony concluded that this had added to the casualty toll and called for better rolling stock. Other recommendations were concerned with the tightening up of procedures for wiring signals and checking the work, but he also called on British Rail to fit a system of Automatic Train Protection (ATP), which went further than the Automatic Warning System, and would automatically apply the brakes if the driver exceeded speed limits or failed to slow down at a yellow signal or stop at a red. The report also said: 'British Rail shall ensure that the organisational framework exists to prevent commercial considerations of a business-led railway from compromising safety.'

By the time there was another major train crash in London, on 19 September 1997, it was no longer British Rail's problem. The railways had been privatised. The Swansea to Paddington service was run by Great Western Trains, though they leased the High Speed Train (HST) pulling it from Angel Train Contracts, the goods train with which it collided at Southall was operated by English, Welsh and Scottish Railways, while the track and signalling were owned by Railtrack. The great irony was that the HST was fitted with both AWS and ATP, which would have prevented the accident even though the driver had missed two amber signals, but neither was working. Seven people were killed and more than a hundred injured. A charge of corporate manslaughter against GWT was thrown out, but the company was fined £1.5 million for health and safety offences.

The criminal proceedings delayed the inquiry which did not get properly under way until July 1999. Soon after, there was another disastrous accident just a few miles away on the same line. This time it was a head-on collision, and in terms of the speed at which the trains hit each other, the worst in British railway history.

On 5 October 1999, in the morning rush hour, a Thames Trains Turbo left Paddington at 08.06, bound for Bedwyn in Wiltshire. It was entering one of the most complex sections of the whole rail system, where the dozen lines leading out of Paddington station converge into four, and drivers have to negotiate a maze of points and signals. The signalling system in the area had been completely redesigned six years earlier, then, two years later, overhead wires had been put in to accommodate the Heathrow express. Within two minutes of leaving the station, the Turbo came to signal SN 87 which was showing a single yellow, meaning that the next signal, SN 109, was at red, but instead of stopping at SN 109, the driver continued at about 40 miles an hour. After it had passed SN 109, the train had 700 yards to go before the track merged with the main line on which, at that moment, the Cheltenham Flyer High Speed Train was approaching the station.

The 700 yards would take about twenty seconds to cover, and there were still two opportunities to stop a disaster. If a set of points had been changed, it would have taken the Turbo off down another line.

If Slough Control Centre had sent an immediate stop message to the radio in the Turbo's cab, it could at the very least have reduced the speed of the impact, but the signal was sent so late it is unclear whether the driver even received it before the crash. When they saw they were on a collision course, both drivers braked heavily, but it was too late to have any significant effect. Two miles from Paddington, at Ladbroke Grove Junction, their trains collided at a combined speed of 130 miles an hour, and both drivers were killed. Michael Hodder, in the Thames train, was the 31-year-old son of a train driver. He had served in the Royal Navy, but had joined the railways because he wanted to spend more time with his wife and two sons. That day, he was hoping to go to his elder son's seventh birthday party when he got home. The HST was being driven by Brian Cooper, a 52-year-old grandfather, who had taken it over at Swindon.

Initially, the Turbo came off worse. It was built of aluminium with its three coaches weighing just 90 tons, and its front coach disintegrated when it was hit by the wedge-shaped HST with 400 tons of train behind it, but the crash was followed by a number of fires caused by spilt diesel igniting. The worst blaze was in the first-class front coach of the HST, Coach H, which reduced the inside of the carriage to a knee-deep pile of ash. Passengers on the HST did not know how to open the doors and could not find hammers to break the windows. Where coaches had tilted over, they could not even open the internal doors. On the Turbo, there were no emergency hammers, but fortunately two Thames Trains workers helped some passengers get out through the driver's cab at the back. All but seven of the thirty-one people who died were travelling in the Turbo, most of them in the front coach. Apart from the driver, all of those killed on the HST were in Coach H. It took nine days to recover all the bodies and remove the last coach from the scene. More than 400 people were injured.

It soon emerged that the driver of the Turbo had only recently qualified. He was two weeks into his job, and on his twenty-first trip out of Paddington. He had not been instructed specifically about signals which had been passed at danger (known in railway jargon as SPADs). Signal SN 109 had been passed at danger eight times since August 1993, and there was evidence from other drivers about how difficult it was to see the signals between Paddington station and Ladbroke Grove, and particularly those on gantry eight, where SN 109 was sited. After first being commissioned in 1993, the signal had had to be lowered to try to give drivers a better view of it, but when the overhead wires were installed in 1995, visibility got worse again. The Turbo driver had to pick SN 109 out from four other signals on the same gantry, and it was also an unusual arrangement, with the red light set not below the other three but on its own to the left.

In November 1995, there had been a collision between two trains near Paddington after a driver became confused as to which signal applied to him, but it happened at low speed and no one was injured. This mishap had been followed by some improvements in training for drivers, but Lord Cullen, who conducted the official inquiry, considered that it was still inadequate.

His report concluded that the driver's poor view of SN 109, combined with the problem of bright early sunlight coming into his eyes at a low angle, led to him failing to see the red light. If he had been told how often this signal had been passed at danger, might he perhaps have taken extra care to ensure that it really was allowing him to proceed? Lord Cullen was also highly critical of what he saw as Railtrack's failure to recognise that SN 109 was badly sited in spite of the number of times it was passed at danger. He complained that although SPADs occurred so frequently in the area around Paddington, the signalling staff did not seem to have any clear idea of how to deal with them. After the crash, Railtrack was instructed to make improvements to more than twenty signals which were the most frequently passed at danger. They were also instructed to investigate SPADs more thoroughly because of what was seen as a tendency to put them down too readily to driver error.

TWELVE

Air Crashes

Heathrow Airport was opened in 1946 and within two years it had experienced its first disaster. At about nine o'clock in the evening on 2 March 1948, a Sabena Airlines DC-3 from Brussels was coming in to land at the airport. On board were nineteen passengers and a crew of three. There was thick fog, with visibility in places down to 20 yards. The aircraft missed the runway, nose-dived onto the grass 50 yards away and burst into flames. In spite of the blaze, rescue crews managed to pull three survivors clear of the wreckage, before they were beaten back by the intense heat. Everyone else was killed.

A similar accident happened seventeen years later, when a BEA Vickers Vanguard was flying into Heathrow from Edinburgh just after midnight on 27 October 1965 in poor visibility. The aircraft had had to abort two landings, and had been in a holding pattern for some time awaiting improved weather conditions. It made a third attempt, but once again the pilot reported they were overshooting. The aircraft then seemed to climb before falling into a steep dive and hitting the runway. The thirty passengers and six crew were all killed.

The worst disaster in Heathrow's history came on a Sunday afternoon, 18 June 1972. It was a turbulent time in British aviation. The pilots' trade union, BALPA, was at loggerheads with British European Airways (later to form part of British Airways) over pay and conditions. The union was threatening strike action and a crucial meeting was due to be held the next day. Opinions were bitterly divided, and in the crew room that afternoon 51-year-old Captain Stanley Key, who was highly critical of the proposed strike action, had an argument described as 'violent', though it seems that

167

his anger quickly subsided. An hour and a half later, he was taking charge of BEA's flight BE 548 from London to Brussels.

The Trident jet took off at 16.08. Key's co-pilot was a rather inexperienced 22-year-old, J.W. Keighley. He was regarded as a promising young man, but lacking in self-confidence and with a tendency to be comparatively slow to react. The other member of the crew was Second Officer Ticehurst, whose job it was to monitor the other two. The three men had been on stand-by duty, and had only been assigned to the flight because the original crew had been delayed.

The weather was blustery, with low cloud and rain, but take-off was normal. After 83 seconds, Captain Key reported 'Climbing as cleared'. As required, 10 seconds later he reduced power to comply with noise abatement rules. After another 7 seconds, Key called 'Passing 1,500 feet'; 1 minute and 48 seconds into the flight, Key said 'Up to 60', acknowledging that he had climbed to Flight Level 60. This was the last that was ever heard from the aircraft. When S/O Ticehurst's log was found in the wreckage, the last entry noted that they had been cleared up to this level.

Moments later, two young brothers out walking the family dog near their home in Staines saw the Trident dropping out of the sky about a hundred yards away in a field by the A30. One said: 'It fell like a stone.' They ran half a mile to fetch help from a woman who was a qualified nurse and a man from the St John Ambulance Brigade. When they reached the aeroplane, they saw that the tail had broken off. There were passengers hanging out of windows, and bodies lying all around. They started pulling people from the wreckage and thought they heard a baby crying. They found three-year-old twin sisters and laid their bodies together under a piece of fuselage. Other people arrived. Some walked around the aircraft looking for signs of life and shouting 'Anybody alive?' but there was a strong smell of kerosene and everyone was afraid it might go up in flames at any moment.

A police constable from Feltham was the first person from the emergency services on the scene. He had been radioed about a plane crash by Scotland Yard. 'The impression they gave me was that it was something like a model plane; no big deal,' he said, 'and then I saw the plane. . . . It was absolutely quiet, utter silence.' He headed down to the aircraft, which was surrounded by debris: 'I started walking over the luggage and then I realised I was walking on dead bodies too.' The aircraft had hit the ground nose first, so that the back was empty while the front was jammed with people and seats. He found a stewardess still strapped to her jump seat, dead. He found a man complaining that his legs were hurting, and dragged him out onto the grass. 'I said, "Don't worry, you'll be all right", but he died within seconds.' Although the impact tore the interior of the aircraft to pieces, a number of passengers had not been killed instantly, and one man was actually taken alive, though deeply unconscious, to hospital. He died three hours later.

At Staines Fire Station, they had heard the crash and wondered what it was. One fireman went outside to look around, but could not see anything. He went back to wait for the phone to ring, but it did not. Then a car stopped outside and a man told them there had been a plane crash by the Staines bypass. They spotted the place easily because there was already an ambulance there and plenty of private cars abandoned on the bypass by sightseers, who were soon congregating at vantage points, often carrying children on their shoulders. Ice-cream vans spotted a business opportunity and rushed to the scene. Even when police shouted 'Ghouls' at them through loud-hailers, the spectators were not deterred. If there had been many survivors, it would have been difficult to get them to hospital through the crowds. In fact, all 112 passengers and 6 crew died.

The Trident had not been fitted with a cockpit voice recorder, but the flight data recorder revealed that 1 minute and 54 seconds into the flight, the droops had been retracted, while the aeroplane was at around 1,750 feet and its speed was 186 miles an hour. Droops are devices on the wing that give additional lift while the aircraft is taking off and climbing to cruising altitude. When they are retracted, the speed at which the aircraft will stall rises by 35 miles an hour. They should not have been retracted until the aircraft had climbed another 1,300 feet and was going another 70 miles an hour faster. To do it at this point was potentially disastrous, but the flight crew had plenty of visual and other warnings to urge them to take remedial action. An amber light would have come on in front of each pilot, a 'droops out of position' warning light would have lit in front of the central pedestal, the steering column would have started shaking, and the control panel would have been pushed forward with considerable force. To correct the problem, they could have applied more power to increase speed, or they could have extended the droops down again, or held the steering column forward. It was not clear who was responsible for retracting the droops, but what was more baffling was why the crew repeatedly failed to recognise what was wrong and take action to correct it. Indeed, 2 minutes and 8 seconds into the flight, the automatic stall recovery system was switched off. The aircraft then lost speed and height, went into a deep stall, and crashed 22 seconds later.

When the Trident was examined, it seemed that all its systems were in working order. So, what of the crew? Captain Key was regarded as a punctilious pilot, as well as a fit and healthy man, but pathologists who examined the bodies after the crash discovered that he had a serious heart problem and had suffered a ruptured blood vessel within the two hours before the crash. It is likely that he would have been suffering chest pains before he climbed into the cockpit. Had this led to errors and misjudgements? The Trident was the first British aircraft to be fitted with droops, so it had two levers, one for the wing flaps and one for the droops, while other aircraft had a single lever. Could Key or Keighley have pulled the wrong lever? Had Keighley misunderstood an instruction from Key? They would have been buffeted and thrown about by the bad weather and for much of the time they would have been in cloud, and unable to see the ground.

Another discovery was made after the crash. A set of offensive remarks, some of them about Key, some about BEA management, had been found scribbled on one of the flight crew's tables. Had there been a row about the pay dispute? The official inquiry by the UK Air Accident Investigation Branch dismissed them as a factor, coming to the conclusion that it was unlikely that either of the other officers had written them and that they pre-dated the flight. It is not clear whether Key ever saw them.

And what of the other two pilots on the flight deck? Did either of them spot that Key was making errors? Had Keighley's fragile self-confidence been further damaged by witnessing Key's outburst in the crew room, making him less likely to question the captain's actions or judgement? And what of Ticehurst, who was supposed to be monitoring the actions of the other two and who should, according to one witness at the inquiry, have been screaming 'Speed!' at the Captain? Was he occupied filling in the log? Or was he distracted by the presence of a passenger on the flight deck, Captain Collins, a freighter captain, who was found after the crash with a can of air freshener in his hand?

The inquiry concluded that Captain Key's heart condition led to a lack of concentration and poor judgement so that he had failed to correct the stall and had possibly confused the droops and the flaps, but that his incapacity was probably not noticed by the others on the flight deck. The absence of a cockpit voice recorder meant, though, that this could only be conjecture. One of the results of the disaster was that from then on, cockpit voice recorders were fitted to all BEA airliners.

The biggest aircraft to come down near one of London's airports was a Korean Air Boeing 747, which had been carrying cargo from Stansted to Milan. The aircraft had arrived at Stansted just after three o' clock on the afternoon of 22 December 1999 from Tashkent in Uzbekistan. At 18.36, it departed again, with a crew of three on board along with a Korean maintenance worker. Staff in the Tower at Stansted considered the take-off normal, and saw the aircraft climb into cloud. Then they saw an explosion to the south, realised that KAL 8509 had crashed, and alerted the emergency services.

The impact, just two minutes after take-off, shook the main terminal. People living in the nearby village of Great Hallingbury dived for cover. One man described seeing the aircraft as it flashed past his window: 'It was so close I ducked. I thought "Oh, my God, it's going to hit me".' Another local resident said: 'There was a massive roar . . . I looked out of the window and the sky was glowing orange with a massive fireball.' A local farmer spoke of a great mushroom cloud erupting into the air, as though a bomb had gone off. The captain of an RAF helicopter that flew over the crash scene described looking down on a giant blazing crucifix created by the aircraft's burning wings and fuselage. In his view, there could have been 'a disaster of immense proportions'. The aircraft missed one farmhouse by only 100 yards, a pub by half a mile, and, alarmingly, it could easily have hit the nearby town of Bishop's Stortford. In fact, the 747 had come down in fields beside Hatfield Forest, scorching trees and leaving wreckage hanging from them. Flames soared 500 feet into the air and debris was thrown on to the M11 motorway, forcing cars to swerve.

On the ground, the crash left a crater 40 yards long, and firefighters had to douse 32 tons of fuel that had exploded. Local people were warned to stay indoors and seal their windows in case of toxic fumes. The four men on board were believed to have been killed instantly. The official inquiry into the accident revealed that a crucial air navigation instrument on the aircraft was faulty.

PART FOUR

Acts of God

THIRTEEN

Plague

London may well have been visited by devastating plagues
during Roman times (see Chapter 5), and during the fifth and
sixth centuries, events some historians believe might account for
the city's failure to thrive at those times, while Bede writes of a
'sudden pestilence' afflicting southern England in 664 and
destroying 'a great multitude'. What is certain is that the city was
struck in the middle of the fourteenth century by a fearful plague
that claimed the lives of perhaps two in five of its population. The
disease was carried by bacteria that normally live in the digestive
tract of fleas, especially fleas of the black rat, a creature that was
happy living close to humans. From time to time, the bacteria
multiplied in the flea's stomach to such a degree that they caused a
blockage. Then, while it was feeding, the flea would regurgitate
huge quantities of the bacteria into its host. If it bit a human, the
human then became infected.

The first symptom was usually a blackish, often gangrenous
pustule at the point of the flea bite, but the most dramatic sign of
the disease were the buboes, inflamed swellings sometimes as big as
an apple in the groin or the armpits of the victim. Then black
blotches would appear on the arm, thigh or other parts of the body,
caused by haemorrhages under the skin. With the swellings would
come a high fever and an agonising thirst. In a small minority of
cases, the buboes might burst and the victim might recover, but
usually they would die within five or six days. This was bubonic
plague. There was another more deadly version where the fever was
accompanied by spitting of blood. Sometimes there were no buboes,
but death came even quicker – within two or three days. It was more
infectious than bubonic plague, because bacteria were sprayed into

the air every time the patient breathed out. This was pneumonic plague, which was able to thrive in the colder conditions of winter, when bubonic plague tended to die out. There was also a third version – septicaemic plague, where the brunt of the infection falls on the bloodstream, and the victim dies within hours, before the buboes get a chance to form. In this version at least, there is so much bacteria in the blood, it can also be transmitted by the human flea. Fortunately, it was the rarest form. Together, the three became known in the fourteenth century as the Black Death. The disease provided a fearfully painful and degrading end. The sweat, excrement, spittle and breath of victims gave off an overpowering stench, and their urine was thick black or red.

The Black Death had appeared in Asia in 1346, from where it began a remorseless advance across Europe. In June 1348, a ship carrying a victim arrived at Melcombe Regis in Dorset, and the next month the port had its first case of the disease, but England had so many important trading links with Europe, it may well have come in through other ports too. Whatever the original source, the disease had reached London by November 1348.

At the time, the capital's population had probably grown to between 60,000 and 70,000, living in crowded, close-packed houses, with rubbish piled up in the streets. Even the aristocracy lived in conditions we would regard as grotesquely overcrowded. An earl and countess might expect to share their bedroom with their daughter and the daughter's governess. Lower down the social scale, it was not unusual to find a dozen people sleeping in one room, perhaps sharing with animals. The warmth and dirt provided an ideal environment for the black rat, and isolation of the sick was practically impossible. The population that awaited the Black Death was already weakened by dysentery, diarrhoea and all manner of other diseases, and, when it arrived, the treatments used for the illness, such as heavy bleeding, if anything did more harm than good. It was generally believed that the infection was passed from person to person through a 'miasma', a poison cloud, so that as far as prevention was concerned, flight was the only really worthwhile measure. If this was impossible, then people carried nosegays of flowers or herbs, sealed windows with waxed cloth, or tried to purify the air by the constant burning of aromatic woods or powders.

During the winter, pneumonic plague was predominant, but then the bubonic strain came into its own with the warm weather in late spring and summer. The Black Death's worst fury was confined to three or four months, but victims were still dying well into 1350. In January 1349, Edward III prorogued Parliament because of fears for the safety of those attending, although he may also have been glad to be spared the inevitable grumbling of MPs about the cost of the French war. As deaths mounted, London's graveyards could not cope and new burial grounds had to be found. A cemetery was opened at Smithfield and hurriedly consecrated by the Bishop of London. In the early part of 1349, some 200 bodies a day were being shovelled into the pits there, but it was not enough. Sir Walter de Manny, one of the King's bravest knights, bought 13 acres of land on the site of today's Charterhouse Square and gave it to the City as a burial ground. Another cemetery was opened in Southwark.

The disaster of the Black Death discredited the civil authorities, the medical profession and the Church. All were seemingly powerless in the face of its horrific progress. It also fuelled resentment against the rich who could afford to flee. In 1349, London got a visit from the Brotherhood of the Flagellants, who had appeared in France, in response to the Pope's order to hold devout processions. In the panicky atmosphere, things soon got out of hand, and before long there would be thousands of people, some barefoot, some covered with ashes, wailing and tearing their hair and lashing themselves with scourges till the blood flowed in a desperate attempt to appease God's wrath. The flagellants' rules forbade them to bathe, wash or change clothes. Crowds would gather, quaking, groaning, sobbing and encouraging the flagellants to even more frenzied excesses. Some believed the Brotherhood could heal the sick, drive out devils, or even raise the dead. The Black Death was seen as the forerunner of the Second Coming of Christ and the flagellants were its harbingers. After they had held a ceremony in front of St Paul's Cathedral, the authorities quickly bundled them out of the country.

Food supplies in London began to dry up as carters grew reluctant to come to the city, so Londoners had to go out into the countryside to search for supplies. Along with those leaving to try to flee the disease they actually helped to spread it. The Black Death proved to be the most disastrous epidemic in the capital's history, probably killing more than 20,000 inhabitants, making the overall death rate for London between 30 and 40 per cent. Most victims came from poor areas, where people were undernourished and could not afford to try to escape, and whole households were often wiped out, but the rich and powerful died too. The new Archbishop of Canterbury, John Offord, was struck down in May 1349 at Westminster, before he could even be enthroned. Thomas Bradwardine was then chosen, but he died in August. A former chancellor was also a victim, along with the royal surgeon. All eight wardens of the Company of Cutters died before the end of 1349, as did four wardens of the Goldsmiths' Company, while six wardens of the Hatters' Company died before July 1350. Religious communities were also hit. St James's Hospital lost most of its brethren, 100 Greyfriars died, and Westminster Abbey lost 26 monks and an abbot, about half the community.

After its first alarming appearance, bubonic plague was to return to London regularly over the next 300 years. There were outbreaks in 1361 and 1369; and in 1394, it is supposed to have claimed as one of its victims, Anne of Bohemia, the wife of King Richard II, sending him into a frenzy of grief. There was a severe outbreak in 1407, and in 1499–1500, it is said to have carried off 20,000 people, making King Henry VII flee to Calais. Then there were a succession of plagues between 1511 and 1518, which kept the court away from Westminster.

In 1518, Henry VIII tried to fight the disease by making the sick carry white sticks and ordering that infected houses be marked. Bills of Mortality were also introduced, so that each week London's parish clerks had to list the number and cause of deaths, but in the 1530s and 1540s, there were seven more epidemics. A policy of trying to isolate those infected proved expensive and difficult to enforce, so that even during the terrible epidemic of 1563–4, which may have killed off a quarter of London's population, it was not introduced until the crisis was almost over, though dogs were killed and fires were lit in the streets to try to ward off the sickness. Queen Elizabeth I, prudently, had withdrawn to Windsor, and is said to have erected a gallows on the market place on which to hang any Londoner who dared follow. Another two plagues in 1578 and 1582, each killing about 6,000, led the authorities to accept the need for measures like improved street-cleaning and the closure of playhouses. Indeed, the epidemic of 1593, which killed 23,000 people, led to the theatres being closed for a year and, in the 1590s, the first pest-house was built. The first year of King James I's reign, 1603, however, was marked by another outbreak, which killed about 30,000, as was that of his son, Charles I in 1625, when the death toll was 40,000. The authorities urged people to stay in the capital so as not to spread disease, but the poet John Donne recorded: 'The citizens fled away as out of a house on fire.' They stuffed their pockets with money and valuables and headed for the highway. However, people outside London were, understandably, not keen to offer them refuge, and some were found dead by the roadside with a small fortune in their pockets. In 1630, the King's physician recommended the imposition of a forty-day quarantine period for sufferers. He also perceptively identified 'rats, mice, weasels and such vermin' as plague carriers, but no one took much notice and there was a further epidemic in 1636 which saw the burial of more than 10,000 victims between early April and mid-December. Plague returned in 1647, killing nearly 3,600, but then the disease began to die away, and between 1650 and 1664 fewer than 14 plague deaths a year were reported.

In 1663, ominous reports had begun arriving from the Netherlands of an outbreak of plague that would kill 35,000 people there. In England, the government promptly imposed quarantine restrictions on ships coming from the infected areas, and only five deaths were recorded in 1664. Reassuringly, the winter of 1664/5 was cold, with the Thames frozen over for two months and the hard frost continuing in London into April. These were seen as unfavourable conditions for the disease. The government had vessels patrol the Thames estuary to enforce restrictions on suspect ships, but in March 1665 war was declared on the Dutch and trade with the Netherlands declined. Perhaps the Privy Council let its guard slip and missed an infected vessel. Certainly, by the end of April, Pepys was recording in his diary: 'Great fears of sickness here in the City, it being said that two or three houses are already shut up.' In fact, only three cases were recorded in April, and although the figure had reached forty-three in May, that still represented fewer than 3 per cent of all deaths, and they had occurred in only 5 out of the 130 parishes covered by the Bills of Mortality. The better off were able to note with relief that it seemed to be the poorest people who were catching the disease in their dingy alleys on the outskirts of the capital, but the Great Plague had arrived.

The Privy Council brought in measures to try to stop the plague spreading, such as closing down ale-houses and putting restrictions on taking in lodgers, so as to reduce overcrowding. They also ordered a general clean-up, making householders responsible for the street in front of their houses and removing rubbish more regularly. They banned street-vendors selling old clothes, and those who visited the sick, such as physicians and searchers (those responsible for finding cases of the plague), were ordered to carry long white wands and were forbidden to attend public gatherings. Not all of these measures were scrupulously enforced.

In spite of the Bills of Mortality, it was not easy to get an accurate picture of the spread of the disease. The Bills did not always reveal the true cause of death, nor did people particularly wish to divulge that a member of their family was suffering from the plague if it meant they were going to be incarcerated in their homes with the victim, which they might reasonably believe amounted to a death sentence. Conveniently, the searchers could often be persuaded or bribed to conceal the cause of death. The government too had an interest in playing down the outbreak so as not to damage trade with other countries, nor did they want to provoke an exodus from London that might damage the war effort. Some may have feared a cover-up was going on, but in May the theatres were still packed. Those old enough to remember 1625, though, foretold a fearful summer.

June was hot and in the first week there were about forty deaths from the plague; Pepys described 7 June as 'the hottest day that ever I felt in my life'. He saw two or three houses in Drury Lane marked with red crosses, and 'Lord have mercy upon us.' Three days later, he heard that the plague had come into the City, and began to think about 'how to put my things and estate in order, in case it should please God to call me away'. A week later, he was being driven in a coach when the coachman was suddenly taken 'very sick'. Pepys found himself torn between concern for the man and fear that he himself had been infected.

At first, the outbreak centred on St Giles-in-the-Fields, around modern-day St Giles High Street, then a big parish of 1,500 households on the edge of the built-up area to the west of the City. Well over half of the 590 victims in June were from here. Neighbouring parishes were told to put warders on the streets and passageways leading from St Giles to try to stop people spreading the infection, but cases were already being recorded in the City in Fenchurch and Broad Streets, and to the east in Whitechapel. As the disease began to appear in Westminster, the King and court moved out.

By the last week in June, the number of deaths had jumped to 270, the theatres had been closed and the streets were full of the coaches of the aristocracy and the grandees on their way to the country. Among those who would stay was the formidable general and admiral, the Duke of Albermarle, who had fought for both sides during the Civil War, and then been the leading architect of Charles II's restoration. He set up headquarters in St James's and handed out orders to Justices of the Peace, trying to stop London's civil government falling apart. Others included the Archbishop of Canterbury, and the Lord Mayor, Sir John Lawrence, who, as a precaution, had a glass case made from which he could receive visitors. Some of those who had nowhere to run took to living on vessels moored in the middle of the Thames.

July was the month when the disease really took hold. There were more than 5,600 deaths in 73 parishes. Pepys, who had already sent his mother to Huntingdonshire, now packed his wife and maids off to Woolwich, where he would spend his nights, though in the daytime he continued to go to his house and office in Seething Lane. Those who did not flee were understandably reluctant to venture out too much, and the diarist John Evelyn was struck by the 'mournful silence'. Pepys, meanwhile, set his affairs in order, sorting out his papers and accounts and redrafting his will, mindful that 'a man cannot depend on living two days to an end'.

He was given constant reminders of the dangers when he passed close to corpse-bearers or discovered that someone with whom he had been in contact had been taken ill, but that did not stop him taking unnecessary risks, like going to see a body buried in a plague pit, or embarking on amorous adventures in areas known to be infected. Anyone who was suspected of having the plague was supposed to be sent to a pest house, where the chances of survival were small, though Pepys did see a group of thirty former inmates walking along the Strand on their way to get a certificate saying they had recovered. In fact, London had only five pest houses, and together they could hold fewer than 600 people.

There were many theories on how to avoid catching the plague. Puffing a pipe or chewing a plug of tobacco was supposed to help, and stories grew up that no London tobacconist had died of the disease. Many potions and supposed remedies were sold and, for those apothecaries who had the courage to stay in town, it was a very profitable time. One idea was to apply a concoction of treacle, rue, fig and onion to a plague sore. Others suggested keeping a piece of gold in your mouth, or wearing an amulet of toad poison, or trying to catch syphilis. At the public health level, fumigation using a mixture of brimstone, saltpetre and amber was supposed to be effective, and it must certainly have created an unpleasant stench for any rodent thinking of moving in. At one point, all the cesspools in London were opened in the belief that the smell might drive away the disease.

As usually happened during epidemics, there was a clampdown on animals, with controls introduced on livestock. The City forbade the keeping of pigs, cats, dogs, pigeons and rabbits, and dog-catchers were ordered to round up and kill strays. The City dog-catcher claimed payment for the slaughter of nearly 4,400. Killing dogs and cats was, of course, a very good way of protecting the rats who were actually spreading the disease, but although the fundamental role of rats in the spread of plague was not established for another two centuries, there was concern about them, and people were employed to catch them too.

During August, the plague advanced remorselessly. In the first week, there were 2,817 deaths, in the second 3,880. Pepys noted on the 12th that the idea of trying to confine plague burials to the hours of darkness had broken down: 'the people die so, that it now seems they are fain to carry the dead to be buried in daylight, the nights not sufficing to do it in'. In week three, 4,237 died, and in the final week, the number leapt again, to 6,102. Now 113 parishes were affected. London was becoming like a ghost town. 'How sad a sight it is to see the streets empty of people,' wrote Pepys, 'and about us, two shops in three, if not more, generally shut up.' On 21 August, the Navy Office was moved to Greenwich Palace and Pepys was given lodgings nearby.

In the 1603 and 1625 epidemics the second half of August had been the peak, but if that pattern was what Londoners hoped for now, their hopes were dashed as the first week of September showed a further increase to just short of 7,000. New measures were tried. Fires were lit in the street, one to every twelve houses, and they burned for three days and nights until they were put out by heavy rain. In the second week, there was a slight fall in the death toll, to 6,544, but then it moved up again to 7,165. Although the last week of the month saw another fall, to 5,533, the Bills of Mortality showed that more than 30,000 people had died during the month. Now Pepys noted that only 'poor wretches' were to be seen in the streets and that if he walked the whole length of Lombard Street, he would see only twenty people. There were no boats on the river and the City was 'distressed and forsaken'.

Many doctors left town, and the Royal College of Physicians was deserted. Some may have felt it poetic justice that its entire treasure worth £1,000 was stolen. Some parish clergy also fled, often to be replaced by ministers who had lost their livings after the Restoration because they were seen as too Puritan. Now they returned to their old pulpits, drawing big congregations with their fulminations against the licentiousness of the court, at which God's wrath seemed so severe. Many of the clergy did stay at their posts, though, and at least eleven Anglican priests died, along with a number of Nonconformists.

The flight of the better off starved the authorities of cash. In some parishes, less than half of what was owed for poor and plague rates was collected. Some individual donors were very generous, but, as the death toll grew and the money shrank, support for the sick, such as it was, was stretched to breaking point. Watchmen, for example, were paid 7s a week for keeping guard over infected houses and were also supposed to deliver food to them. Increasingly, there was no money for food, and there was also a shortage of people available to perform the duties of watching and nursing. Normal decency began to break down. Nurses often robbed, or left to starve, the victims they were supposed to be looking after. Apothecaries were accused of strangling patients so they could ransack their homes. Searchers were suspected of theft. Gate keepers were meant to turn away from the City those who did not have certificates of health, but in fact they took bribes to let them in. Not surprisingly, attempts to quarantine the sick increasingly ran into resistance. The Privy Council was told of a case where a building in St Giles-in-the-Fields had been forced open 'in a riotous manner'. By mid-August, the parish of St Giles, Cripplegate had stopped confining plague suspects to their houses, and in September Pepys noted that the practice had been abandoned.

It was important to bury corpses to try to restrict the spread of the disease, but from mid-August at St Dunstan's-in-the-West and St Bride's there were so many dying that victims had to be put in common graves, while St Botolph's, Aldgate, where nearly 5,000 deaths were recorded, had a great pit in which more than 1,100 bodies were buried. Often the mass graves were lined with quicklime. Pepys came across a body in a coffin lying in a yard with nobody to bury it. 'The plague,' he wrote, 'made us as cruel as dogs one to another.' The City acquired a walled burial place at Bunhill Fields and another for the pest house at Soho Fields, but the coffin makers could not keep up with demand and from the end of July, St Bride's, for example, had to bury the dead in shrouds. When shrouds ran out, in many plague pits bodies were dumped naked. The predominant sounds of London now were the incessant tolling of church bells and the rolling wheels of carts collecting corpses, with the cries of 'Bring out your dead', or the oaths and curses of the ruffians who manned them. The bodies of the dead, or nearly dead, were tied in shrouds at foot and head and flung aboard. They were despoiled of rings, and subjected, it was said, to sexual assaults.

The City now was so quiet that the rush of water beneath London Bridge could be clearly heard, and there was so little traffic that grass grew in the streets. The air was full of smoke from the bonfires that had been lit to try to halt the disease, and death dominated everything. The Puritan minister Thomas Vincent thought he had heard of the death of someone he knew almost every day for a month, while in mid-October, Pepys wrote: 'Lord, how empty the streets are, and melancholy, so many poor and sick people in the streets, full of sores, and so many sad stories overheard as I walk, everybody talking of this dead, and that man sick, and so many in this place, and so many in that.'

By then, though, the death rate was beginning to fall. The number declined to 4,327 in the week ending 10 October, and by the end of the month was down to just over 1,000. There was a blip in the first week in November, when the total went up again, but later in the month, a heavy frost brought growing hopes that the disease would be killed off. On 24 November, Pepys visited his old oyster shop, and 'bought two barrels of my fine woman of the shop, who is alive after all the plague – which now is the first observation or enquiry we make at London concerning everybody we knew before it'. As the disease waned, those members of the clergy who saw it as a divine punishment were not always pleased; they felt the burden was being lifted before the lesson had been learned. Views as to who was being punished for what tended to differ. The Puritans saw the crime as being the immorality brought in by the Restoration court, while the High Church Anglicans thought it was the Civil War – a rebellion against the King.

Londoners got an unpleasant shock as the number of deaths rose again in the middle of December, but it was only a brief interruption to the downward trend. On Christmas Day, Pepys saw a wedding, 'which I have not seen many a day, and the young people so merry with one another', and in the first week of January, his wife returned to Seething Lane as, the diarist noted, 'the town fills apace'. Evelyn was still unwilling to bring his wife and family back to Deptford, though, even after ice had begun to form in the Thames, and they did not return until February, by which time the King and court were back at Whitehall. Even during March and April 1666, though, there were still on average 30 plague victims buried each day, and the first three weeks of May brought another increase. There was little alarm, and the numbers fell again. Still, in June, July and August, there were an average of 36 victims a week, while over the whole of 1666, 1,800 Londoners died of the disease.

For the whole of 1665, the official total for plague deaths in London was more than 68,000, but the disruptive effect of the disease had made it difficult to keep accurate records and there were plenty of incentives to conceal the true cause of death if plague was responsible. Many contemporaries, therefore, believed it was an underestimate, and one of the few grandees to stay in London, the Earl of Clarendon, believed the true number was 160,000. Nowadays, historians tend to accept a figure of anything up to 100,000, out of a population of about 500,000. What is clear is that the number who died was much greater than in the Black Death 300 years before, but that the proportion of the population carried off, dreadful though it was, was not as high as in the previous epidemic.

The areas that had been worst hit were around the edge of the City – places like St Giles-in-the-Fields, St Giles, Cripplegate and St Botolph, Aldgate. Southwark too suffered severely with more than 15,000 deaths, just less than a third of its population. In St Giles, Cripplegate, four children from one family had been buried within six days, and in the space of four days the parish clerk recorded the burial of a married couple, the son and two daughters, and a journeyman who worked for the husband. The areas that got off lightest tended to be the wealthiest, like Cheapside. Clarendon noted that 'the lowest and poorest sort of people' formed most of the victims, and that 'not many of wealth and quality' had died.

The last individual plague death recorded in the Bills of Mortality was at Rotherhithe in 1679, but 1665–6 was the last epidemic in London, despite the fact that the disease continued to ravage Europe throughout the eighteenth century, and that, as far west as Provence, tens of thousands were killed in 1720–1. The popular explanation for the end of the plague was that the Great Fire of 1666 destroyed the black rats' habitats. Those buildings of timber and thatch in which it was so comfortable, were burned down and replaced with houses of brick and tile. In fact, rats can colonise brick buildings, and, besides, the area of London that was burned down was not the part where the plague had been most devastating. In addition, the plague also disappeared from other parts of England where there was no great fire.

One explanation may be that the brown rat began to drive out the black rat, though this did not happen until well into the eighteenth century. The brown rat is supposed to shun humans and rarely to act as a host for the flea that carries the plague bacteria. Another possibility was that the black rats may themselves have built up immunity to the plague bacteria. If the rats were no longer dying, there would be no need for the fleas to migrate to human hosts. Some historians now consider that the most important factor was more stringent quarantine regulations in England and in other countries, though they did not prevent the many serious outbreaks in Europe over the next century, nor were the intellectual and organisational resources of the British Empire sufficient to prevent 12 million plague deaths in India in the first half of the twentieth century.

FOURTEEN

Cholera, Flu and Fog

Just as trade brought the plague to London, so, in the nineteenth century, it introduced a disastrous new disease, cholera. Once again, it came from the East, spreading from India in the 1820s, and arriving in England in 1831. It could kill with frightening speed, carrying off by nightfall those who had breakfasted in good health, causing acute diarrhoea, draining the body of nutrients and fluids, and producing dehydration and kidney failure. Its cause was a mystery.

Cholera arrived in the docks of Rotherhithe in the second week of February 1832, and crept along the south bank of the Thames to Southwark and Lambeth, before leaping across the river to Ratcliff, Limehouse, Whitechapel and Hoxton. As with any new disease, all sorts of preventives were suggested. The *Lancet* reported that a community of Jews in Central Europe had escaped by rubbing their bodies with liniment containing wine, vinegar, camphor, mustard, pepper, garlic and ground beetles. More rationally, Emergency Boards of Health were set up with the power to close cesspools and order the scouring of sewers and the cleaning of slaughterhouses. This first cholera epidemic killed 6,500 in London, but by autumn the outbreak was dying away and the Emergency Boards were disbanded.

The conditions in which many Londoners lived were appalling: A report for the Poor Law Commissioners said Bethnal Green's main thoroughfare was full of 'masses of putrefying matter'. 'There is no drain,' it added, 'the water runs off as it can, and now and then the parish authorities send round a mudcart to gather up what becomes so thick as to block the way.' Dr Hector Gavin from Charing Cross Hospital conducted his own survey of the area. He found that some people lived fourteen to a room, that privies were shared by forty to fifty, and that thirty houses could depend for their water supply on a

188

single standpipe which operated only intermittently and delivered water with 'highly coloured deposits'.

In 1848, cholera returned. By now, a new General Board of Health had been set up, but with strictly limited powers. It could only advise the Poor Law Guardians, and when it recommended those in Whitechapel and Bethnal Green to cleanse infected houses and open emergency dispensaries for the sick, its recommendations were ignored. Dr Gavin, by now Medical Inspector of Bethnal Green, Hackney and Shoreditch, found the filthiest areas were the worst hit by the disease, but by identifying those most at risk and getting them prompt treatment, he managed to reduce the death rate to about one in ten. Overall, this epidemic was much more severe than the first. Altogether in London there were about 30,000 cases in four months, and nearly half, 14,000, died. With the best of intentions, the authorities had ordered the flushing out of sewers, but the effect of this had been to fill the Thames and its tributaries with infected excrement.

The problem was that they were working in the dark; although there were many theories circulating, still no one knew what caused cholera. During the eleven years between 1845 and 1856, some 700 works on the disease were published in London. The *Lancet* mused: 'Is it a fungus, a miasma, an electrical disturbance, a deficiency of ozone, a morbid off-scouring of the intestinal canal? We know nothing; we are at sea in a whirlpool of conjecture. . . . ' Many believed cholera was spread by bad smells, others thought moral depravity must play a role, but a Soho doctor, John Snow, who was to become Queen Victoria's gynaecologist, was already wondering why, when cholera was a disease of the intestines not the lungs, it should be spread through the air. In 1849, he published a paper suggesting that cholera might be transmitted by polluted water.

When the disease returned in 1853, he got a chance to test his theory. Snow noticed how high its incidence was among people who drew water from a well in what is now Broadwick Street, close to his surgery. His suspicions were further aroused when he found that a sewer passed close to the well. Snow persuaded the parish council to remove the handle that operated the pump – and the death rate immediately fell. Today, the pump is marked with a granite stone, and the site of his surgery is occupied by a pub that bears his name.

Snow's views were far from being generally accepted, but in 1852 a new law had been brought in requiring water companies to filter any supplies drawn from rivers. It did not prevent the outbreak of 1853–4 that killed nearly 11,000 people, and when the new Metropolitan Sewers Commission removed cesspools from the cellars of hundreds of dwellings, that did not seem to help either. Snow provided an answer. In 1857, a year before his death, he published a study of mortality rates during the last two cholera outbreaks in two South London parishes. Both got their drinking water from the Thames, but in Lambeth it was supplied mainly by the Lambeth Water Company, while Southwark was served by the Southwark and Vauxhall Water Company. In the 1849 outbreak, the rates were similar, with Lambeth slightly higher, but in the 1853–4 epidemic, there were six times as many deaths in Southwark. Snow's explanation was that after 1849, the Lambeth company had started taking its water from Thames Ditton, which was above Teddington Lock and so could not be reached by sewage carried upstream on the tide from London, while the Southwark and Vauxhall continued to draw its supplies from the contaminated tidal stretch near Vauxhall. The action of the Sewers Commission had probably made things worse. When houses had their cesspools removed, the sewers to which they were connected spewed their contents straight into the Thames.

In June 1866, cholera appeared at Bromley-by-Bow and then at Poplar. Within days, it was spreading along Mile End Road and Whitechapel Road. The following week, half a dozen people an hour were dying in Tower Hamlets. By the end of July, it was becoming clear that there was a remarkable correlation between the areas in which people were dying, and those supplied by the East London Water Company from the River Lea. Sewage was still being discharged into the river at Bow Bridge, half a mile below the company's reservoir at Old Ford, which meant the incoming tide would have carried sewage back upstream towards the reservoir. This should not have mattered, because, under the law of 1852, the company was supposed to filter the water – indeed, its chief engineer claimed that 'not a drop' was unfiltered – but in one house where two children died, their father found a putrid eel 14 inches long blocking the pipes, and there was at least one other similar incident. Investigations revealed that, although the company's new reservoirs had filters, water was getting into them from its old reservoirs which did not. In July and August, more than 4,300 Londoners died of cholera; nearly 3,800 of them in areas supplied by the East London Water Company. A private government inquiry confirmed that the company had committed a breach of the new laws, but no one was ever prosecuted and even if they had been, the maximum punishment was a fine of £200. By now, resistance to Snow's theory was crumbling and most people were coming round to the view that cholera was spread by water. In 1868, Sir Joseph Bazalgette's new sewage system was completed, and London had no more cholera epidemics. In fact, by 1896 it was rare enough to be classified as an 'exotic disease'.

The last year of the Wars of the Roses, 1485, had seen the first appearance of an apparently new illness in London, the 'sweating sickness', which, it was said, could carry off its victims within twenty-four hours. It killed the mayor, Sir Thomas Hille, then, four days later, it took his successor. In the same week, six aldermen died, and altogether 'a wonderful number' of people, perhaps thousands. There were five further epidemics over the next seventy years, and the one of 1551 was serious enough to drive King Edward VI and his court away to Hampton Court. Nowadays, it is thought that at least some of these epidemics were caused by some kind of influenza.

It was certainly flu that brought a public health disaster to London in the final year of the First World War. In February 1918 King Alfonso XIII of Spain caught the disease, as did millions of his countrymen, though there were relatively few deaths. It became known as 'Spanish flu', but this may simply have been because the country was not involved in the war, and so had sufficiently relaxed press censorship for news to get out. In fact, like so many strains of flu, this one may have originated in Hong Kong or China, or

American troops may have brought it with them as they crossed to Europe in huge numbers.

Whatever its source, after its first appearance in London in the spring, it seemed to die away, only to return later in the year in a much more deadly form. From mid-June to the beginning of August, official estimates put the number who died in the capital at between 1,600 and 1,700, and there was also a big increase in deaths from bronchitis and pneumonia, many of which could probably be attributed to the infection. One of the striking things about the illness was that the death toll was higher for those aged between five and forty-five than for those above, while flu was normally a bigger killer of the old. The symptoms were headache, backache, and a 102-degree fever. The disease was highly infectious, being spread through coughs and sneezes. One sneeze could distribute more than 85 million bacteria. In a high number of cases, flu turned to pneumonia within a few days, or even a day, of symptoms appearing, with the skin becoming a deep plum colour. It could be a horrible end, with victims gasping desperately for breath, their lungs full of fluid.

In October, the disease strengthened its grip. By the end of the month, essential public services were under threat. Some 500 employees of the London General Omnibus Company were off sick. More than 1,400 police had the disease, and 30 had died; 100 firemen had fallen victim. Half the London Hospital's nursing staff of 150 were absent. At Edmonton Military Hospital, 2 nurses died after catching flu from patients they were tending. In East Ham, 200 teachers were ill, and there as in Wood Green the schools were closed; 1,000 telephone operators were away from work, and the Postmaster-General asked people to make phone calls only if it was strictly necessary.

In Greater London, 761 people died in one week, 371 of them in the London County Council area. All over London, people were collapsing in the street. Nearly 60 had to be rushed to hospital by ambulance during the last weekend in October. At the Middlesex Hospital, the resident Medical Officer complained he did little more than 'direct the traffic', speeding victims to emergency wards or the mortuary, so that BID (brought in dead), became a routine entry in the Administration Book. At the London Hospital, they had 55 cases of flu complicated by pneumonia in a week; half of the patients died. The hospital had seen nothing like it since the cholera epidemic, and was running out of beds, while many nurses were off sick. At London Zoo, the chimpanzees were protected with glass cages.

Two young women working near St Paul's caught the disease and were both buried on what should have been their wedding day. In Edmonton, gardeners from local parks had to be pressed into grave-digging duties. In Stroud Green, there were twenty-nine deaths in one road. It seemed especially cruel that so many who died were soldiers who had survived the horrors of the First World War. Sometimes, the disease was also supposed to produce severe psychological symptoms. At St Marylebone Police Court, a man charged with stealing a car produced a doctor's certificate to say the after-effects of flu had 'clouded his moral sense'. In a more extreme case, a crane-driver at London docks, who had had a severe case of the illness, cut his throat with a razor after killing his two-year-old daughter.

In St Pancras, notices were posted advising people to keep warm and stay in bed at the first appearance of symptoms, and recommending gargling with a solution of salt and permanganate of potash. The medical correspondent of *The Times* suggested a precaution reminiscent of the advice meted out during the SARS outbreak of 2003 – wear a mask of gauze across the mouth and nose. The writer advised smoking 'in moderation', a measure that found considerable favour, with a number of workplaces dropping 'no smoking' rules, and he also recommended moderate drinking, especially of port and Burgundy. One Harley Street specialist favoured 'drenching' his patients with big doses of aspirin.

On 11 November, unparalleled scenes of rejoicing in London greeted the end of the First World War, but there was no let up in the epidemic. Now half of the city's ambulance staff were sick, and Croydon's schools were closed. In the first week of the month, deaths had leapt to 4,163 in Greater London, including 2,458 in the LCC area. 'The visits of the raiding Gothas (see Chapter 3) to London were but a summer shower compared with the deluge of germs we have just received,' commented *The Times*. 'The air raids cost

London some hundreds of lives; the influenza has cost it upwards of 10,000.' There were more than 360 school classes without teachers, and things must have really been getting serious when the Launderers' Association warned that 'the public must be prepared for delay and irregularity in collection and delivery of laundry work'. As colder weather came in for the rest of the month, the number of deaths for Greater London fell to 1,487 in the first week in December; by the end of the year, they were down to 186 a week. Still, *The Times* lamented what it saw as the number of unnecessary fatalities. It maintained that if only people had been told to wear gauze masks in the street, 'there is not much room for doubt that hundreds, if not thousands, of lives might thus have been saved'.

Even when it seemed the worst must be over, Spanish flu resurfaced in early 1919, when three nurses and eighty patients died at the London Hospital. Among those who had lost their lives in the epidemic were Captain William Leefe Robinson VC, who brought down a Zeppelin at Stanmore, the first over Britain, and Sir Charles Wyndham, founder of Wyndham's Theatre. King George V and the Prime Minister, David Lloyd George, both caught it but survived. Overall, it was estimated that 18,000 Londoners died, though worldwide the number killed was 20 million, including more than 12 million in India, representing about 4 per cent of the population. The exact nature of the organism that caused Spanish flu remains a mystery and is still the subject of energetic research.

Complaints that smoke from coal fires was polluting London's air go back at least to the reign of Queen Elizabeth I, and were frequently repeated. In 1661, John Evelyn wrote a pamphlet lamenting the 'Hellish and dismal cloud of sea-coal' which was wrecking the lungs of Londoners. In the eighteenth century, Tobias Smollett complained about the city's acrid atmosphere and, in the nineteenth, Dickens described a classic London fog in the opening chapter of *Bleak House*. Occasional attempts were made to clean up the air, but things only seemed to get worse.

One great fog began two days after Christmas Day 1813 and lasted until 3 January 1814. It was so bad that few Londoners ventured out. One who did was the Prince Regent, who decided to visit the Marquess of Salisbury at Hatfield House, only to be forced to turn back at Kentish Town. Coachmen had to lead their horses, and the London to Birmingham mail took nearly seven hours to get as far as Uxbridge, while the Maidenhead to London coach got lost and overturned. Even worse, though, was the fog that began in November 1879 and lasted right through to March 1880.

Apart from the disruption they caused, fogs also killed people through lung and heart disease. During the one of December 1873, the death rate was estimated to be 40 per cent higher than normal. The problem was the sulphur dioxide and the dust, soot and other solid airborne pollutants given off when coal was burned. These could trigger a whole range of illnesses like emphysema, asthma, bronchitis and heart disease.

On 5 December 1952, the densest fog since 1873 descended on London. The air was yellow, with smoke and sulphur dioxide levels ten times higher than usual. Visibility was often down to 20 yards, sometimes even less. Road, rail and air transport were brought almost to a standstill. Drivers simply had to ditch their cars; when the fog cleared, some could not find where they had left them. One man told the story of brushing against what he thought was a person and asking for a light for his cigarette, only to discover he was talking to a lamppost. The smog even got inside buildings. A performance at Sadler's Wells Theatre had to be stopped because the audience could not see the stage. High humidity and lack of wind meant the fog did not clear until 9 December, during which time it was estimated to have caused 4,000 deaths in London.

The government set up a committee to examine air pollution; its findings resulted in the Clean Air Act of 1956, introducing smoke-control areas and beginning the process of change from coal to smokeless fuel. It was seven years, though, before the Act came fully into effect, which left time for more pea-soupers, like the one of December 1957 that killed 1,000 Londoners through illness as well as causing the Lewisham train crash (see Chapter 11), while the smog of December 1962 claimed another 750 lives.

FIFTEEN

Wild Weather

Among the first instances of extreme weather recorded in London were the violent storms said to have wracked the Roman city in AD 253 and 277, destroying many dwellings. Then, in 548, Saxon London was supposed to have been hit by a tempest that killed many people. After the Norman Conquest, there was another fierce storm, in November 1091. It lifted the roof of St Mary-le-Bow clean off, as well as blowing down hundreds of houses, and sending so much flotsam and jetsam along the Thames that London Bridge, then built of wood, was swept away, while the White Tower at the Tower of London, which was still being built, was 'sore shaken'. London Bridge was damaged again in 1281 when a severe cold spell caused so much ice to build up under it that five of its arches were demolished. In 1362, a fierce gale lasted for a whole week, knocking down trees, houses and towers.

The steeple of Old St Paul's was the tallest in Europe and so, not surprisingly, was often struck by lightning. It was damaged by a strike in 1230 and then, on the afternoon of 1 February 1444, it was struck again and set on fire. The story goes that local people thought they had managed to put it out with vinegar, but that the flames burst out again in the evening and this time the mayor had to come along to direct operations. The fire was extinguished, but not before it had done a lot of damage.

In 1561 came another violent thunderstorm, and the steeple was struck by 'marvelous great fiery lightning', setting timbers on fire. Lead flowed like lava from the roof and long pointed flames licked the steeple. The Lord Mayor, the Bishop of London, the Lord Treasurer and the Keeper of the Great Seal were called to the scene. There followed a lively and interesting discussion – should they

196

shoot the steeple down with cannon, or hew a gap in the roof to act as a firebreak or, since the lightning strike must be a sign of God's wrath, should the fire be left to burn? Meanwhile, the flames got on with their work, bringing the golden cross and eagle crashing through the rafters and setting fire to the interior. Eventually, as fears grew that whole streets might be set on fire, an Admiralty official appeared and took charge of the situation. Ladders and axes were sent for and a volunteer army of 500 men and women was marshalled to fight the blaze. It still took a long time to subdue the flames, and damage was severe. The roof of the nave was restored, but the spire was never replaced before the whole church was destroyed in the Great Fire of 1666 (see Chapter 5).

In November 1703, London was shaken by what the novelist Daniel Defoe, then living in Cripplegate, described as the 'Dreadful Tempest', but which became known as the Great Storm. There had been a week of disturbed weather. On the evening of the 24th, Defoe had almost been buried by a house that collapsed in a fierce squall. The next day, thunder and hail storms hit the City then, on the 26th, the wind really got up. When Defoe looked at his barometer that night, the reading was so low he thought his children must have been playing with it, but around midnight, he was woken by a shrieking, moaning wind accompanied by the sound of falling objects and breaking glass. By two in the morning it had reached a frenzy.

People cowered in their homes, many believing it was the end of the world. When Defoe ventured out, he found a fierce gale still blowing, rain lashing down and chimneys, metal piping and timber crashing into the streets. In some places, tiles were being flung 40 yards through the air, to be embedded inches deep in the ground, and everywhere gates and fences were blown down. A house near Islington belonging to the Earl of Northampton lost thirteen chimney stacks. Defoe himself knew of twenty houses that had been completely demolished, and there were many more. Near Moorfields, a whole row was levelled. Church steeples were razed to the ground and the lead on top of Westminster Abbey was rolled up like parchment and blown clear of the building. Twenty-seven vases were blown down from the steeple of St Michael, Crooked Lane, and among the other churches damaged was St Mary Overie. Many trees were brought down: 70 at Moorfields and 100 in St James's Park, and rows of Queen Anne's acacias, elms and limes were uprooted.

A total of 21 people were killed on the streets of London; 2 boys died in Hatton Garden, and 2 more people in Aldersgate when their house collapsed. A man was crushed by a falling chimney stack in Fetter Lane. A distiller and a maid were killed in St James's, and a carpenter in Whitecross Street. Altogether it was estimated that 200 Londoners were injured by falling debris, but there were also some miraculous escapes. At three o'clock in the morning, a furious gust of wind blew a stack of chimneys onto a house in St Martin's Lane, where there were 17 people. A nurse, a maid and a baby fell through three floors to the kitchen. The baby was found unharmed hanging in the curtains and the other two escaped with slight bruises. Indeed, everyone in the house got out without serious injury.

The storm also wrought havoc on the Thames. Defoe saw 700 ships 'crushed together' between Shadwell and Limehouse. Many were torn from their moorings and driven ashore, barges smashed against the arches of London Bridge, and more than 60 wherries were sunk. In addition to the 21 people killed on land, another 22 were drowned, including 2 watermen at Blackfriars and 5 people at Fulham when a boat capsized.

Overall, the damage was estimated at £2 million, a colossal sum for the time. Queen Anne declared a general fast on 19 January 1704, marking a calamity 'so dreadful and astonishing that the like hath not been seen or felt in the memory of any person living in this our Kingdom'. It was, of course, to be seen as 'a token of the Divine displeasure', and while the storm may have seemed bad enough to those caught up in it, the Queen felt they should be grateful it had not been much worse, and that 'it was the infinite mercy of God that we and our people were not thereby wholly destroyed'.

London saw nothing like it for the best part of another three centuries, though there were plenty of episodes of extreme weather. In October 1780, for example, two people died when a fierce storm flattened a house near Barnes Common. In addition, a workhouse lost its chimneys, a windmill was turned upside down and smashed to pieces, and Hammersmith church was badly damaged. Many trees were flung down, including a walnut that was uprooted and thrown 22 feet.

In October 1898, Camberwell was struck by a tornado accompanied by a terrific downpour. It lasted only a few minutes and was confined to an area about half a mile square, but many people were injured and practically every building in the area was damaged. Doors were wrenched from their hinges, lampposts were twisted like corkscrews and roofs were torn off, leaving the streets strewn with debris.

In the twentieth century, lightning claimed the lives of six Londoners in May 1911, then, three years later, seven were killed by a thunderbolt while they were sheltering under a tree on Wandsworth Common.

Nearly seventy-five years later, just before half past one on the afternoon of 15 October 1987, BBC weatherman Michael Fish said on television: 'Earlier on today, apparently a woman rang the BBC and said she'd heard that there was a hurricane on the way. Well, if you're watching, don't worry, there isn't.' About nine o'clock, though, a normal October night was transformed by an invasion of sub-tropical air forced over southern England by a storm. The temperature rose an unprecedented 13 degrees Fahrenheit in less than half an hour. As the winds grew more fierce, at half past one on the morning of 16 October, the Meteorological Office sent a warning to the Ministry of Defence that a storm of such ferocity was expected that the civil authorities might have to ask the military for assistance.

In the capital, the winds brought the most destructive night since the Blitz (see Chapter 3). In South London, concrete balconies fell 30 feet from two flats in Peckham, while the roof of a block in Stockwell had to be held on with tarpaulins weighted down by sacks of salt. Police found a car perched on top of a tree in Upper Norwood. Pubs and schools lost their roofs. At Biggin Hill, one private aircraft was cut in half and three others were written off. At Beckenham, a newspaper boy was rescued after being crushed under a fallen tree.

Salt blown in from the sea was found caked to the windows of London tower blocks. At Kennington, all eighty-four families living in Strinham Point had to be evacuated after brick walls were sucked out of a thirteenth-floor flat, leaving a gaping hole just feet from where a couple had been sleeping. They watched in horror as their stereo and drinks cabinet disappeared into the void. Another resident was awoken by the noise. 'I switched my bedroom lights on,' he said, 'and noticed the lampshades were actually swinging from one side of the ceiling to the other. At that point, my bed started to move across the floor.' He got dressed and went outside: 'It was the kind of feeling I imagine people would have after a bomb had dropped. Everybody was quiet. It appeared they were just wandering around not knowing what to do.' The flats were so badly damaged, it would be eight months before it was safe for the residents to return.

One Streatham police officer said: 'Thank God it happened at night.' If the storm had struck during the day, the casualty list would surely have been much higher than the two people who died – a tramp dossing down in Lincoln's Inn Fields and a motorist in Croydon, both killed by falling trees. The storm sent corrugated iron sheets flying through the air, and scaffolding poles were hurled like javelins. As it was, many Londoners simply slept through it all, including the family in Putney Heath whose chimney stack fell through their roof and into the kitchen and the tramp who lived in a bus shelter at Gospel Oak. A tree missed him by inches, but the first he knew of it was when a policeman woke him at nine o'clock the next morning. The tramp asked who had been chopping down trees in the night.

To the west, in Ealing, more than 200 cars were damaged, as well as 80 out of the borough's 90 schools. In North London, a Kentish Town woman had an astonishing escape when her bed plunged 40 feet from her second-floor bedroom into the basement. It took firemen three hours to rescue her, but she suffered nothing worse than severe bruising. Another North London householder found that a strange greenhouse had been blown into his back garden. In East London, a tower block at Lower Clapton had to be evacuated because it was swaying so much in the wind, and on Chingford Plain, a circus big top was torn to shreds.

A fire service controller who finished work in the early hours said that when she went out into the street, her first impression was 'there are no trees'. Altogether, a quarter of a million were uprooted. In terms of those felled in public places, the worst-hit boroughs were Bexley and Croydon, which lost 75,000 each, while Sutton lost 50,000. Many rare and valuable trees were destroyed. Kew Gardens lost 1,000 as well as sustaining damage to buildings, like William IV's temple, hit by a falling tree of heaven. A team of horticulturalists from Oregon flew in with chainsaws to help clear the mess. Chelsea Physic Garden lost a number of notable specimens, including a honey locust tree that crashed through the roof of the curator's house, while a rare Judas tree was felled in the grounds of Dulwich Picture Gallery. At St Mary's Church in South Woodford, a 400-year-old yew came down. Altogether, 5,000 trees were brought down in the royal parks, with Kensington Gardens suffering particularly badly. To the west, at Syon Park Gardens, the London Butterfly House was smashed. More than 300 exotic specimens escaped, though some were later found in nearby potting sheds. At Richmond, one casualty of the storm was a 200-year-old copper beech under which Thackeray was said to have written parts of *Vanity Fair*. Buckingham Palace's gardens were damaged, but central London's tallest tree, a 130-feet-high London plane, escaped.

To many Londoners, it seemed like a disaster, but some naturalists argued that periodic storms of this kind are actually beneficial, clearing out old vegetation and making way for new growth. Richard Mabey, chairman of the London Wildlife Trust, wrote that the storm was 'an integral part of the workings of the environment, not some alien force'.

The cost of the damage, though, ran into many millions of pounds, and disruption the next day was dreadful. Nearly 2 million homes, shops and offices had their electricity cut off, and the Metropolitan Police received more than 12,000 emergency calls. In Croydon, 100 roads were blocked, in Camden, there were 70, while in Wandsworth the number was more than 40. About 60 trees had fallen on to the Epping to Ongar section of the Central Line. There were precious few buses or trains, and no flights from Heathrow. On the Thames, barges had been torn from their moorings and hurled into the middle of the river. The City was a ghost town. Not only was hardly anyone able to get to work, dealing screens and telephone exchanges were out of action through power failures. When the Stock Exchange did reopen, it was for Black Monday, with the FTSE 100 falling 22 per cent in two days. Meanwhile, the disaster acquired its own poetic memorial in *Hurricane Dub*, a radio drama in verse by the rap poet Benjamin Zephaniah: 'Breeze blowing hard, breeze blowing hard / Things start moving in the backyard / Breeze blowing hard, breeze blowing hard / This must be a hurricane from abroad.'

Now that word 'hurricane' struck a raw nerve at the Met Office. Some may have regarded the storm as perfectly natural, but the boss of the Met Office found his home besieged by reporters demanding to know why the nation had not been warned. The government weighed in too, with Environment Secretary Nicholas Ridley describing what he saw as the failure to predict the storm as 'unbelievable'. Ten years afterwards, the memory still rankled with a senior Met Office staff member. 'It was', he told a television documentary, 'an enormous embarrassment. It was perhaps the blackest day the Met Office has had.'

Officially, Michael Fish was right. There was no hurricane. It was true that at ten to three in the morning, a gust of 94 miles an hour was recorded across High Holborn, the highest since records began in 1940, but hurricanes are tropical storms and involve sustained winds of 75 miles an hour or more that can reach 160 miles an hour. What London experienced were some gusts of wind of hurricane force. Still, the Met Office conducted an inquiry. It pointed out that various severe weather warnings were given during the evening, culminating in a warning of severe gales at 01.20, but it recognised that its television forecasts had tended to concentrate on rain rather than wind, and acknowledged that the use of the word 'hurricane' had been 'particularly unfortunate'. And the Met Office did make changes, like bringing in more powerful computers and a new severe weather warning system. It also expanded its observation network and improved the training of forecasters.

Michael Fish did not actually give the late forecasts on the evening before the storm, but his was the one that stayed in the popular memory, and he insisted vigorously that he did not get it as wrong as people thought: 'The day before, I was on the television saying "batten down the hatches, there's some very, very stormy weather on the way". Unfortunately the little low pressure area that caused all the problems just changed course at the last minute.' Whatever the Met Office might say, his overall judgement was: 'I shouldn't think I'll ever live it down now. I won't be able to read my obituaries, but I'm sure it'll be in them.' Still, at least everyone could relax and think there would not be another storm like it for another 300 years.

So was it global warming or malign coincidence that set the corrugated iron and scaffolding polls flying again less than three years later? Whatever the reason, on 25 January 1990, Burns' Day, the winds were back. At eleven o'clock in the morning, gusts of 87 miles an hour were recorded in London. Nearly all the capital's mainline stations were closed and, when they reopened, services were severely disrupted because of damage to power lines and fallen trees blocking tracks. Seven Underground lines were partially closed, and Waterloo Bridge was blocked for more than three hours by a lorry that had been blown over. Edgware Road and the Embankment were shut because of fears that buildings were going to collapse, and flying debris forced the closure of Heathrow for a time.

At half past three in the afternoon, the Central Lobby at the Houses of Parliament had to be evacuated after masonry fell from the roof. Many buildings had their roofs torn off, cars were crushed by trees or fallen scaffolding and, once again, many homes and businesses were without electricity. A quarter of Barking and Dagenham's council houses were damaged, and the total number of houses needing repairs in the borough was more than 25,000, at a cost approaching £4 million. The new developments in London's Docklands were particularly badly hit, as construction materials were blown around and dashed into buildings.

Though the winds were not as strong as they had been in 1987, there were more deaths and injuries because they came during the daytime when people were out and about. Four people were killed in London. One man died when his car ran into debris; another was hit by a tree. One woman was killed by a falling wall; a second was blown under a car. Ambulance crews, who were locked in a bitter pay dispute, called off their industrial action to help the many who were injured. The actor Gordon Kaye, star of the television series *'Allo, 'Allo*, was hit on the head by a plank of wood that crashed from a hoarding near his home by the Thames at Hounslow, and had to undergo brain surgery.

Once again, the trees suffered. Kew Gardens lost 100, including some that had been weakened in the 1987 storm. In London's royal parks, the toll was 300, but the Met Office had a better storm this time. Thanks to those improved computers, and clearer understanding of an 'explosive depression', they were able to give warnings of severe gales likely to cause structural damage more than 14 hours before the winds hit the Cornish coast. Their verdict: 'We got it right this time.'

SIXTEEN

Earthquake, Famine and Flood

The only death known to have been caused by an earthquake in London came on 6 April 1580, when an apprentice cobbler named Thomas Gray was hit by masonry falling from Christ's Hospital in Newgate Street. The earthquake caused a number of chimneys to collapse, and so great was the shock that stallholders at the Royal Exchange packed up for the day. There were a number of other reported earthquakes in the capital. One in 1247 is said to have destroyed many houses in the City, while another, twenty-eight years later, is supposed to have damaged houses and churches.

On 8 February 1750, there was a minor tremor that caused little damage. That was followed by a slightly stronger one on 8 March. As usual, there was no shortage of suggestions that this was a manifestation of God's wrath at the depravity of Londoners. There was also dreadful foreboding as to what might be in store for 8 April, and a guardsman was sent to gaol for inflaming people with his wild prophecies. On the fateful night, thousands slept in the open at Highgate, Hampstead and Islington, but nothing happened.

Famine was a regular blight in London in the Middle Ages. In 1258, people are supposed to have fought over carrion and dead dogs, and to have drunk pig swill. The hunger also brought disease, and the Bishop of London died, along with an alleged 20,000 others, though this figure was almost certainly an exaggeration. Hunger returned in 1270, when heavy rain ruined crops, while famine also stalked the city from 1314 to 1317, when there was serious drought and hundreds are said to have died from heat and starvation.

For centuries, the Thames was London's principal artery for transport and trade, but it also caused regular havoc when it flooded. In 1236, there were two major inundations. One, early in the year, was caused by heavy rain, and struck Westminster, which was always vulnerable, flooding the Palace so that lawyers had to row around the Great Hall in boats. The second was produced by a high tide in November, which turned Woolwich Marshes into a sea, drowning many people as well as hundreds of cattle. In 1240, after days of continuous rain, floods were said to have extended for 'above six miles' at Lambeth. In the late thirteenth century, the authorities improved river defences, but in both 1324 and 1326 they were breached, causing major floods at Greenwich, Woolwich and Wapping.

In 1377, the Abbess of Barking Abbey asked to be excused the tax then being imposed to finance the war with France because her lands at Barking and Dagenham had been inundated by the Thames. They were flooded again three years later. By the sixteenth century, stronger dykes were being built along the river using slabs of Essex clay, but that did not save the Great Hall at Westminster from flooding in 1515, 1555 and 1579. In 1651, it was the turn of Deptford, where the Thames flooded during a violent storm. Within half an hour, some streets were 10 feet deep in water and residents had to be rescued from rooftops and upper windows. Twelve years later, the waters burst into the House of Commons during a debate. Pepys recorded: 'there was last night the greatest tide that ever was remembered in England to have been in this river, all Whitehall having been drowned'. Some modern authorities believe it was the highest tide in 200 years.

In 1707, Dagenham got its worst ever flooding, with 1,000 acres inundated, and before the end of the century, Fulham was flooded, as were Westminster and Southwark, three times. In 1791, not only were the lawyers having to go to and from court in boats, but St James's Park, Bankside, Tooley Street, and Wapping High Street were all under water too. Altogether, between 1209 and 1840 the Thames is reckoned to have flooded London and its surroundings thirty-six times; thirteen times largely because of high tides, and on most other occasions due to heavy rain or rapid melting of snow.

In 1875, a gale-force wind whipped up the river and it burst through an 11-foot-high embankment wall. Around Nine Elms, 600 houses and shops were flooded. Wandsworth, Putney and Fulham were also hit, along with Princes Square in Lambeth, a low-lying area that was home to many poor Irish immigrants. In January 1881, a severe storm caused flooding at Bankside and Upper Ground, and at Woolwich, where two men were drowned, as were two more at the Royal Albert Dock. The waters also swept over the wall by the government powder magazines at Plumstead Marshes. Two police constables were reported missing there; their bodies were never found.

In 1927, London enjoyed a white Christmas. Snow began to fall on Christmas night, and a blizzard raged all of Boxing Day. In central London, it lay 6 inches deep and in the suburbs up to 2 feet. Fierce gales threw up huge snowdrifts and roads were sometimes blocked for days, with cars buried and lost. On New Year's Eve, the snow began to melt, but, unfortunately, as the thaw set in, heavy rain began to fall. By 3 January 1928, there was flooding at Willesden, Greenford, Ealing and Golders Green, with hundreds of people marooned in the upper floors of their houses. By the 4th, nearly 1,000 houses in the Lea Valley had been flooded. Two days later, a gale began blowing over the North Sea, whipping up the Thames as the river was having its highest tide in fifty years. Just after midnight, water came up onto the terraces of the Houses of Parliament, and filled the moat at the Tower of London. Temple Pier and Upper Thames Street were flooded, and soon the Embankment by Temple was covered with water for 200 yards. Lorries coming through the waters created a wash like ships steaming through the sea. Witnesses reported waves 20 feet high or more as the river overflowed or broke its banks all the way up from Woolwich to Richmond. On the Thames, two barges sank.

In the early hours of the morning, a man living at Hurlingham Court in Putney heard shouts for help. When he looked out of his bedroom window, he saw a girl swimming in fast-rising waters. She had got out through the window of the basement flat directly below his, where she had been staying. The man made a rope from the sheets on his bed, lowered it down and pulled her up. The girl's fifteen-year-old brother had broken a window and got out of the flat with another boy, aged nine. With the help of his wife and the maid, the man managed to pull them up to safety too, along with another woman, but two other women in the flat were trapped and drowned. After the rescue, the girl said she had been awake and had heard the sound of water pouring in 'like the waves of the sea'. She saw the two women who were drowned knocked down by its force. One local man escaped by clambering onto the top of a shed that was floating in his garden, and climbing to one of the upper windows of the house.

In a house right by the river at Upper Mall in Hammersmith, two maids, aged twenty and twenty-two, were sleeping in one of the basement bedrooms. Apart from them the house was empty and no one in the neighbourhood knew they were there – their bodies were found only when the butler arrived at seven o'clock the next morning. One eye-witness said the flood had done so much damage that the house looked as though it had been hit by a shell.

It was in Pimlico, though, that the worst loss of life occurred, with ten people drowned. The Embankment wall between Lambeth and Vauxhall Bridges gave way in three places, with a sound like an explosion, and huge quantities of water poured into Grosvenor Road, tearing up the wooden paving blocks and filling the basements of houses in a few seconds, then dashing in torrents along Page Street and Horseferry Road. Police ran along the streets banging on doors with their truncheons trying to get people out of basements into higher rooms. Some were swept off their feet as they tried to raise the alarm.

Much of the area was occupied by working-class families crowded into small flats, or domestic servants. The bodies of two maids who drowned in Grosvenor Road were recovered only after the water was pumped out. Another resident of Grosvenor Road, Mr Harding, had eight children. A few days before, he had moved his four daughters, aged two to eighteen, from their bedroom to the basement kitchen because he thought they would be warmer. He said goodnight to them at half past eleven. Then two hours later, he heard a loud noise as the embankment wall gave way and a mass of water came across the road and rushed into the basement. 'There were iron bars in front of the window, and I could not get the kitchen door open owing to the force of the water inside the room which was keeping it firmly closed,' he said. 'The girls were caught and drowned in something like 20 seconds.'

In Horseferry Road, a youth was sleeping in a basement room when the flood waters came. He tried desperately to push open the door, but the weight of the water made it impossible. Then he tried the window, but it was barred. He shouted for help to his neighbours. With the water in his basement now well up to his neck, they tried their best to prise the bars open. Then just as they had almost done it, the room filled with muddy water and the youth's cries for help died away. Seven policemen held hands across the raging torrent in the street and managed to break in, but it was too late.

Meanwhile, a similar struggle was going on to try to save a 76-year-old woman trapped in a basement room in Causton Street, near Vauxhall Bridge. When the waters broke in, her lodger, who lived on the floor above, fought his way down to the basement where his head was just above the water. Inside his landlady's room, he could see her lying motionless on the bed, which was floating close to the ceiling, but water was still flooding in, and the bed disappeared beneath it. He fought his way back to the ground floor and, out of the window, he saw the landlady's daughter lying exhausted on the scullery door, which was floating in the backyard. He climbed onto a window ledge and held out a stick to her, which she caught, enabling him to drag her in through a window. The daughter, who slept in an adjoining room, had been swept out through her bedroom window. A policeman managed to dive into the landlady's room through a window and push her bed into the street, but she was already dead.

In Grosvenor Road another man went to try to rescue his neighbours from their basement room. A door that he had got through was slammed shut by the rising waters, knocking all the breath out of his body, and trapping him half in and half out of the room. The people he was trying to help could only watch in horror

209

as he drowned. At the Tate Gallery, a nightwatchman escaped by swimming along dark corridors as the waters poured into offices and storerooms. A number of works of art were damaged, including a collection of Turner's sketches.

On the south bank, between Blackfriars and Southwark Bridges, the river poured into the narrow streets and alleyways. In Sumner Street, it was 4 feet deep. Police got residents out of their houses, and carts were used to take them to safety. In Wandsworth and Battersea firemen brought dinghies and home-made rafts to evacuate residents, while in Rotherhithe policemen rowed in boats along the streets to warn people of the danger. Six hundred homes were ruined and many poor people lost their few possessions, but no one died.

To the east, Woolwich Arsenal was under water and, on the Isle of Dogs, the electricity failed and people had to struggle in darkness through the waist-high tide. To the west, water filled the auditorium of Fulham Theatre and flooded the stage to a depth of 2 feet. At Kew Green it was several feet deep, and houses were flooded at Barnes, Chiswick and Putney. Altogether, 14 people were killed in London and 2,000 homes were wrecked. After the flood, Parliament authorised the raising and strengthening of most of the Thames river defences and a new Storm Tide Warning service was also introduced.

What London did not get at this point was a flood barrier, even though the idea had been mooted for 150 years, and a quarter of a century later, in 1953, the capital again faced a serious threat. On Sunday 1 February, high tide was due at London Bridge at just after three o'clock in the morning. On its way, whipped up by a violent gale, it had wreaked havoc in eastern England, flooding 150,000 acres and killing more than 300 people, including 58 on Canvey Island in Essex.

As they reached the capital, the waters began to lap over the top of the river defences between Greenwich and London Bridge, and there was widespread flooding at West Ham. At Canning Town, the streets were flooded to a depth of more than 3 feet and people had to take refuge on the upper floors of their houses, while nightwatchmen clambered onto the roofs of lorries and caravans. During Sunday afternoon, members of the armed forces were brought in to rescue people in boats. Woolwich Arsenal was awash, as was Plumstead, and the swollen river carried debris into ground-floor rooms of houses at Blackwall and Wapping. Kew and Richmond were also hit. At Putney, swans swam in the street, while in Barnes a 73-year-old man, who had been sleeping in an air-raid shelter, was drowned. Altogether 1,000 families were flooded out of their homes.

Fortunately for London, the surge produced by the gale, which added an extra 9 feet to the water level, did not coincide with a spring tide, but there was widespread realisation that things could have been much worse and that the capital had probably got off lightly, so the government set up a committee of inquiry which recommended that a flood barrier should be built as soon as possible. Inevitably, it turned out to be not quite as simple as that. Work did not actually start until 1974, and the barrier was not finished until 1982.

During its 2,000 year history, London had been the scene of some of Britain's worst disasters – the sinking of the *Princess Alice*, the Harrow train crash, the Silvertown explosion. Looking back, one could argue that the first was the worst, in that only Boudicca and her army managed to destroy the city completely, though, it was then, of course, by modern standards, a tiny place. The Great Plague probably killed more Londoners than any other disaster, accounting for anything up to 100,000, but the Black Death, though it carried off far fewer was more deadly in that the number of victims represented up to 40 per cent of the population, double the proportion accounted for by the Great Plague.

The six years of the Second World War represented London's longest ordeal, with the air-raid alert sounding every forty hours, the destruction of more than 100,000 houses and the damage to more than a million others. The ravages of the Great Fire, on the other hand, were much more concentrated. Only 75 acres inside the City walls escaped and one house in three was burned down, along with eighty-seven churches and more than fifty livery halls. But what all of the disasters had in common was that, terrible though each one seemed at the time, London always recovered, and went on to thrive and prosper as one of the great cities of the world.

BIBLIOGRAPHY

Books

Ackroyd, P., *London, The Biography*, London, Chatto & Windus, 2000

Barker, F. and Jackson, P., *London, 2000 Years of a City and its People*, London, Papermac, 1983

Bede, *Ecclesiastical History of the English Nation*, London, J.M. Dent & Sons, 1954

Bowyer Bell, J., *The Irish Troubles. A Generation of Violence 1967–92*, Dublin, Gill & Macmillan, 1993

Brazell, J.H., *London Weather*, London, HMSO, 1968

British Railway Disasters, Shepperton, Ian Allan, 1996

Charlton, J., ed., *The Tower of London: its Buildings and Institutions*, London, HMSO, 1978

Clark-Kennedy, A.E., *The London. A Study in the Voluntary Hospital System*, 2 vols, London, Pitman Medical Publishing, 1963

Collier, R., *The Plague of the Spanish Lady. The Influenza Pandemic of 1918–19*, London, Macmillan, 1974

Davison, M. and Currie, I., *London's Hurricane*, Westerham, Froglets Publications, 1989

Dillon, M., *The Enemy Within. The IRA's War against the British*, London, Doubleday, 1994

Edwards, A. and Wyncoll, K., *The Crystal Palace is on Fire. Memories of the 30th November, 1936*, London, The Crystal Palace Foundation, 1986

Faith, N., *Black Box. Why Air Safety is No Accident*, London, Boxtree, 1996

——, *Derail. Why Trains Crash*, London, Channel 4 Books, 2000

Gottfried, R.S., *The Black Death. Natural and Human Disaster in Medieval Europe*, London, Robert Hale, 1983

Grieve, H., *The Great Tide. The Story of the 1953 Flood Disaster in Essex*, Chelmsford, County Council of Essex, 1959

Halliday, S., *The Great Stink of London. Sir Joseph Bazalgette and the Cleansing of the Victorian Capital*, Stroud, Sutton Publishing, 1999

Henham, B., *True Hero. The Life and Times of James Braidwood, Father of the British Fire Service*, Romford, Braidwood Books, 2000

Holloway, S., *Courage High. A History of Firefighting in London*, London, HMSO, 1992

——, *Moorgate. Anatomy of a Railway Disaster*, London, David & Charles, 1988

Inwood, S., *A History of London*, London, Papermac, 2000

Kee, R., *The Bold Fenian Men*, London, Quartet, 1976

212

Bibliography

King's Cross 18th November, 1987. How London's Firefighters Answered the Call, London, London Fire and Civil Defence Authority 1988

Kolata, G., *Flu. The Story of the Great Influenza Pandemic of 1918 and the Search for the Virus that Caused It*, London, Macmillan, 1999

Latham, R., ed., *The Illustrated Pepys. Extracts from the Diary*, London, Bell & Hyman, 1978

Lloyd-Elliott, M., *City Ablaze. Life with the World's Busiest Fire-fighters*, London, Bloomsbury Publishing, 1992

Mallie, E. and McKittrick, D., *The Fight for Peace: the Secret Story behind the Irish Peace Process*, London, Heinemann, 1996

Marsden, P., *Roman London*, London, Thames & Hudson, 1980

Merrifield, R., *London. City of the Romans*, London, B.T. Batsford, 1983

Milford, A., *London in Flames*, West Wickham, Comerford & Miller, 1998

Milne, A., *London's Drowning*, London, Thames Methuen, 1982

Neal, W., *With Disastrous Consequences. London Disasters 1830–1917*, Enfield Lock, Hisarlik Press, 1992

Ogley, B., *In the Wake of the Hurricane*, Brasted Chart, Froglets Publications, 1987

Ollard, R., *Pepys. A Biography*, London, Sinclair-Stevenson, 1991

Palmer, A., *The East End. Four Centuries of London Life*, London, John Murray, 2000

Pierce, P., *Old London Bridge. The Story of the Longest Inhabited Bridge in Europe*, London, Headline, 2001

Pollard, M., *North Sea Surge. The Story of the East Coast Floods of 1953*, Lavenham, Terence Dalton, 1978

Porter, R., *London, A Social History*, London, Hamish Hamilton, 1994

Porter, S., *The Great Plague*, Oxford, Isis, 1999

——, *The Great Fire of London*, Stroud, Sutton Publishing, 2001

Richardson, J., *The Annals of London*, London, Cassell & Co., 2000

Rolt, L.T.C., *Red for Danger*, London, Pan Books, 1966

Sheppard, F., *London. A History*, Oxford, Oxford University Press, 1998

Thurley, S., *The Lost Palace of Whitehall*, London, Royal Institute of British Architects, 1998

Vaughan, A., *Tracks to Disaster*, Shepperton, Ian Allan, 2000

Weightman, G., *Rescue. The History of Britain's Emergency Services*, London, Boxtree, 1996

Weinreb, B. and Hibbert, C., eds, *The London Encyclopaedia*, London, Macmillan, 1983

White, J., *London in the Twentieth Century*, London, Viking, 2001

Wolmar, C., *Broken Rails. How Privatisation Wrecked Britain's Railways*, London, Aurum, 2001

Wragg, D., *Bombers: From the First World War to Kosovo*, Stroud, Sutton Publishing, 1999

Ziegler, P., *The Black Death*, Harmondsworth, Penguin, 1970

——, *London at War 1939–45*, London, Sinclair-Stevenson, 1995

Bibliography

Newspapers and Journals

Fire. The Journal of the British Fire Services
The Fireman and Journal of the Civil Protection Forces of the UK
The *Stratford Express*
The Times

Reports

Air Accidents Investigation Branch, *Report No. 3/03 – Boeing 747–2B5F, HL–7451 near Great Hallingbury*, Department of Transport, 2003

Buller, P.S.J., *The Gales of January and February 1990. Damage to Buildings and Structures*, Building Research Establishment, 1993

Department of the Environment, *Report on the Accident that Occurred on 28th February 1975 at Moorgate Station*, London, HMSO, 1976

Department of Transport, *Investigation into the Clapham Junction Railway Accident*, London, HMSO, 1989

——, *Investigation into the King's Cross Underground Fire*, London, HMSO, 1988

——, *The Ladbroke Grove Rail Inquiry Part 1 Report*, London, HSE Books, 2001

——, *Marchioness/Bowbelle Formal Investigation under the Merchant Shipping Act 1995*, London, The Stationery Office, 2001

Ministry of Transport and Civil Aviation, *Report on the Collision which Occurred on 4th December, 1957 near St Johns Station, Lewisham*, London, HMSO, 1958

——, *Report on the Derailment that Occurred on 5th November, 1967 near Hither Green*, London, HMSO, 1968

——, *Report on the Double Collision which Occurred on 8th October, 1952 at Harrow and Wealdstone Station in the London Midland Region British Railways*, London, HMSO, 1953

——, *The Southall Rail Accident Inquiry Report*, HSE, 2000

UK Air Accident Investigation Branch, *Report of the Public Inquiry into the Causes and Circumstances of the Accident near Staines on 18 June 1972* http://www.dft.gov.uk/stellent/groups/dft_avsafety/documents/page/dft_avsafety_502559.hcsp

INDEX

Index